Art, Experience and Criticism

Third Edition

William T. Squires

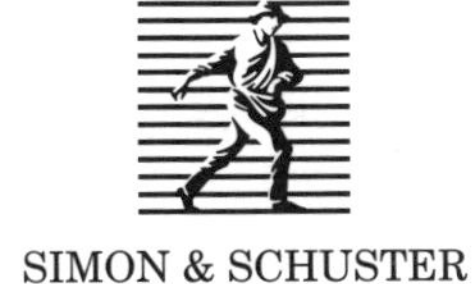

SIMON & SCHUSTER

Cover art: "Untitled," by Dale Cooper.

Printed in the United States of America

10 9 8 7 6 5 4 3 2 1

ISBN 0-536-59833-9
BA 96327

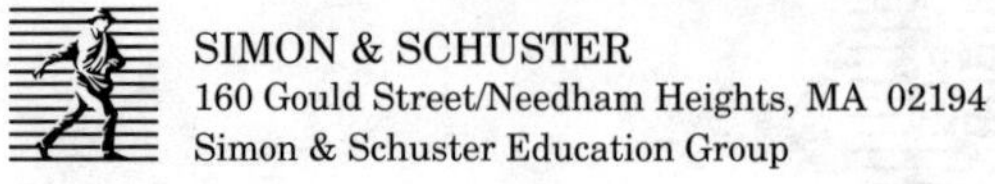

To

Ivan E. Johnson

TABLE OF CONTENTS

List of Illustrations

CHAPTER IV: TOWARDS A CRITICAL METHODOLOGY

FIGURE

CHAPTER V: MEANING: A SERIES OF INTERPRETIVE MOMENTS

CHAPTER VI: RATIONAL CRITICISM AND CENSORSHIP

CHAPTER VII: THE ELEMENTS OF ART AND COMPOSITION

7-7 *Autumn Rhythm,* Jackson Pollock, 1950, oil on canvas, 105" x 207", The Metropolitan Museum of Art, NY.

7-8 *Flemish IX,* Al Held, 1974, acrylic on canvas, 72" x 60", Collection High Museum of Art, Atlanta; Purchased with funds from Edith G. and Philip A. Rhodes and the National Endowment for the Arts, 1979.134.

7-9 *Madonna with Peaches,* Mary Ruth Moore, photograph, 1984, Cortona, Italy.

7-10 *The Three Crosses,* Rembrandt van Rijn, 1653, etching, 15 1/8" x 17 3/4", The Metropolitan Museum of Art, NY.

7-11 Color wheels of Brewster, Ostwald, and Munsell.

7-12 *Still Life: Helmet, Books, Trumpet, and Sheet Music,* William Harnett, 1883, oil on wood panel, 10 5/16" x 13 3/4", The High Museum of Art, Atlanta, Georgia.

7-13 Collage, Tree Collins, student project: cut paper, fabric and fiber collage based on the tempera painting *Carpenters* by Ben Shahn, 1940–1942.

7-14 *David,* Gianlorenzo Bernini, 1623, marble, lifesize, Borghese Gallery, Rome, Alinari/Art Resource, NY.

7-15 Exterior view, *The Solomon R. Guggenheim Museum,* NY, Frank Lloyd Wright, 1959, (photo: Robert E. Mates).

7-16 Interior view, *The Solomon R. Guggenheim Museum,* NY, Frank Lloyd Wright, 1959, (photo: Robert E. Mates).

7-17 *The Miracle of the Loaves and Fishes,* c. A.D. 504, mosaic, Sant' Apollinare Nuovo, Ravenna, Italy, Alinari/Art Resource, NY.

7-18 *Laila and Majnun in Love at School,* 1524–1525, miniature from a manuscript of the Khamsa of Nizami, colors and gilt on paper, Metropolitan Museum of Art, NY.

7-19a When drawn in perspective, all parallel lines recede to a point of convergence (the "vanishing point").

7-19b This 15th century painting "View of an Ideal City" by Piero della Francesca and Luciano Laurana demonstrates the Italian Renaissance fascination with linear perspective. Scala/Art Resource, NY.

7-20 *The Oxbow (the Connecticut River Near Northampton)*, Thomas Cole, 1836, oil on canvas, 51 1/2" x 76", The Metropolitan Museum of Art, NY.

CHAPTER VIII: THE MEDIA AND METHODS OF ART

FIGURE

CHAPTER IX: WRITING ABOUT ART

FIGURE

FOREWORD

THE ROLE OF CONCEPTS IN ART EDUCATION

E.F. KAELIN
FLORIDA STATE UNIVERSITY

When art educators began the process we all now recognize as an examination of conscience,[1] it became *de rigueur* to refer to their discipline as a triple-T system. We were all familiar with the teachers or art, or what passed as such, in our public schools; and we readily admitted that these individuals themselves had teachers ensconced within the university system. What was not so clear was the relationship between these teachers—the second T of the system—and their teachers—the third T of the system—, who were presumably either "art educators" or individuals from other disciplines, such as psychology, philosophy, sociology, or the like, upon whose work our art educators borrowed to fulfill the demands of their own calling—which was to educate teachers of art. At least in principle, that was the status of the profession until the middle fifties of this century, when art educators, such as Fred Logan of the University of Wisconsin, began pushing philosophical aesthetics as the *conditio sine qua non* of art education.

I am not arguing here that Fred Logan was right or wrong in his contention, only that I was the chief beneficiary of his movement to ground the work of art educators—those teachers of teachers of art—in a philosophical aesthetics. He sent all of his graduate students to my classes in aesthetics, and they went on to wreak the havoc Fred had predicted, should his advice have been followed as he was then dishing it out. The Penn State Seminar of 1965,[2] the Ohio State Institute of 1966,[3] largely benefitted from this advice, if only one keep in mind the proviso that aesthetic language is not only theoretical or metatheorical as it usually turns out to be under the tongues of practicing philosophers, but critical, art historical, and metacritical as well.[4] These roles were already clearly observable in the institutions of art education, and it ultimately came as no surprise that the Getty foundation would unite these three disciplines to a fourth, concerned with the productive values in art activity, to create its own concept of what aesthetic education should be when the values in art are thought to transcend creativity itself.[5]

But even within the Getty system a problem, which nonetheless loomed large, remained largely unsolved. For if our system of education in the arts were truly of the triple-tiered process outlined above, it made no difference how many sub-disciplines were to be subsumed under the rubric of art education, one would still have to show, in order ultimately to manage the process, how something that started out as an idea in the head of a theorist actually ended up in the activities of our students of art.

It is to that question that I now turn.

How does a concept turn up as an activity? Surely it may turn up as an activity because it was never anything else. Concepts are concepts in so far as they permit us to recognize the nature or quality of a situation, and we tend to use the marks (or string of characters) by which we name the concept, in preference to the qualities or natures to which they refer, because of the greater ease in manipulating them as compared to the relative difficulty in manipulating situations. We are lazy; concepts are easy—at least easier to manipulate than the situations to which they refer.

Note that I am not entering the discussion opened up by Henri Bergson, in "Introduction á la mètaphysique" (1903),[6] where he distinguishes "images" from "concepts" and devalues the latter because of their generality, their separation from reality, and their mere "utility" as opposed to the "truth" of the images that may be said to be true in that they are not separated from the reality they present to us, and indeed are individual rather than general or universal. My claim is valid even for the invalid claims of Bergson's bifurcation of the ways of knowing into intuition and science. Let us accept science and its concepts: we still must show how our instruction in or through these concepts has succeeded to transmit into action the knowledge of these concepts.

Careful readers will already have perceived the repetition of a prior claim: if we are to succeed as art educators, then we shall have to bring our concepts to the level of those individuals who are meant to use our concepts and thereby prove that they have understood them.

This process is not one of diminution as we descend the ladder of educational stages. The teachers of our teachers must be led to understand our concepts; they must convey this knowledge to their students; and these latter must pass on this same information to our children who are indeed their students. The catalogue seems endless, but that doesn't influence the matter. Whether we are attempting to describe what makes a situation aesthetic, or how one is to criticize objects found in such situations; or to describe what is to count as an element of that situation, or how these elements are related to create the same situation; or indeed, how to make a work of art, and to appreciate it—all of these considerations are motivated by a set of concepts. The smaller the set, of course, the better.

Where philosophers may write for themselves or for other philosophers, that interchange constitutes the cognitive value of an epistemological situation. But where they write for art educators, they must not only exchange information; they likewise must communicate to their counterparts in art the necessity of using the concepts they propound. These concepts must be transferred through the two "lower levels" of the communicative process; and when they are, the initial concepts would have undergone the transformation

I have been hinting at: what began as an idea in someone's head ended up as the ground for a concrete action.

That, indeed, is what I have found in the first edition of William T. Squires' *Art, Experience and Criticism.*[7] The book does what all good handbooks should do: it reduces a very complex set of concepts to the level of action required of the participants in our aesthetic institutions. He does this admirably: clearly, simply, and without ostentation. A second edition of this text should readily make its appearance. I am happy to be able to supply this foreword to that edition.

In order to do so, I have merely assumed that the whole system of teachers—of teachers and of students—has its head somewhere within the university system at the same time its feet are firmly planted within the actions of the individuals whose acculturation within our social system is completed in our public schools. Professor Squires is one teacher who seems to have carried off the trick.

References

1. I was first introduced to this notion of art education by Professor Harlan "Rip" Hoffa, who was then with the arts division of the U.S. Office of Education; he later became professor of art education at the Pennsylvania State University.

2. See Edward L. Mattil, Project director, *A Seminar in art education for Research and Curriculum Development,* co-operative research project V-002, The Pennsylvania State University, University Park, PA, 1966.

3. See David W. Ecker, Project director, Institute for Advanced Study in Art Appreciation, Columbus, Ohio, The Ohio State University, Summer, 1966.

4. See D.W. Ecker and E.F. Kaelin, *The Limits of Aesthetic Inquiry: A Guide to Educational Research,* 71st Yearbook, National Society for the Study of Education, Part 1, 1972, 258–86.

5. See Getty Center for Education in the Arts, *Beyond Creating: The Place for Art in America's Schools and the Journal of Aesthetic Education* edited by Ralph A. Smith. Vol. 2 no. 2, Urbana, Ill.: University of Illinois Press, 1968.

6. See Bergson, *La Pensée et le Mouvant,* Paris: Presses Universitaires de France, 1950, pp. 177–227. Original, 1903.

7. William T. Squires, *Art, Experience and Criticism,* (Needham, MA: Ginn Press, 1991).

E.F. Kaelin,
Florida State University, Tallahassee

Preface

The development of analytical and critical thinking skills and of intelligent appreciation is the aim of *Art, Experience and Criticism.* While acquisition of analytical and critical thinking skills might seem contrary to the subjective matters of taste we often associate with art, a knowledgeable appreciation frequently depends on rationality and plain good sense.

Art, Experience and Criticism is designed to cultivate visually "literate" viewers of artwork. Application of the idea of literacy to vision assumes that art may be understood as language. A language of vision is one built upon an understanding of visual images just as a child's early linguistic education is built upon the ABC's. The major concepts in this book are introductory yet they are intellectually challenging. Those who are new to art will learn to clearly organize their perceptions of and reflections about artwork. Students are taught to translate experience of artwork into written form. Paradigms of descriptive art criticism are provided for study.

I would like to thank all of those who have contributed to this volume. I thank Dr. Eugene F. Kaelin, my former professor of aesthetic philosophy and the best scholar I know. Dr. Kaelin very constructively examined the manuscript and encouraged its publication. Dr. Ivan E. Johnson, my friend and major professor at Florida State University continues to bolster my spirit and encourage my work.

— *William T. Squires*
University of Georgia
Athens, Georgia

Chapter I: Having an Aesthetic Experience

. . . the creative act is not performed by the artist alone; the spectator brings the work in contact with the external world by deciphering and interpreting its inner qualifications and thus adds his contribution to the creative act.

—Marcel Duchamp, *Le Surrealisme* (1957)

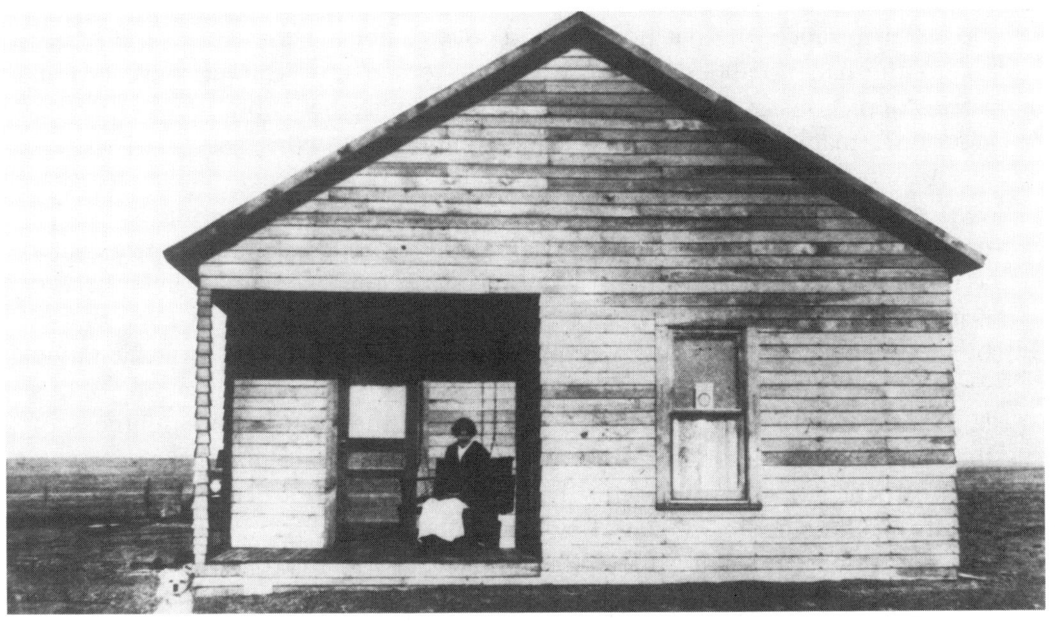

Figure 1-1: *Smith Ranch House*, 1918, Ordway, Colorado (photograph by Elza D. Smith).

WHAT MAKES A SITUATION AESTHETIC?

This photograph, The Smith Ranch House (Figure 1-1) of all those from the family album, unites my memory, experience and imagination. Depicted is a bare, clapboard house built by my grandfather in 1918. The house stands alone in the hard, unforgiving landscape of the Colorado plains. My grandmother Gladys sits on the narrow front porch. Her dog sits at attention in the yard.

I have been told that not long after my grandfather recorded this moment, my mother was born in the house. A year or so later the small house and farm were swept away by the winds of the dust bowl, driving my grandparents with their young family back east to Missouri.

The grandfather of my memory was not a rancher of the western plains who carried a six gun and herded cattle. When I knew him, he was a Missouri business man with four grown children. He and my grandmother lived in a neat, two-story Victorian style house, drove a Hudson and went to church every Sunday.

This photograph unites a young boy's imagination with the reality of a family's history. By enjoying art we unite memory and imagination with experience. The kind of "experiencing" offered by my enjoyment of the photograph is nostalgia. Nostalgia alone is not aesthetic. However, the object of nostalgia may be aesthetic; the photograph objectifies the personal through an arrangement of formal visual elements and takes on an aesthetic dimension. For instance, the flat horizon and severe, linear geometry of the house reflect the harsh realities of life on the western plains. Traditionally, it is an artist's depictions of experience that are labeled aesthetic, but the aesthetic is not only a matter of experiencing or responding to artwork.

Aesthetic emotions are not confined to the art galleries, museums, theaters and concert halls of the world. Feelings associated with aesthetic experience are repeated in our lives many times in a variety of settings. Even now as I sit on a large gray rock, a cool lake before me and a light breeze bringing the characteristic odor of boats and fishing toward me, I am drawn by the deep rich colors of the setting sun and I am filled with an exhilarating sense of vital well being. I may not remember the particular sensations of this late summer afternoon a year from now, but the beauty and rightness of these sensations is a familiar experience I will enjoy again in other places.

Aesthetic experiencing turns up in unlikely places. There is aesthetic beauty in the smooth, powerful swing of the hitter driving a baseball deep into the center field stands for a home run. There is artistry in the moves of a great shortstop going deep in the hole behind second to make a diving grab of a sinking line drive. Even politics may have an undeniably aesthetic dimension when a leader from one part of the world galvanizes diverse populations through charisma and a message of universal harmony and peace.

A great artist may discover aesthetic experience even in a modest cup of tea and a bit of "petite madeleine." Marcel Proust wrote:

> *No sooner has the warm liquid, and the crumbs with it, touched my palate than a shudder ran through my whole body, and I stopped, intent upon the extraordinary changes that were taking place. An exquisite pleasure has invaded my senses, but individual, detached, with no suggestion of its origin. And at once the vicissitudes of life had become indifferent to me, its disasters innocuous, its brevity illusory—this new sensation having had on me the effect which love has of filling me with a precious essence; or rather this essence was not in me, it was myself. I had ceased now to feel mediocre, accidental, mortal. Whence could it have come to me, this all-powerful joy? I was conscious that it was connected with the taste of tea and cake, but that it infinitely transcended those savors, could not indeed, be of the same nature as theirs. Whence did it come? What did it signify? How could I seize upon and define it?*[1]

Proust's tea and cake took him on an extraordinary inward journey, a journey of self-examination, a journey into the past.

Appreciation and Aesthetic Experience

This book is about aesthetic experiencing, or perhaps more accurately, it is devoted to enriching your understanding of the experience of art. While it is true that having an aesthetic experience cannot be taught, a greater capacity for in-depth appreciation of art can be developed.

We may not assume that we already understand all that is implied by "appreciation." If we like a thing, do we not therefore appreciate it? Not necessarily. Webster's dictionary defines appreciation as, first: "sensitive awareness; especially: recognition of aesthetic values." In the pages that follow we will examine the nature, definition and major forms of art, and we will introduce aesthetic theory and art critical practice. In short, we will examine everything about art that contributes to aesthetic valuing, understanding and judgement.

The appreciator of art does not know the thoughts that were involved in making an artwork. Since he cannot enter the artist's mind, the appreciator must rely upon direct perception and upon any ancillary information which assists understanding of the work. How does this operate in the real world?

Philosopher Curt J. Ducasse suggested a connection between art appreciation and consumerism.[2] He proposed that appreciators are consumers of art or consumers of the work created by artists. As consumers/appreciators we may hang pictures we like on the walls of our homes. We may occasionally attend concerts or visit museums. We may watch television dramas and comedies and enjoy movies. We may read novels and poetry. Our homes may be decorated with furniture which we have selected. Our closets hold the clothes we wear. And, we own special pieces of jewelry which reflect our taste.

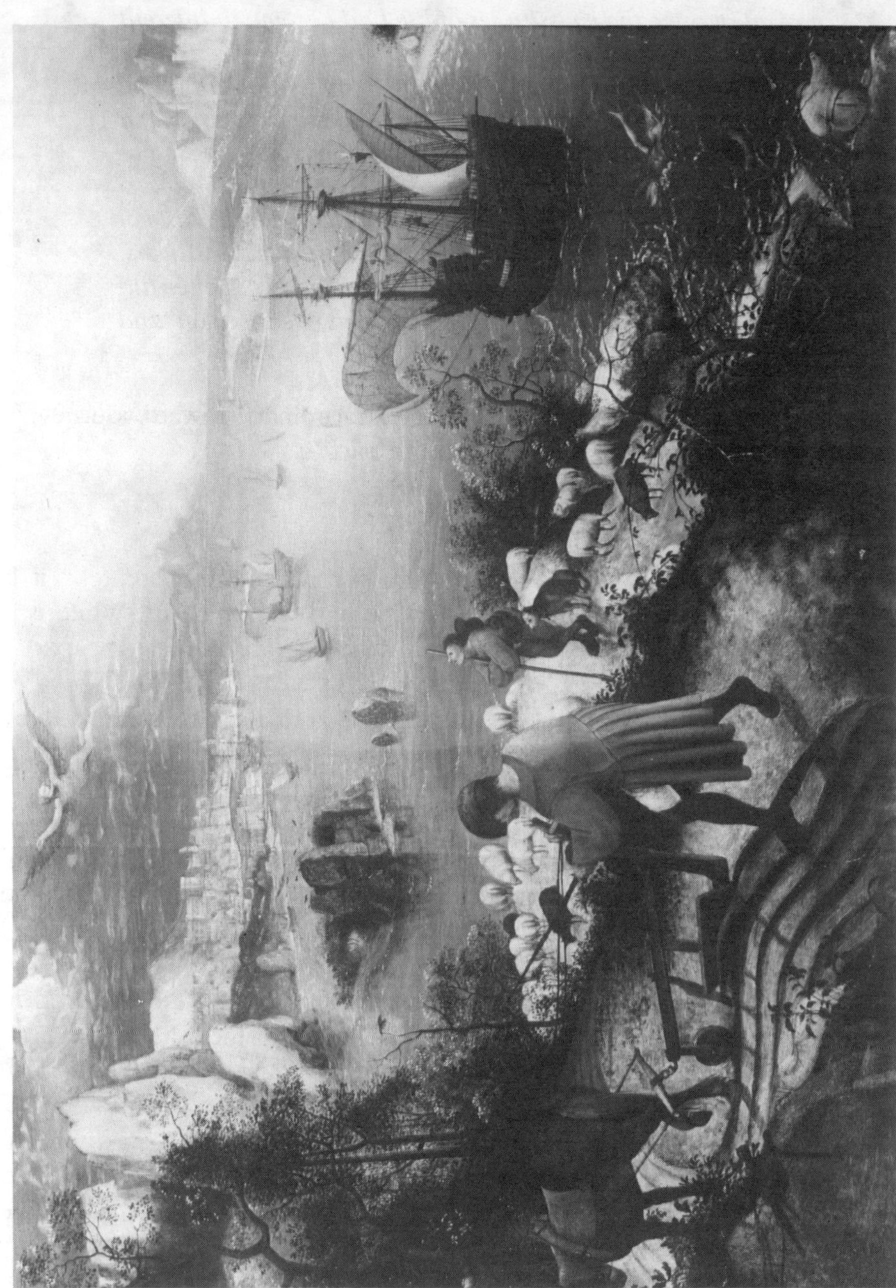

Figure 1-2: *Landscape with the Fall of Icarus*, Pieter Bruegel the Elder, 1554–55, oil on canvas, 29" x 44 1/8", Musées Royeaux des Beaux Arts, Brussels, (Giraudon/Art Resource, NY).

What is the nature of the aesthetic interest of the appreciator/consumer? What is it that motivates people to visit museums or to hang a particular picture on the wall? In the course of daily life we come into contact with a profusion of conflicting visual images. We see things we enjoy or detest. We have an idea of what we prefer, and we naturally gravitate toward our preferences. We may visit a museum because there are works of art on display which we think we might enjoy seeing. We may purchase a picture because looking at it gives us special pleasure. It is the nature of this special pleasure which is the concern of art appreciation.

Artistic or aesthetic pleasure might be described as "a 'listening' for the feeling impact—for the emotive reverberations—of the object attended to."[3] How does the appreciator "listen" for this feeling impact? Listening is a kind of attending. The appreciator may be said to be an attentive, contemplative observer. In the role of aesthetic observer, the appreciator functions in a manner which is almost the reverse of the artist's function. For example, the artist has certain emotions which are infused into the work. The appreciator looks at the artist's work and tries to extract those emotions which are inherent in the work. This is not to imply that the emotional state of the contemplative viewer would or should duplicate that of the artist at work.

In appreciating artwork the viewer savors what is enjoyed. The modern British poet W. H. Auden expressed his appreciation of Pieter Bruegel's painting *Landscape with the Fall of Icarus* (Figure 1-2) in a beautiful poem, "Musée des Beaux Arts."

Musée des Beaux Arts

About suffering they were never wrong,
The Old Masters: how well they understood
Its human position; how it takes place
While someone else is eating or opening a window or just
walking dully along;
How, when the aged are reverently, passionately waiting
For the miraculous birth, there always must be
Children who did not specially want it to happen, skating
On a pond at the edge of the wood:
They never forgot
That even the dreadful martyrdom must run its course
Anyhow in a corner, some untidy spot
Where the dogs go on with their doggy life and the torturer's horse
Scratches its innocent behind on a tree.
In Bruegel's "Icarus," for instance: how everything turns away
Quite leisurely from the disaster; the ploughman may
Have heard the splash, the forsaken cry
But for him it was not an important failure; the sun shone
As it had to on the white legs disappearing into the green
Water; and the expensive delicate ship that must have seen

Something amazing, a boy falling out of the sky,
Had somewhere to get to and sailed calmly on.[4]

Auden indeed savors the imagery and meaning of this poignant myth painted by Pieter Bruegel. The savoring and enjoyment of imagery and meaning in art might be compared to the pleasure of a gourmet tasting a culinary masterpiece. The gourmet is sensitive to and discriminating about subtle nuances of flavor. If this analogy seems frivolous, recognize that there is a point to the comparison. The gourmet is neither a chef nor a food critic; the art appreciator, like the gourmet, is not obliged to qualify aesthetic responses and satisfactions in terms of either the canon of the critic or the discipline of the artist. It may appear, at first glance, that the appreciator is no more than a curiosity, sensation or pleasure seeker, but the example of Auden contradicts such a superficial characterization of the appreciator.

A case can be made for the validity of "knowledgeable" art appreciation; certainly most college art appreciation courses try to instill knowledge and provide information. A seemingly contrary old adage declares, "a little knowledge is a dangerous thing." If we bend meaning to serve our present purpose, what the saying tells us is that the knowledgeable appreciator should aspire to substantial knowledge rather than a little. However, knowledge can be dangerous to the appreciator if its acquisition inhibits direct experience of the work. It is direct experiencing of art that is the essence of appreciation.

Novelist and critic Henry James wrote: "To criticize is to appreciate, to appropriate, to take intellectual possession, to establish in fine a relation with the criticized thing and to make it one's own."[5] Art criticism can provide the appreciator with a methodology for understanding more fully the artwork experienced. This text is based on the rationale that the appreciator's experience of artwork grows when critical understanding increases empathy and identification with the work. The appreciator's aesthetic satisfaction can also grow as a result of sharing in the experiences and discoveries of art professionals and other knowledgeable viewers.

In this text, particular attention is paid to the emotive impact of art on appreciators. Underlying these discussions is a conscious effort to communicate means of analyzing and understanding art in order to foster appreciation.

FOR DISCUSSION

1. How does aesthetic experience differ from other kinds of experience such as religious, business, or political experience?
2. Are certain conditions or circumstances necessary or helpful for aesthetic experience? Cite examples to support your position.
3. Describe the relationship between aesthetic experiencing and art appreciating.

CHAPTER II:

THE NATURE OF ART AND CREATIVE PROCESS

"Art is not just 'the expression of the age': it is the work of people who have to find approval if they want to live."

—E. H. Gombrich, *Meditations on a Hobbyhorse, (1963)*

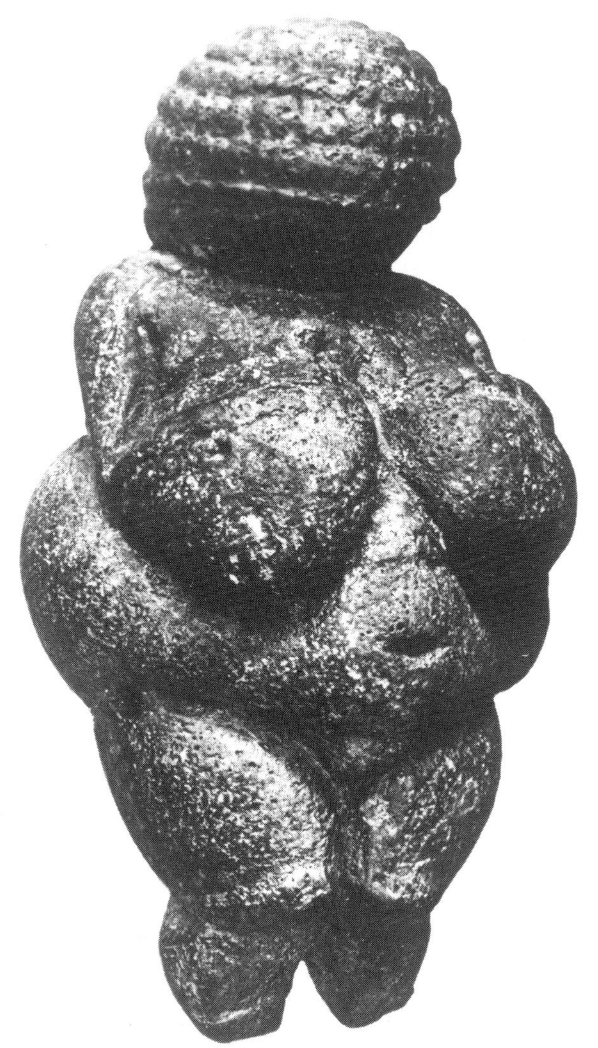

Figure 2-1: *Venus of Willendorf,* Upper Paleolithic, stone, height 4 3/8", Museum of Natural History, Vienna, (Giraudon/Art Resource, NY).

WHAT IS ART?

Art has always been influenced by practical, religious and social values which demanded the creation of objects designed specifically to express those values. Art has always been present in socially significant ceremony and ritual. The ancient shaman, magician or witch doctor used objects to give meaning, force and truth to ceremony and ritual. Although the art and aesthetic value were originally subordinated to societal function, the actual shape and pattern of objects created for ceremony and ritual were, in some measure, at the discretion of the maker. Although they are generically similar, even Paleolithic Venus figures were uniquely varied and expressive (Figures 2-1 and 2-2).

To use a mundane example of art's service to utility, consider the design of a spoon. The use of the object is clear: it conveys food to the mouth. In general, the size of the spoon, shape of the bowl, and necessity for a handle are prescribed by the fact that a spoon is held in the hand and usually fits the mouth conveniently. Beyond these requirements the artist, or the maker, is free to shape the spoon in any way. This point illustrates how an artwork may be a practical and genuinely aesthetic product of imagination and individual preference.

Utilitarian objects, primarily made to fulfill some functional need, are potentially enjoyable or beautiful. Look at the things with which we surround ourselves, objects of ordinary daily use: our house, car, clothing and furniture. While all of these things are useful, we also value them for their decorative qualities. In fact, we expect and require that these things give pleasure by their conformation and employment of materials. Industry expends much effort and money to design functional forms which will please the consumer by their appearance.

Art and beauty are fundamental to humans, as basic, perhaps, as science, religion and trade. If so, then, why is art viewed by many people today as strictly a luxury which may be enjoyed but also may be happily and successfully lived without? What is the luxury so readily labeled "Art" with a capital "A"?

If we can name art's functions or describe its nature, will we know what art is and value it properly? Many writers of art books devote chapters to describing art's functions in society. Those same writers often devote many pages to identifying art's nature. They ask such questions as, What qualities are there which are characteristic of all art? Is art a describable activity? Is it play? Is it language? Is it emotional release? These questions lead to definitions of art offered by philosophers, critics, collectors, artists and, generally, anyone who happens to have an opinion.

One definition offered by the dictionary calls art a species of human activity, a process. If that is true, we cannot hold up our favorite paperweight and declare, "This is art!" We have, perhaps, shown a result of art, a by-product of art making, but not art itself. Another definition, the reverse of the first, identifies art as a product. Art, according to this view, does not reside in

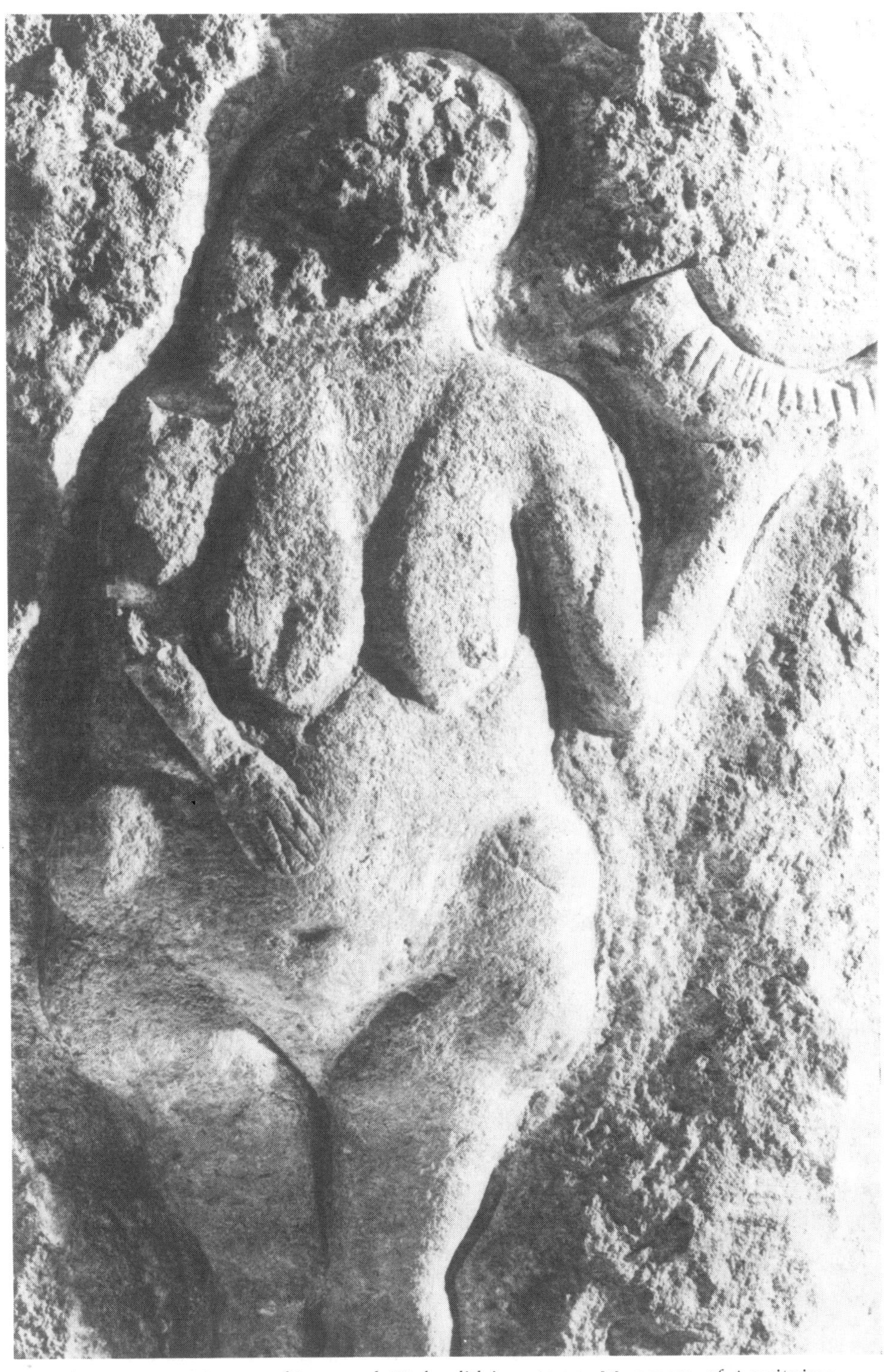

Figure 2-2: *Venus of Laussel,* (Paleolithic, stone, Museum of Aquitaine, Bordeaux. Scala/Art Resource, NY).

production processes, but in the object produced. Presumably, you can call an object art if it meets certain specified criteria. An "art as product" definition leads, inevitably, to questions concerning the requirements an object must fulfill in order to be labeled "Art." And, who sets the requirements?

Art seems to defy a single, meaningful, universal definition. Varied definitions exist. Plato wrote that art is imitation.[1] Presumably the artist was to imitate the appearance of things. Art was destined always to copy the look of reality but never to capture the essential truth of reality. This definition would satisfy few people today simply because much art work today makes no attempt to create likenesses. Abstract art may start with a model drawn from nature, but its final product may bear no apparent relation to its origin.

At times, religious institutions, such as Christian churches, have been quite dogmatic about labeling art. Churches have contended that art, or beauty, resides only in the mind of God, never in objects. Art, according to this view, is revealed to Man as God's gift but is never completely revealed because man is an imperfect vessel (receptacle of truth and beauty).[2] At best, what Man can experience through contemplation of imperfect corporeal existence is a sense of awe and mystery. Artwork may elicit a sense of awe and mystery from some viewers, but some religions contend that pleasure is a more typical response to physical beauty. From this point of view, art and beauty are therefore inevitably debased because they are identified with sensuousness rather than spirituality.

Art has been described as play. Play, like entertainment, makes no demand of us; art on the other hand demands a great deal of us both intellectually and emotionally. We engage in play purely for the enjoyment it provides. The play definition of art is inadequate because play is externally stimulated, whimsical and often non-directed. If art is understood as internally motivated and purposeful, it is clearly distinguished from the pure freedom and pleasure of play.

Art is sometimes defined as whatever a museum or gallery collects and displays. The presumption is that if it is art, it is in a museum collection somewhere. Such a way of defining art is, of course, absurd, because it implies that any object that is not housed in a museum is not art. This logical absurdity would imply that an object moved from the studio to the museum undergoes a transformation from non-art to art as a result of the move. Another fault inherent in the definition of art as that which is in a museum is that the definition would be subject to inconsistency and bias at each specific museum. The bias might stem from manipulative marketing strategies used by art dealers who wish to artificially inflate the value of the artwork. Bias could grow out of collusion between museum officials and collectors or changes in government tax policies.[3] So, the museum as a constant and definitive arbiter of art is a myth.

Like so many sand castles, no formal definitions of art stand long against the ever rising tides of conflicting opinion from artists, scholars and laymen. Visual art and our perception of it are intuitive and basically indefinable, since it is non-discursive in character. Resorting to the worst sort of tautology, it may be said that art is art. Defining art, even informally, is difficult. Each one of us who has the interest eventually defines art in a usefully personal way.

This text is written from the point of view that art communicates expressive impact or effect. This impact is conveyed via the senses, and as we are concerned here with the visual arts rather than the performing arts, it is through the visual sense that this aesthetic, expressive impact is transmitted. Mental and emotional information is conveyed to the viewer through his or her perception of expressive objects (artworks).

If we agree with the philosophy that art communicates and expresses, how does it do so? How is expression transmitted through art? Perhaps communication and expression unite in the aesthetic object to evoke a visual language.[4] This language may operate in the same way that ideas and thoughts are converted into words through writing and speech. Art, then, would objectify thought and feeling. Perhaps it would be useful to analyze the syntax and semantics of art. Just as by listening to and contemplating a dramatic performance, we could come to comprehend certain inherent ideas and feelings, by viewing a bronze sculpture we could know its feeling impact.

Expression that is objectified through art should be distinguished from expression which is simply chaotic. The expression of physical passion, for instance, has aesthetic value only when it is expressed through artistic means. If we happen to see two people passionately making love on a park bench, we may note certain gestures and movements which we identify as characteristic of passionate lovemaking. However, as passing observers, we do not ourselves feel love as a result of the impromptu display. An artwork may empathetically elicit from the viewer feelings reminiscent of those which led to the passionate physical display observed. The case is the same when anger is impulsively indulged. A show of anger is art only when it is staged (or controlled) in such a way that an audience is allowed to reflect upon it and thereby comprehend its origins. A good actor is the link that transmits, through art, the feeling content inherent in the play.

How does the artist transmit a unique vision and thereby forge a link of understanding with the audience? The answer is through "style." The artist's style is a means of communication. It is a "manner of speaking." When the word style is applied to an artist's work, a unity of vision is implied. Style also suggests a unique or individually characteristic way of acting, performing or expressing oneself. Typically, if we say, "That person has style," we use the word style in a complimentary way, but style may also be used for derogatory labeling of art. If we describe an artwork as overly stylized, we mean the work is stiff, mannered and lacking in naturalism. Stylization need not be a negative quality however. At the beginning of this discussion we related ceremony and ritual to art, referring to the role of created objects in traditional ceremonial practice. Such objects are almost always generically similar and therefore stylized. Their form and function is handed down from generation to generation, often remaining virtually unchanged. In such instances style insures continuity and preserves the intent of traditional ceremonial practice.

The Creative Process

The processes attending stylistic development and artistic creation continue to fascinate scholars of art. Writers for centuries have tried to describe the process of creating art. At times, these descriptions of the artist at work resemble melodramatic, chauvinistic fiction more than observed practice.

> *The painter feels a need or desire to paint. . . . Faint though this need may seem initially, it grows and, at times, may become overwhelming. This need is stimulated by the artist's perception of the world and by a sense of internal, personal necessity. He confronts a blank canvas; this is the mute, neutral material through which he will transform emotion into expression. Whatever pleasure the plain surface of that canvas may afford in and of itself, the painter is not satisfied with it, nor can he accept it as it is for very long. The canvas is a means, a surface to be coaxed, even goaded into realization and fulfillment.*
>
> *The painter does not proceed with his painting unhampered. There is resistance, hence modification. Sometimes the canvas seems unwilling to yield to the painter's mind and hand. His most careful calculations, his most eloquent applications are resisted. At times the painter's efforts are totally rejected, and he strikes out against his frustration, even smashing his work in rage.*

We may not have much sympathy with the foregoing romanticized vision of the artist at work because it is overly dramatic and trivializes the creative process. However, there is a widely shared misconception that artists create in a state of mental anguish and even physical frenzy. Art, such as the Abstract Expressionist works of Jackson Pollock (Figure 2-3) or Franz Kline (Figure 2-4), may appear angry, aggressive, even chaotic, but that does not mean that they were executed in a rush and flurry of muscular exertion by an angry artist. Most art originates with a certain degree of thought and deliberation. The poet Wordsworth traced the origin of his art to "emotion recollected in tranquillity"; the same phrase may be applied to visual art.

Henri Matisse described his making of a painting in an analytical, workmanlike manner. The passage that follows describes the way in which Matisse weighed one quality of tone and color against another as his work moved forward.

> *If, on a clean canvas, I put at intervals patches of blue, green, and red with every touch that I put on, each of those previously laid on loses in importance. Say I have to paint an interior; I see before me*

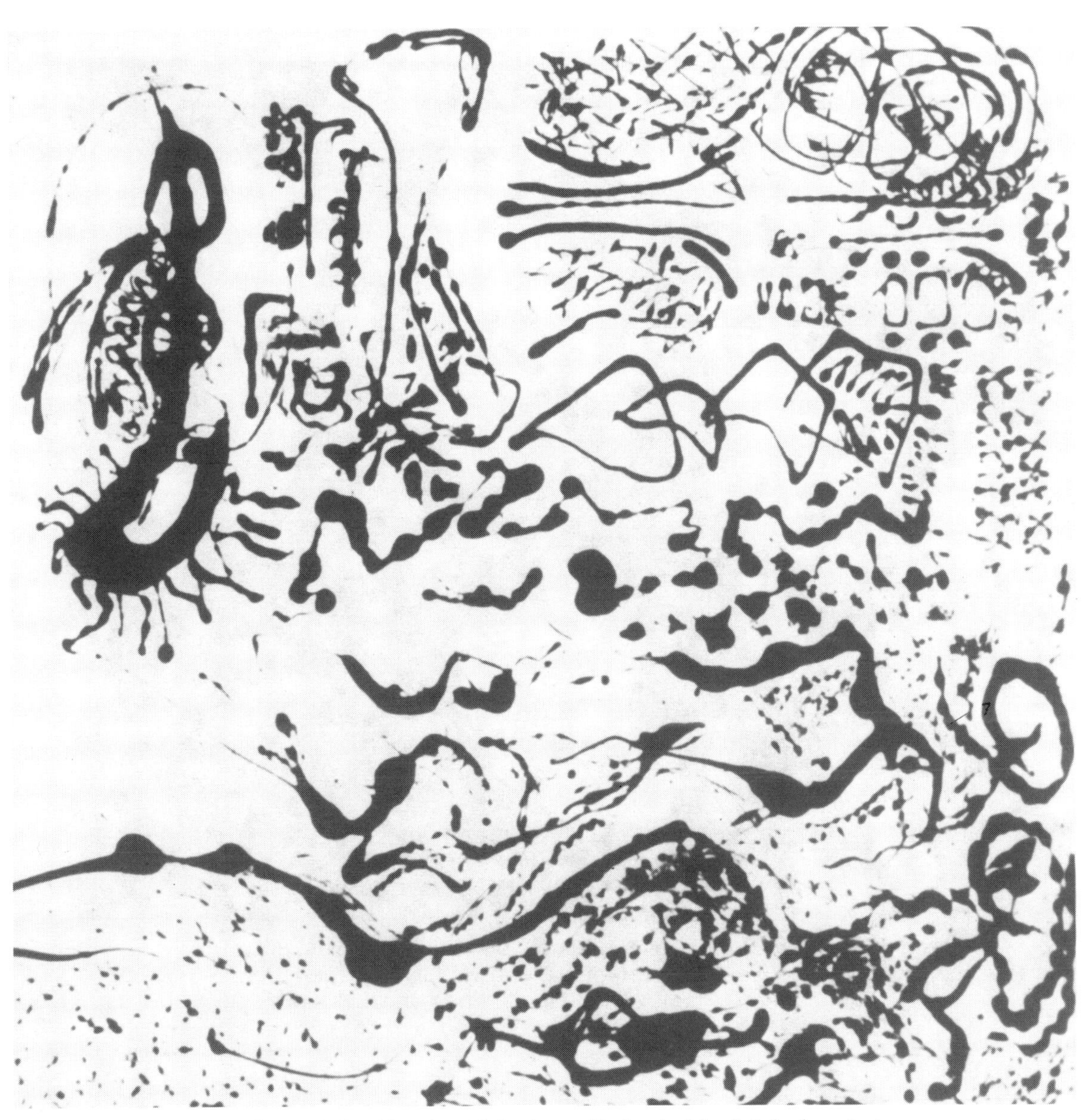

Figure 2-3: *Number 5,* Jackson Pollock, black ink drawing, (ESM/Art Resource, NY).

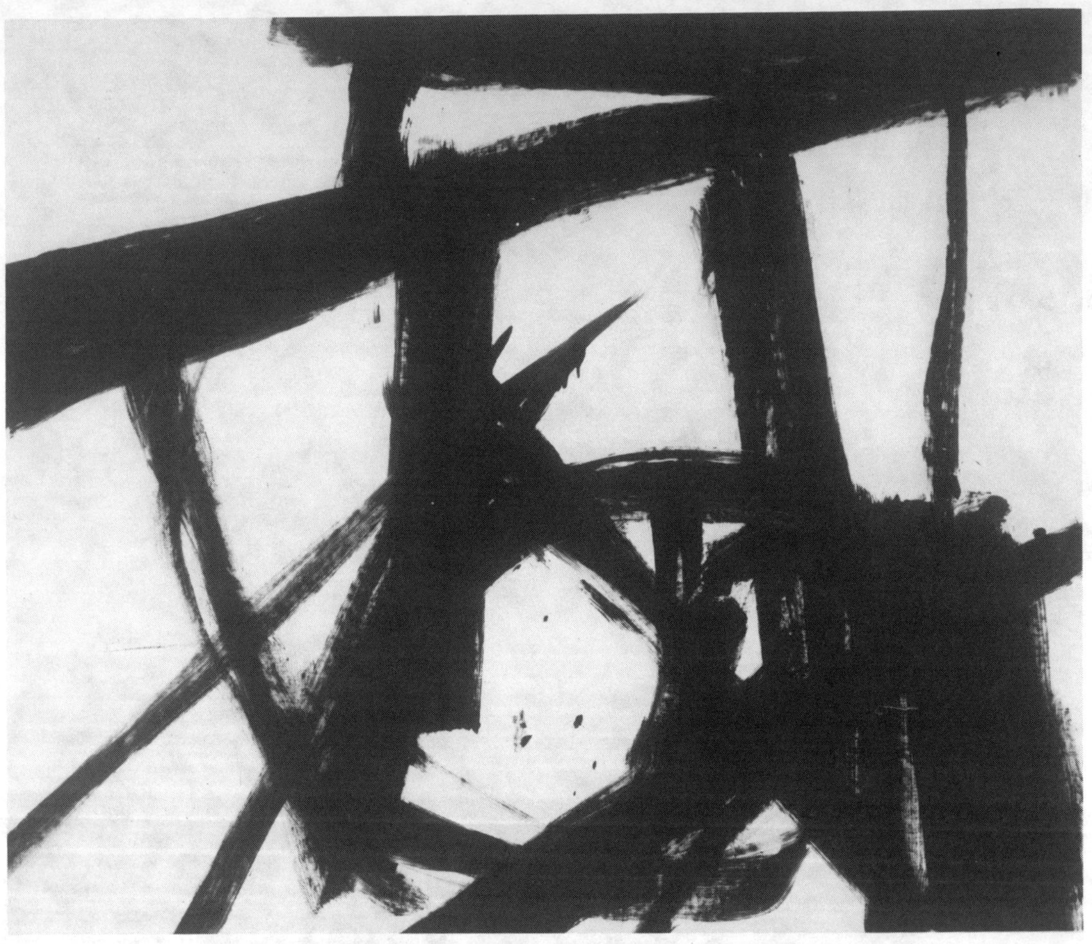

Figure 2-4: *Turin,* Franz Joseph Kline, 1960, oil on canvas, 80" x 95", The Nelson-Atkins Museum of Art, Kansas City, Missouri (Gift of Mrs. Alfred B. Clark through the Friends of Art) F61-23.

> *a wardrobe. It gives me a vivid sensation of red that satisfies me. A relation is now established between this red and the paleness of the canvas. When I put on besides a green and also a yellow to represent the floor, between this green and the yellow and the color of the canvas there will be still further relations. But these different tones diminish one another. It is necessary that the different tones I use be balanced in such a way that they do not destroy one another. To secure that, I have to put my ideas in order; the relationships between tones must be instituted in such a way that they are built up instead of being knocked down. A new combination of colors will succeed to the first one and will give the wholeness of my conception.*[5]

Matisse's conception was never simply a matter of the craftsman plying his trade. Something other than technical adjustments seemed to attend the process of creating. That something has been called insight, intuition, inspiration, imagination and the unconscious. No one knows very much about intuitive insight. The artist may be tentative, even totally unsure, yet still proceeds. Finally, success or rightness of the completed work depends upon the painter's perception of its wholeness or "rightness." A work may be completed without the artist sensing any obvious intuitive direction, but sometimes artists feel that an element of intuitively conveyed intelligence or insight permeates the work and process. The Russian painter, Wassily Kandinsky, described this insight as a prophetic "secretly implanted power of 'vision'."[6]

TWO SOURCES OF INSPIRATION

To explore the nature of inspiration, you may initially think of the artist's path to inspiration as stemming from two different sources: drawn from without or generated from within. Inspiration from without occurs through observation of the objective world or when a particular thing in the objective world becomes suddenly significant. Inspiration from within is a revelation that emerges subjectively from within, owing no apparent debt to conscious reality.

The first path to inspiration leads the artist to pay special attention to some aspect of external reality. Perhaps Leonardo Da Vinci had this in mind when he instructed a young painter to discover ideas for his work by fastidiously studying the weather stains on old buildings or the veins of marble.[7] According to the biographer/historian Giorgio Vasari, inspiration would overtake Piero di Cosimo and render him senseless when he would occasionally "stop to contemplate a wall at which sick people had for ages been aiming their spittle."[8] Vasari wrote that di Cosimo described inspired visions of "battles between horsemen, and the most fantastic cities, and the most extensive landscapes ever seen: . . . [di Cosimo] . . . experienced the same with clouds in the sky." Perhaps it was to such visions that di Cosimo owed his ability to create perfectly convincing monsters. These examples hold one key to the origin of ideas attending the creative process. The artist's work begins, not in sensation alone, but rather in the response of imagination to stimuli.

A second path to inspiration seems to spring from within the artist's subconscious mind free from attachment to any external stimuli. Piet Mondrian, an artist who in mid-career began painting totally abstract geometric works wrote, "Intuition enlightens and so links up with pure thought. They together become an intelligence which is not simply of the brain which does not calculate, but which feels and thinks."[9] Inspiration, for Mondrian, originated from within his unconscious mind. At times, for the artist, this intuition or inspiration occurs in the form of a sudden illumination. It is as if the creative worker is struck by a conceptual bolt of lightning. The mathematician Jacques Hadamard reported such a spontaneous intuitive experience when he wrote that:

> *On being very abruptly awakened by an external noise, a solution long searched for appeared to me at once without the slightest instant of reflection on my part . . . the fact was remarkable enough to have struck me unforgettably . . . and in a quite different direction from any of those which I had previously tried to follow.*[10]

Spontaneous, inspired solutions to creative problems are not as unusual as we might think. Such solutions often present themselves to artists after much conscious, rational effort has been unsuccessfully expended to find a solution to a difficult problem. We may think of inspiration as the wild card in the creative process. Despite its illusiveness, its presence or absence is often credited for the success or failure of creative work.

For Discussion

1. Of what use is a definition of art?
2. Should art describe realities, express emotions, teach lessons, tell stories or do something else?
3. Discuss the two sources of inspiration suggested in this chapter.
4. Are artists naturally inspired or can anyone potentially be trained as an artist?

Chapter III: Art Critical Theory

"Criticism, rather, is to art what history is to action and philosophy to wisdom: a verbal imitation of a human productive power which in itself does not speak."

—Northrop Frye (1957), *Anatomy of Criticism*

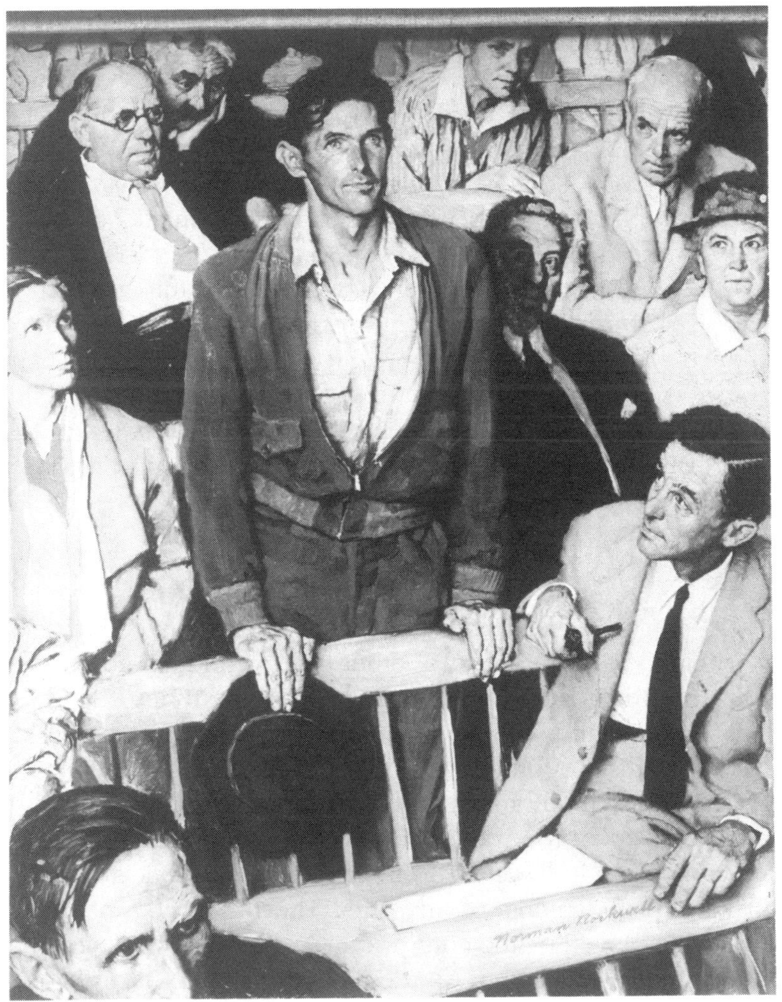

Figure 3-1: *Freedom of Speech,* Norman Rockwell, 1943, Metropolitan Museum of Art, NY.

Introduction to Art Criticism

While artworks are created by artists, they are contemplated by many of the rest of us, by appreciators and critics. We are interested in the nature of the process by which artists produce their work. What attracts people to pay special attention to the artist's products? What stake does the professional critic have in the artist's work?

Why do people bother looking at artworks? They do bother; according to recent surveys, every year in the U.S. as many people attend art museums as attend pop music concerts.[1] It is also fact that virtually every college and university in the country offers art instruction of some sort.

Besides makers of art and contemplators or appreciators of art, there are critics. Critics are professionals who discuss, analyze and pass judgement on the merits of art. When he says that a work is good or bad, better or worse, what does the critic mean? Who is qualified to judge the merits of artwork? Are there valid and objective standards of judgement to be used by critics? If so, how are these standards determined?

Some people say, "I may not know much about art, but I know what I like." Our likes and dislikes are a good starting place for understanding art. Too often, however, preferential statements are followed by, "I like this, and it's good." Or, "I don't like this, it's bad, and that's all there is to it!" Those who are unfamiliar with art tend to prefer highly representational works such as Norman Rockwell's painting, *Freedom of Speech* (Figure 3-1). Statements such as "I don't like this!" all too often refer to twentieth-century abstractions such as De Kooning's *Woman I* (Colorplate 1). "Liking" and "disliking" should lead us to question the nature of the art to which we pay attention. Our curiosity should move us to account for our responses by probing and questioning. What is it that we like about Rockwell's painting? What is it we dislike about abstraction? The formalized process of accounting for our responses to art is called art criticism.

Approaches to Criticism

It may help you to better understand art criticism if we discuss the critic's position within the larger context of other types of inquiry about art.[2] Imagine, if you will, an upright ladder with several ascending rungs (Figure 3-2). At the foot of this ladder stands the artist and artwork. The artwork is the empirical evidence of the artist's effort and the object of inquiry. On the first rung up our imaginary ladder of inquiry stands the art critic. The critic studies and comments on the artists' work. Above the critic on our ladder is the critic of critics (the meta-critic). This individual, a philosopher or aesthetician, studies the way critics make their judgments of artworks. The meta-critic inquires about the methodology employed by the critic and may offer his own suggestions for the practice of art criticism. Further up the ladder of inquiry is a philosopher who develops broadly based theories about the nature and purposes of art. And, at the very top of our ladder stands the meta-theoretician who thinks about the

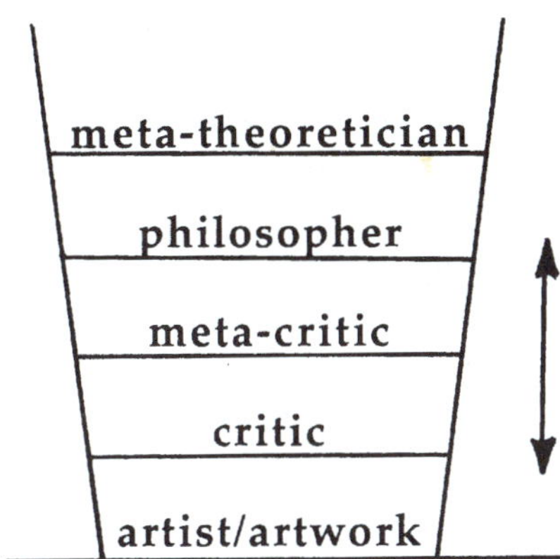

Figure 3-2: Ladder of Inquiry

adequacy of theories and the way theories about art are evolved. Our ladder of inquiry, as you can see, is one of rising generality. As one ascends the ladder, the breadth of inquiry increases. It is important to stress that these levels of inquiry overlap since they may be pursued by the same individual at different times. The ladder may be descended as well as ascended. The theoretician may at times function as a critic; occasionally a critic is also an artist and vice versa.

The art critic always has the artwork as the focus of attention. The critic may not practice criticism by consciously applying a formal method or theory of art. On the other hand, some critics do consciously apply criteria to their deliberations about the merit of artwork.

In his distinguished book, *Art as Experience*, the American philosopher John Dewey classified art criticism prevalent in 1932 into two types.[3] He labeled these types judicial criticism (formalism) and impressionistic criticism. In rejecting these approaches, he laid the conceptual groundwork for a third type of criticism, analytical criticism.

According to Dewey, the judicial school of criticism substituted rules for direct experience of artworks. These rules were applied in a legalistic fashion to aesthetic situations in order to pass judgement on the merits of art. Dewey felt that judicial criticism arbitrarily set standards for artworks which may have had virtually nothing to do with the works themselves. Eighteenth-century Neoclassical painters and sculptors who used ancient classical models as a standard of excellence were viewed by Dewey as an example of the judicial approach.

In his opinion, impressionist criticism offered no rules. Instead, it relied upon the personal and subjective taste of the critic. According to the impressionist ethos, the critic who had seen the most art and the critic who felt the most and emoted the most were the best critics of art.

Dewey advocated a third critical approach which he labeled analytical and synthetical criticism. This critical approach was experientially based and was a logical outgrowth of his philosophy of rational empiricism.

Dewey's critical types still provide a useful framework within which to understand the practice of art criticism today. We will examine each type and find where and with whom art criticism originates. We will look at several expressions of the judicial approach to criticism and then explore the impressionistic approach. Finally, we will explore Dewey's analytical and synthetical approach to art criticism.

JUDICIAL CRITICISM

Judicial criticism/formalism represents one approach to critical judgement which results in a rigidly framed analysis. The term formalism is used to mean a theory of judgement based principally on study of an artwork's elemental and compositional structure. The formalist critic might look for an approved use of materials and craftsmanship. An approved use of materials and techniques would probably be based on traditional or academic criteria. The formalist critic would probably develop an idea of harmonious linear, shape and color relationships which would be superimposed on every aesthetic situation. The perceived quality of an artwork would depend upon the critic's apprehension of some overriding unification of all the work's constituent parts. For the formalist critic, there is an ideal way in which art's elements and compositional principles combine to produce good art. Achievement of this standard of excellence may be based on the critic's belief that the relationships in the artwork meet *a priori* criteria. Achievement of the critic's ideal standard may also be based upon perception of an artwork's "good Gestalt." A Gestalt standard is one wrongly extrapolated from Wolfgang Kohler's classic discussion of experimental psychological discoveries concerning sensory organization and characteristics of organized entities.[4] A misapplication of Gestalt theory to art critical practice would reside in the critic's superimposition of some configurational ideal or pattern upon artwork.

To some extent, every critic is a formalist because formal relationships, in certain situations, demand attention. However, for formalism not to be myopic it must be only one aspect of the critic's wider repertoire of analytical considerations.

IMPRESSIONIST CRITICISM

An impressionist critic is one who relies almost totally upon emotional responses to art as the source and content of critiques. Feelings evoked by artworks not only initiate criticism but often replace the artwork as the subject of criticism. Impressionist critics eschew the use of objective standards of judgement. Instead, they cite their personal credentials as sufficient justification for passing judgement on artwork. One popular contemporary critic who relies to an extent upon her personal vitae for critical license is Barbara Rose. She has written that, "The critic can discriminate value, then, only by means of his own sense of quality, which he has developed by looking at a wide variety of works of art. His reaction is entirely subjective and intuitive."[5] Ms. Rose does not say so, but the clear implication of her view is that her judgement of an artwork may be challenged only by someone who has looked at as many, or more, artworks than she and by someone who feels as much as she does. It would be logically absurd to consider settling a critical disagreement by collecting, counting and comparing two critics' museum receipt stubs and travel records. Impressionist critics generally place a high value upon what they consider their superior experience and sensibilities. The truth is that a widely traveled viewer of art may understand little of what is experienced. The experience of viewing great art may be totally lost on certain individuals. On the other hand, a perceptive student who has never traveled further than the local library may glean from art books with good reproductions far more than the museum-hopping traveler who has actually stood before countless numbers of the world's most treasured masterpieces.

Some impressionist critics emerge from the ranks of connoisseurs, collectors and gallery owners. These critics, surrounded by the purchased testament to their personal taste, may pass judgement on whatever is self-serving. Their judgments may be quite sincere; they may be honestly altruistic. However, these critics may, with their arbitrary dicta, rely for legitimacy upon a self-sanctioning judgmental process.

The foregoing description exposes impressionist criticism at its worst. A more moderate view must recognize that Barbara Rose's writings, for instance, are among the most sensitive, thoughtful and widely read since the Second World War. The most widely read, widely published art critics are those who, like Ms. Rose, write for newspapers and magazines. Additionally, television has exposed many people to critiques of film and theater. The popular media lend themselves well to impressionist criticism because the public requires little rationality and few standards to govern what is stated. In fact, much that passes for criticism in the press is probably not criticism at all.

If Edmund Feldman's comment, "art criticism is talk about art"[6] is narrowly interpreted, this statement might qualify almost any comment as art criticism. If, on the other hand, there is validity in Dewey's statement that criticism is judgement, criteria are necessarily tied to any expression which is really critical. Given an absence of criteria for judgement, what is the nature of the art talk and writing we encounter on television and in magazines and newspapers? Such expressions are byproducts of impressionist criticism and frequently take the form of semi-critical reviews. A review should serve several purposes: to be factually informative, to summarize and, at times, to excite patron interest through controversy.

Art reviews, well written or stated, give readers or listeners a good idea of what they will encounter if they attend a concert or see an exhibition. This type of reporting may be little more than a spot advertisement, or it may take an extended form, telling us about the nature of the work's subject matter, providing quotes from the artist or even describing biographical data. A reviewer may include quotes from other reviews or critiques of an artist's work, but the reviewer/reporter who seeks primarily to inform does not offer opinions.

Often reviewers go beyond informing their audience and air their views of the art under consideration. The motivation for such a venting of opinion may be purely egocentric, or it may be the critic's desire to generate interest where little or none exists. Reviewers who are employees of media corporations are not necessarily above trying to increase sales of media through antagonism and sensationalism. Such expostulating represents, at best, a subjective impression, and, at worst, it is damaging to the arts and personally injurious to artists.

Another expression of impressionist criticism is that offered by the general public. We may not think of ordinary people as art critics (usually they are not), but at certain times the public expresses, in no uncertain terms, its judgement of artworks.

In the early 1980s a huge steel sculpture by Richard Serra (Figure 3-3) incensed more than 7,000 New York city workers who signed a petition for the sculpture's removal from a public plaza. This public outcry eventually did result in the sculpture's removal.[7] Such public wrath is not new. Artists like Auguste Rodin, Diego Rivera, Pablo Picasso, Claes Oldenburg, Alexander Calder and Robert Arneson have all had work scorned, mutilated and removed from sites as a direct or indirect result of popular opinion. Majority rule seems to be the guiding principle of popular criticism and the public seems to like its art sentimental, simple and familiar. This translates into a widespread public preference for representational painting and figurative sculpture. However, representation and figuration are not enough to insure acceptance by the public. Diego Rivera's frescos painted during the 1930s in Detroit, Michigan, were criticized for their satire and socialist propagandizing (Figure 3-4).

Analytical and Synthetical Criticism

When he wrote *Art as Experience* in the early years of the Depression, John Dewey proposed a type of criticism which promised change in American critical tradition. First, Dewey directed the attention of critics to specific aesthetic objects. Previous American art criticism, generally, had been written in response to group exhibitions. In depth criticism of individual artworks was virtually non-existent.[8] Dewey provided guidelines for engaging in such an object oriented critical approach, and called for a methodology involving analysis and synthesis.

By analysis Dewey meant analytical judgement based on an initial discrimination of the parts of the artwork. Critics needed to know what they were looking at; therefore, having a "consuming informed interest"[9] was requisite. This informed interest meant that critics needed a knowledge of both historical tradition, style, techniques and materials. Critics would also benefit from knowledge of the artist's development through exposure to a succession of works. With such a background the critic might be expected to understand the parts and the interrelations of the parts that constitute the whole artwork.

Synthesis, for Dewey, was that aspect of criticism which would unify all the critic's analytical perceptions. Without synthesis the critic would be bogged down in a meaningless recitation of descriptive detail and unrelated tidbits of knowledge. Synthesis or unification was to be achieved through "insight." Dewey did not try to explain how the critic achieved this insight. He said that it was at this point (at the moment of insight) that the practice of criticism became an art. He suggested that the formulation of hypotheses explaining threads of continuity would bring about unity in criticism and therefore result in synthesis. Apparently Dewey felt that the critic had an insight cloaked in the shape of a theory or a thesis. The critic was to try theories out, so to speak, by

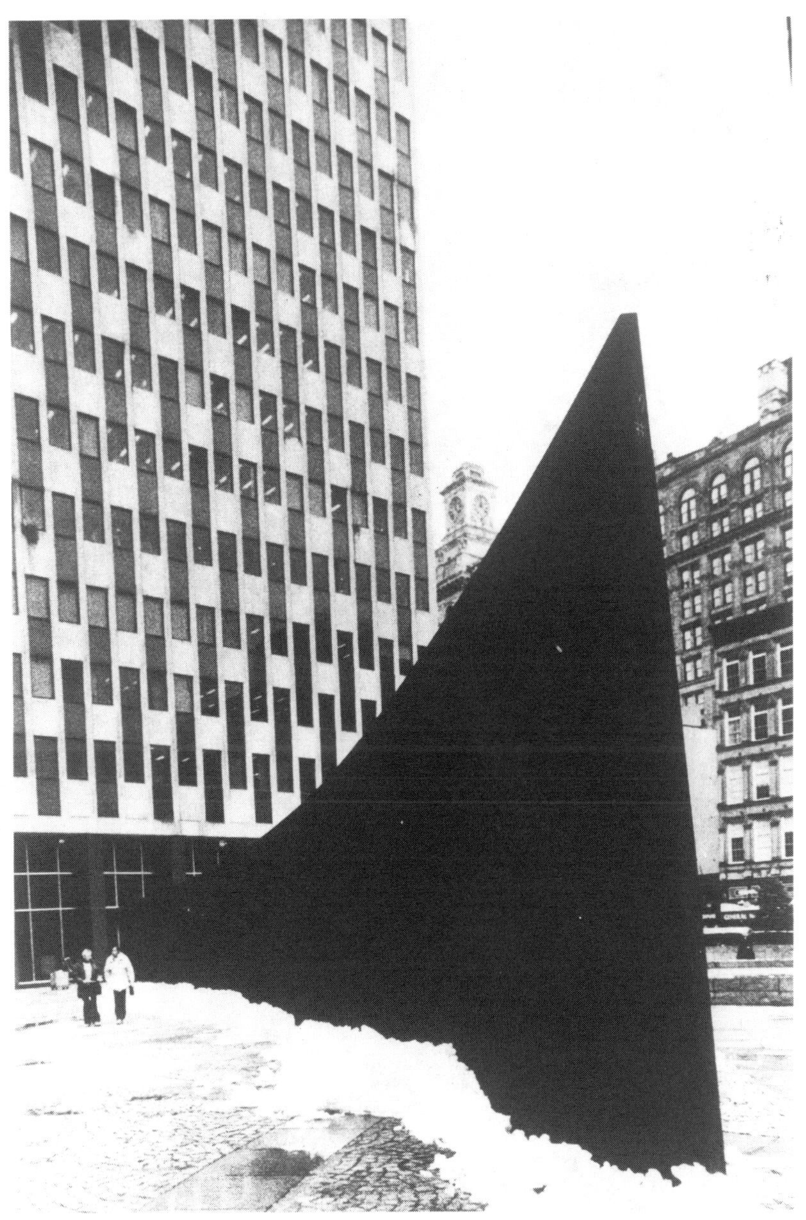

Figure 3-3: *Tilted Arc*, Richard Serra, Federal Plaza, NY, (photo: Edward Hausner, New York Times Pictures).

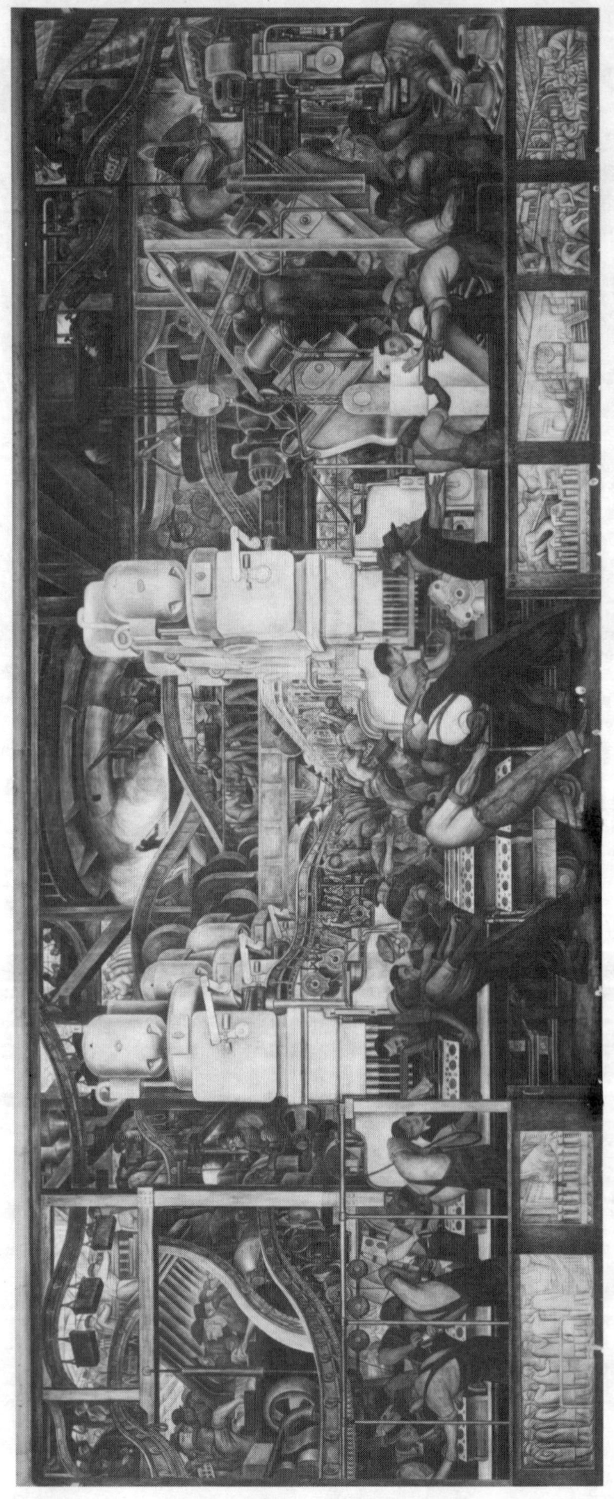

Figure 3-4: *Detroit Industry*, Diego Rivera, 1932–33, central panel on the north wall, fresco, 17' 8 1/2" x 45', Detroit Institute of Arts.

plugging them in at each stage of the development of the criticism; if the theories fit the facts, synthesis and closure resulted. At closure the critic achieved full or total explication of the art in question.

From this summary description of Dewey's critical approach you may get the misleading notion that he advocated a linear, almost lock-step critical methodology, but, to quote Dewey, "There are no rules that can be laid down for its performance."[10] Advocacy of a critical methodology which proceeds according to steps or is hierarchial in any degree would negate Dewey's divergent sympathies. A stepped methodology would be reductive and legalistic. Dewey held that a critical procedure must be fallible and therefore, correctable; that a good method should allow for self-adjustment; and that a sequential ordering of what the critic does would inevitably result in disingenuous analysis.

FAULTS IN SEQUENCED METHODS OF ANALYSIS

For many years determination of a right or correct sequencing of critical methodological inquiry has been a goal of many aestheticians, critics and art writers. With the ubiquitous use of computers in education and the popularity of behavioral psychology many art educators have been the willing followers of a kind of technological, structural formalism. Before suggesting an introductory critical methodology which will avoid such pitfalls, we will examine the problems posed by ordering a critique in steps.

There is a widespread affection for prescriptive, sequenced methodology among teachers of art criticism. The popularity of a stepped critical methodology owes much of its appeal to its progression from simplicity to complexity. Typically, a stepped methodology starts with description or observation, moves to analysis, then interpretation and finally arrives at judgement or evaluation.[11]

It might be argued by advocates of stepped critical methods that there is a natural or inherent pattern which governs what the viewer sees first, second, third . . . etc. This inherent perceptual viewing pattern, then, should govern what is evaluated first. Our examination of art criticism rejects the claim of a natural or an inherent sequence of seeing. It is only reasonable to assume that the complicated nature of the art and the unpredictable personality of the viewer will determine what is noticed first. This would cause the viewing pattern to change with the introduction of a different viewer or artwork.

Ordering an analysis in a progression of increasing complexity would seem a plausible approach. However, upon inspection, we find that relative complexity is too often a matter of personal opinion which fails to control perception by external evidence. A critical analysis based on increasing importance would fail for the same reason.

The most valid ordering of an analysis might deal first with the physical or tangible aspects of a work and then with the philosophical or intangible aspects. This idea is appealing because it is logical and avoids questions of relative importance. Unfortunately though, even this idea has its problems.

Dealing first with the tangible and then with the intangible might prescribe a method which is unnatural to a particular critic or work. Even using the most traditional art as a source, we can find many examples for which it is highly likely that the meaning of the work reaches the viewer's conscious mind long before considerations such as shape and color are even noticed. Another problem posed by this method would be in defining the areas of value that are or are not philosophical. Many would say that color, texture, form, composition and use of materials are tangible qualities, while meaning, universality and form-function balance are intangible. Some would argue that behavior and energy relationships are physical; some would argue that composition and use of materials are philosophical. There would seem to be little point in generating endless debate about such considerations.

Possible rank ordering of the questions asked in criticism is rejected for the reasons just stated. An order or hierarchy of questions is unnecessary. Each critic is advised to use no specific order or to use multiple ordering or simultaneity, whichever suits particular personal needs. Maximum flexibility is proposed because the artwork must be experienced as a whole. It is quite probable that, as the critic discriminates and seeks analytical interrelations, any external pattern of organization will be abandoned. The critic will find that in experiencing an artwork the elements, composition and interpretive meaning are inextricably and simultaneously interwoven. As a result, any structure suitable to both the critic and the artwork is justifiable if it helps the critic in reaching synthesis.

FOR DISCUSSION

1. What are the weaknesses of formalist criticism?
2. When are age and experience inadequate preparation for developing the ability to criticize art?
3. In your own words describe what is wrong with art criticism done by steps?
4. Read and analyze two published art reviews. First, find a writer who uses a formalist approach. Second, find an impressionist art reviewer. Specifically compare the two approaches, then contrast each with the analytical and synthetical approach of John Dewey.

Chapter IV: Towards a Critical Methodology

"I am bound by my own definition of criticism: a disinterested endeavor to learn and propagate the best that is known and thought in the world."

—Matthew Arnold (1861), *On Translating Homer*

Openness and Receptivity

How do we experience an artwork? And how do we critically evaluate art? Openness is a primary precondition for any knowledgeable appreciation of art. An attitude of openness implies a willingness to pay attention to art, or to "let a work happen." Preconceived notions bias the viewer's attention. The open viewer must allow the work to succeed or fail on its own terms. In fact, openness on the part of the viewer makes one receptive to the aesthetic experience offered by the artwork. It is not suggested that the viewer become a perceptual drainage ditch into which any sort of flotsam and jetsam may pass. The openness advocated is not mindless, but rather meditative and reflective, and supports the sort of response and speculation that accompany full understanding. This attitude of openness accompanies a desire to examine, know and verify our experience of art. Openness and receptivity should not be considered the first steps in a sequence of processes required for criticism; instead, they are continuous conditions that must be maintained throughout the critical process.

We respond to artworks according to our view of the world and reality itself. Our response to art is ultimately a matter of who we are and what we value. We are in some sense what we have experienced in life. At times we all carry a heavy baggage of memories with us. Our responses to art are filtered through our personal storehouse of memory and experience. In this way, we attempt to rationally comprehend our responses.

Stimulus for Criticism

When we look at an artwork, what do we see? We may see color, shape and line; identifiable forms or subject matter may also be present. Whatever the exact nature of the artwork, our responses to it are instantaneous, not thought out and measured.

In short, we respond emotionally to the artwork. That emotion may be very positive, very negative or neutral, but we do respond to perceived color, shape and line. We may begin to weigh one quality of the work against another according to some pattern of thought, but our initial like or dislike of the artwork is a matter of our emotional and spontaneous responses. If we are pressed to justify our first response to an artwork, we may only be able to reply in confusion that we "really have not thought it out."

Let us assume that we are looking at an artwork, and the work evokes a response. What has actually happened? We have begun experiencing the work. Our responses may raise more questions than they answer. If the artwork interests us sufficiently, we go beyond our initial response. We attempt to answer our questions and account for our interest. This accounting may be mostly intuitive, or it may take the more sophisticated, systematic form of a specific critical methodology. Whether the appreciator/critic relies on intuition or logic for understanding artwork, it should be remembered that no recipe or method can replace the value of the whole, interrelated experience of the art itself. Whatever mental and/or emotional processes govern the creation and appreciation of art, they are still mysterious and will probably remain so, at least until electrophysiologists, neurologists and psychologists learn much more about the human brain.

This text does not postulate critical analysis by logically necessary sequential steps. Instead, criticism is recognized as multidirectional, non-procedural, non-linear and, perhaps, simultaneous.

The critic, as an adjunct to the direct experience of art, should depend on knowledge which is indispensable for judgement. Three sources of information are sufficient for critical practice: knowledge of the defining properties of the art in question, knowledge of the areas of possible critical evaluation and a knowledge or sense of aesthetic value. Admittedly, the last source is subjective, but this text rejects the possibility or desirablilty of a fully prescribed, sequential, objective methodology.

Knowledge Required for Criticism

Good critical or analytical practice depends on three primary sources of knowledge. First, knowledge is required to identify the defining qualities of any work in question. For instance, a paleolithic artifact has certain characteristics which distinguish it from a neolithic artifact or from anything else. An etching and a drawing possess qualities which identify each as unique. The distinguishing factors or defining qualities of any work to be evaluated must be clearly understood and articulated. Second, knowledge of the possible areas of critical evaluation is required to engage in effective criticism. Although the possible areas of critical evaluation may vary from one artwork to another, most works can be analyzed in terms of the art elements, use of materials, meaning and other factors. Third, knowledge of artworks and a knowledge or sense of aesthetic value is also requisite to critical practice. The development of a knowledge of aesthetic value may be enhanced by study and experience.

DEFINING QUALITIES OF THE ARTWORK

A historical illustration of the significance of defining the artwork by its inherent properties may prove useful. Former President of the United States, Theodore Roosevelt, wrote a critique for *The Outlook* in March, 1913, after he attended the famous New York Armory Show. It is important to understand that Roosevelt was responding to a show of experimental European art. The 1913 Armory Show was the first large scale exhibition of modern European art to be shown in America. Roosevelt wrote as follows:

> *In this recent art exhibition the lunatic fringe was fully in evidence, especially in the rooms devoted to the Cubists and Futurists, or Near-Impressionists. There is no reason why people should not call themselves Cubists, or Octagonists, or Parallelopedonists, or Knights of the Isosceles Triangle, or Brothers of the Cosine, if they so desire; as expressing anything serious and permanent, one term is as fatuous as another. Take the picture which for some reason is called "A naked man going down stairs."* [Nude Descending A Staircase *by Marcel Duchamp] There is in my bathroom a really good Navajo rug which, on any proper interpretation of the Cubist theory, is a far more satisfactory and decorative picture. Now if, for some inscrutable reason, it suited somebody to call this rug a picture of, say, "A well—dressed man going up a ladder," the name would fit the facts just about as well as in the case of the Cubist picture of the "Naked man going down stairs." From the standpoint of terminology, each name would have whatever merit inheres in a rather cheap straining after effect; and from the standpoint of decorative value, of sincerity, and of artistic merit, the Navajo rug is infinitely ahead of the picture.*[1]

The President was pointed and witty in his criticism. However, from the standpoint of sound analytical practice, he failed to sufficiently define what he saw. He compared Duchamp's work, (Figure 4-1) an oil painting on canvas, with a Navajo rug, a hand woven textile (Figure 4-2). The qualities that characterize or define an oil painting are quite different from those which define a hand woven textile. These differences would necessarily invite a different approach to subject matter and composition in each instance. The painter has freedom within the Cubist framework. The Navajo weaver, given the warp and weft of the loom, explores the breadth of tribal tradition. Each art form imposes limits and liabilities, and each offers a certain latitude and

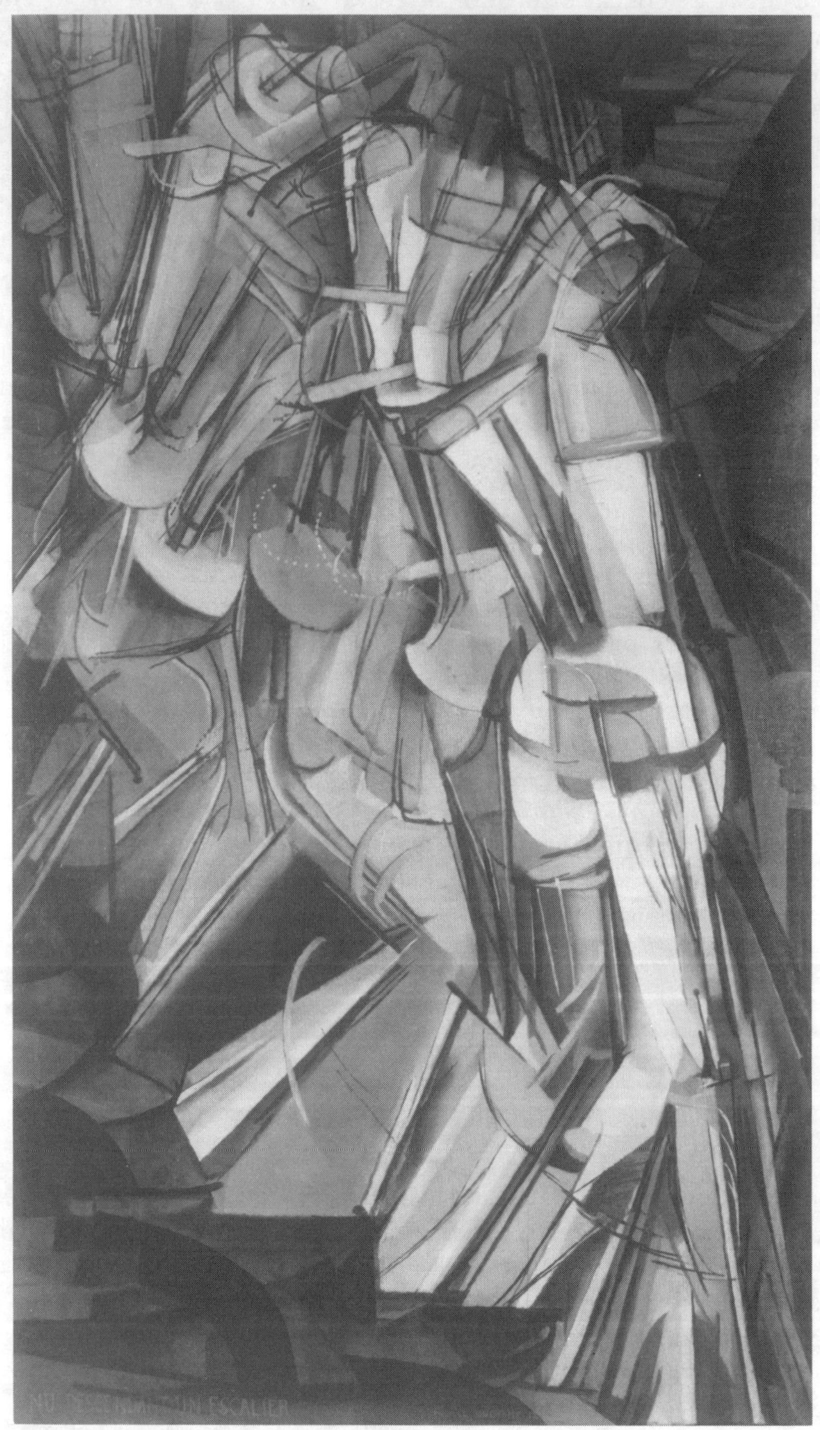

Figure 4-1: *Nude Descending a Staircase, No. 2,*
Marcel Duchamp, 1912, oil on canvas, 58" x 35",
Philadelphia Museum of Art.

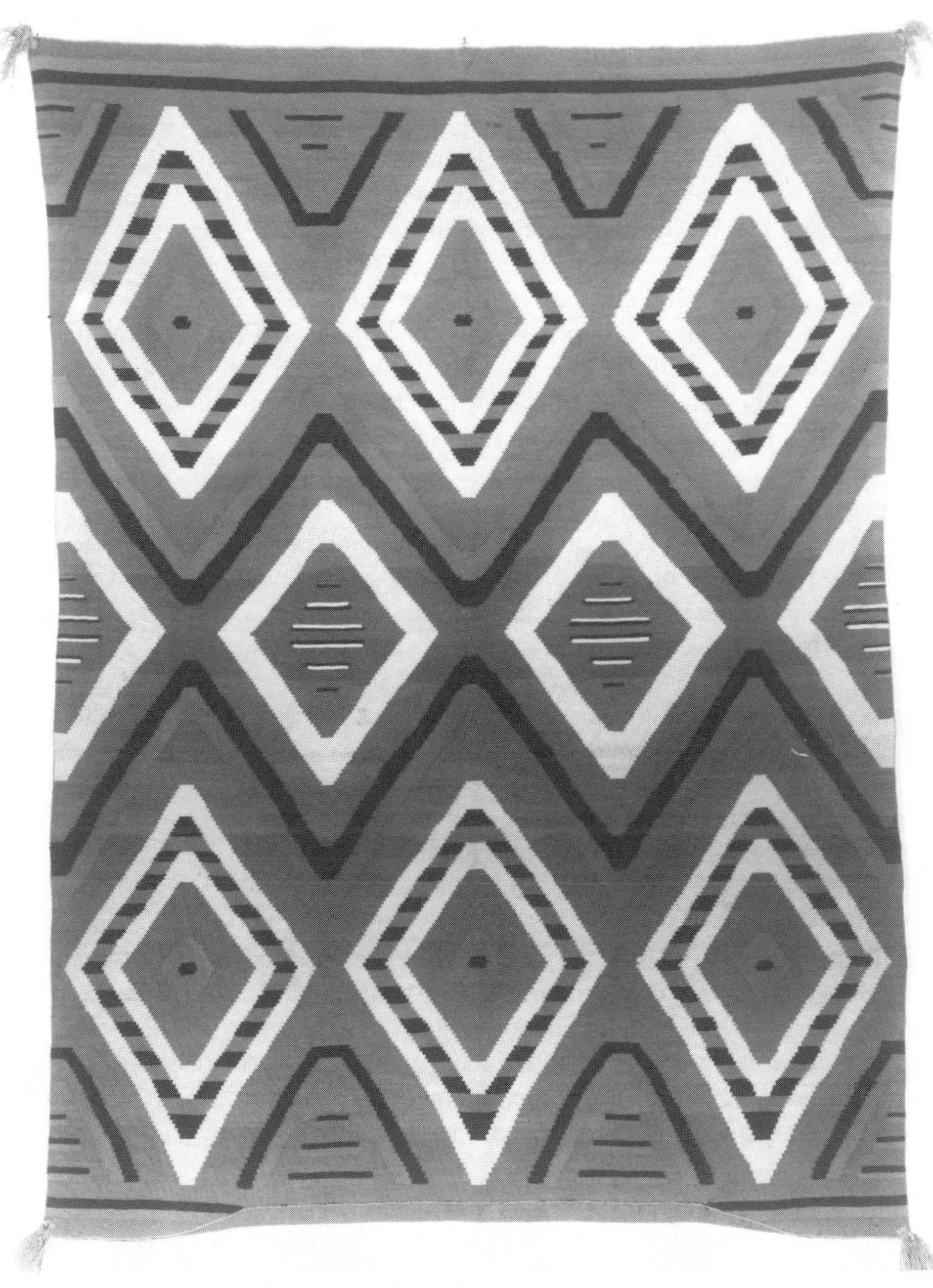

Figure 4-2: Navajo, Arizona, 1860–1870, serape, Late Classical, wool, 69 3/4" x 52 1/4", The Nelson-Atkins Museum of Art, Kansas City, Missouri (Nelson Fund) 33-1431.

advantage. To ignore the distinctive qualities of each art form answers the question of value and artistic merit based on little more than subjective and emotional liking and disliking. This is exactly what Roosevelt did when he labeled Duchamp's *Nude Descending a Staircase* as "rather cheap" and the rug as sincere.

What defines an artwork? Those qualities that make a work particularly and distinctively what it is are the qualities which define it. Two basic sources of information can serve as references for identifying an artwork's unique qualities: studies of (1) media and techniques and (2) cultural milieu and history.

Study of art media and the technical processes employed by artists can be a daunting enterprise. However, rational appreciation and the critic's judicious temperament frequently depend upon a knowledge of the advantages and limitations of materials and techniques. The advantages of technical knowledge to intelligent appreciation and criticism can hardly be over estimated. Given the impracticality, for most of us, of a lifetime of technical education, the appreciator of art can gain adequate knowledge from an introductory-level study of the processes of traditional and newer forms of art. The traditional art forms are architecture, sculpture, crafts, drawing, graphics and painting. Each of these art forms has been radically altered by technological developments. The nineteenth-century genesis of the Industrial Revolution in Europe and then in America fostered research into new art forms and materials. The so-called second Industrial Revolution, a revolution of automation, has resulted in the current eminence of high technology in photography, cinema, television, computation and the design disciplines.

Artistic practice is indelibly marked by the interface of cultural milieu and historical circumstance. A knowledge of historical periods, countries, social and political institutions, religious movements and traditional uses of materials and techniques helps define artwork and provide the groundwork for analysis. The critic is cautioned, however, about the potential irrelevancies of historical knowledge during criticism. Historical references are useful only when they relate directly to something perceptible in a specific work being analyzed. The fact that Vincent Van Gogh mutilated himself would be of only incidental relevance to an analysis of any of his paintings, except possibly a self-portrait. During analysis, all references to history, media and techniques are meaningful only when they are seen within the context of the work itself.

THE EVALUATIVE CRITERIA

The critical areas which apply to most forms of expression in the arts might be described as follows:

- The elements of visual art structure: line, shape, color, texture, value, and space.
- The compositional principles of art: form, balance, rhythm, repetition, dominance, and subordinance.
- The use of materials, techniques, craftsmanship.

- The balance of form and function (especially useful for utilitarian art forms such as ceramics, architecture and furniture).
- The energy relationships or movement.
- The meaning or universal significance.

In Chapter VII we will discuss the elements of art and the compositional principles of art. At this point we will discuss the aesthetic qualities of additional areas: use of materials, techniques and craftsmanship, form-function balance, energy relationships and meaning and universality. Each of these evaluative areas is indispensable for fully understanding specific aesthetic situations.

Use of Materials, Techniques and Craftsmanship

The use of materials in a work of art has been a traditional point of assessment. Is the choice of material suitable to the work? To answer this question the viewer must know the properties and applications of materials. The material determines the appropriateness of its use. For example, the use of steel as a primary structural unit for building suspension bridges is fitting and necessary because of the bridge's function and because of steel's tensile strength. Using glazes in painting that requires transparency is better than diluting a fundamentally opaque painting medium such as egg tempera.

An example of the appropriate material for an artwork is Andrea Del Verrocchio's choice of bronze for his *Equestrian Monument of Colleoni* (Figure 4-3). Bronze was the only material that would have provided the tensile strength Verrocchio needed to successfully cast his thirteen-foot, freestanding sculpture. If the sculptor had chosen to work in marble, he would have courted disaster. The weight and inadequate compressive strength of brittle stone would have made the material useless. It is inconceivable that a horse's thin legs carved in any stone could support a massive body weighing tons. Only a carving in relief would make stone the best material for a large scale equestrian subject. The monumental granite equestrian relief carving on Stone Mountain, Georgia, (Figure 4-4) represents an appropriate marriage of material and concept. A clumsy and insensitive handling or poor selection of materials inevitably mars an artwork.

Technical analysis is an important tool of art criticism. A study of how a work was executed provides the viewer with clues to understanding. When judging a work's quality in terms of craftsmanship, it is good to remember that a well-crafted work may lack expressive power or that a powerfully expressive work may lack technical finesse. The viewer must ask, "Does the workmanship in this work add to or detract from its overall effectiveness?"

Form-Function Balance

In traditional critical analysis form-function balance usually has been applied to architecture and crafts. Critical analysis of form-function balance has

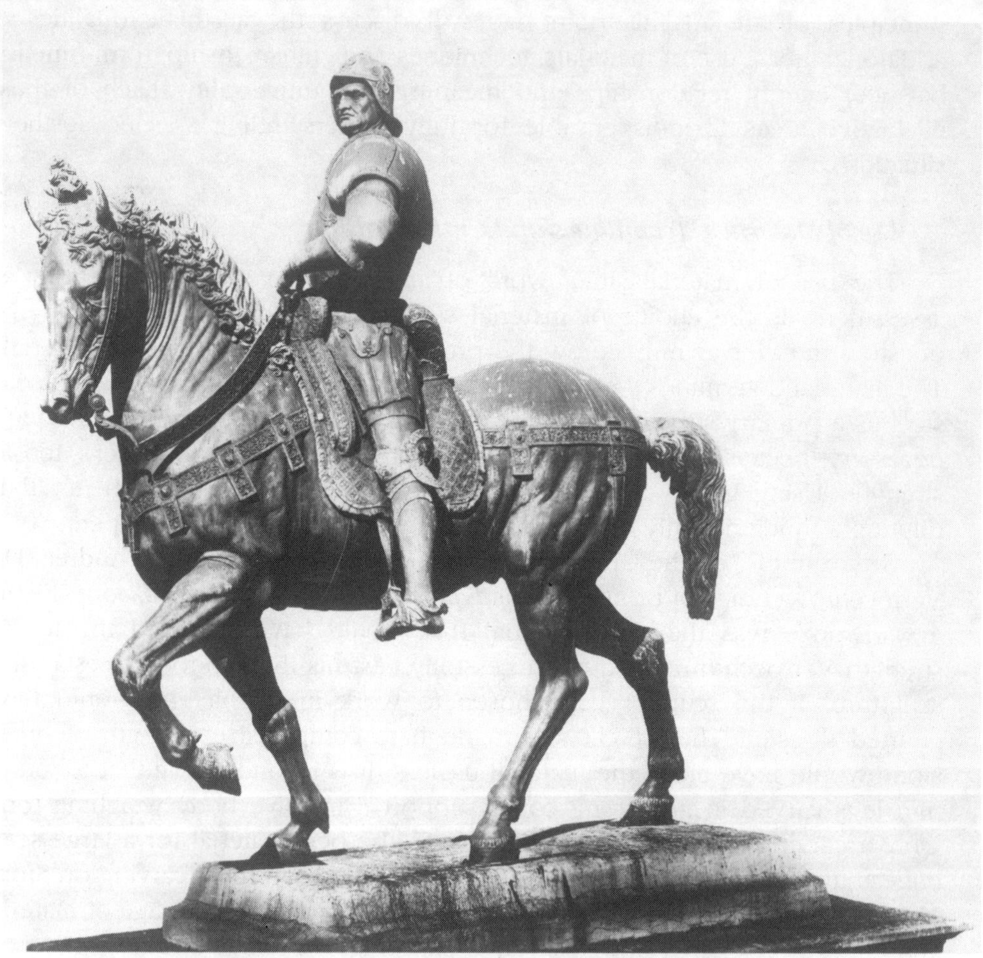

Figure 4-3: *Equestrian Monument of Colleoni,*
Andrea Del Verrochio, 1483–88, bronze, height c.13',
Campo SS. Giovanni e Paolo, Venice, (Alinari/Art Resources, NY).

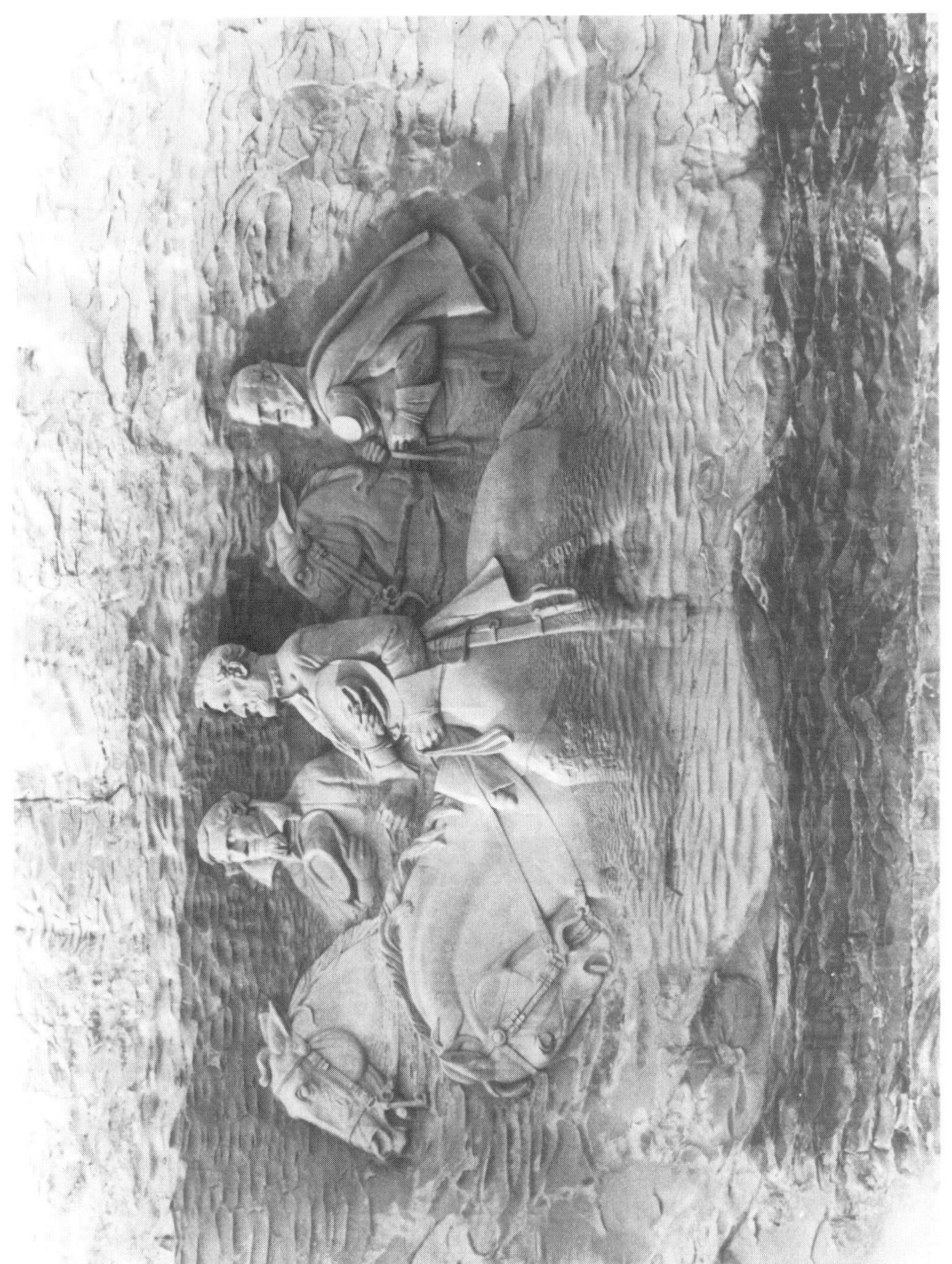

Figure 4-4: Stone Mountain Memorial, Augustus Lukeman, Walter Hancock, and Roy Faulkner, 1915–1970, Stone Mountain, Georgia, 90' x 190'.

wider applicability today and must include art media such as sculpture, graphic design and environmental design. To judge the balance of form and function in a work of art the viewer must determine the extent to which the form complements the function for which the work is intended. A convenient illustration of form-function balance is building design construction. A building designed for the purpose of warehousing huge crates should not resemble a wedge-shaped high-rise apartment building. The difficulty of moving crates in and out of elevators and up and down levels would waste effort and resources. A ground-level, rectilinear structure is more functional for warehousing needs. Unfortunately, the relationship of form to function is not usually such an obvious one. If the form of a Gothic church, for instance, was meant to give our sensibilities spiritual uplift, the precise nature of that spiritual uplift might be a very personal matter, and therefore judgement of the adequacy of the form for the function could be difficult to assess. To the extent that this same church was built to meet objective specifications such as, a hall for singing, an arena for weekly rituals, or an educational center for the community's youth, the building's adequacy can be judged.

Energy Relationships

Perception of energy relationships in artwork should be considered a potential area of analytical depth in criticism. To understand energy relationships in art we need to envision art occurring along an energy continuum. This means characterizing our perception of artwork in terms of the work's degree of movement. At one extreme of this energy continuum would be artwork expressing implied movement, while the opposite extreme of the continuum would include artwork which is operatively active. The traditional distinction between potential and kinetic energy used in physics provides a useful analytical tool for the critic.

Implied energy, or potential energy, results from a work's conformation or its composition. An artwork usually does not actually move, but it often suggests movement through its organization of mass or shapes. Myron's sculpture, the *Discus Thrower* (Figure 4-5), expresses or suggests a great deal about physical motion by virtue of its conformation. A Cubist painting such as Marcel Duchamp's *Nude Descending a Staircase* (Figure 4-1) suggests the movement of a form sequentially descending from the upper left corner of the composition to the lower right. The implication of movement and energy in an artwork may have much to do with our perception of the work's organization and coherence.

Operational energy, or kinetic energy, is expressed in certain works of art, principally sculpture, through physical motion. For instance, the mobiles of George Rickey are actually moved by external forces such as currents of air or the touch of a hand (Figure 4-6). High technology systems art also moves, but the movement is generally driven or controlled internally. Kinetic movement in art is primarily a contemporary expression of a technologically based aesthetic and, as such, provides an orientation for critical evaluation.

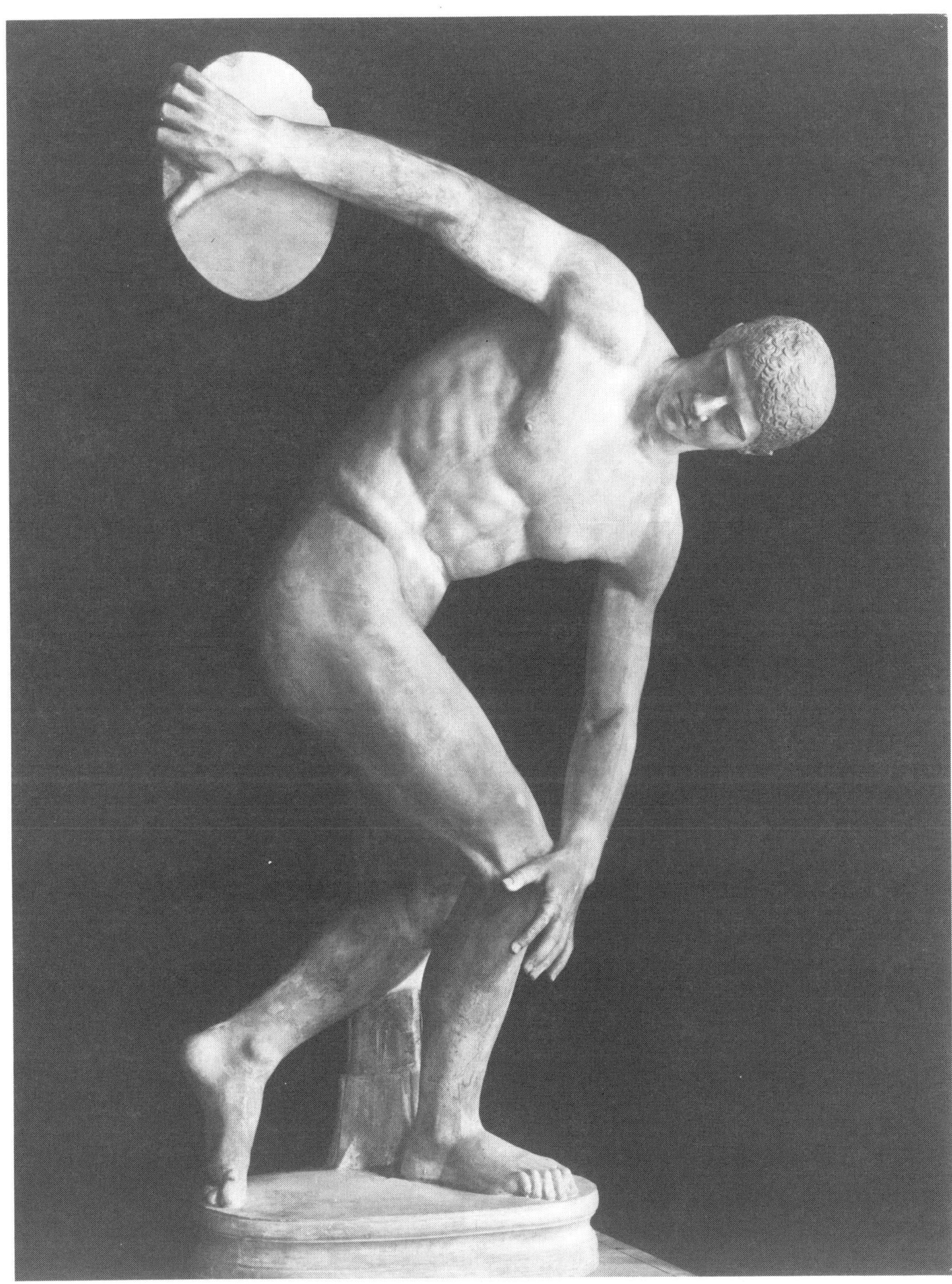

Figure 4-5: *Discobulus (Discus Thrower),* Myron, c. 450 B.C., Roman marble copy after a Greek bronze original, Museo delle Terme, Rome, (Alinari/Art Resource, NY).

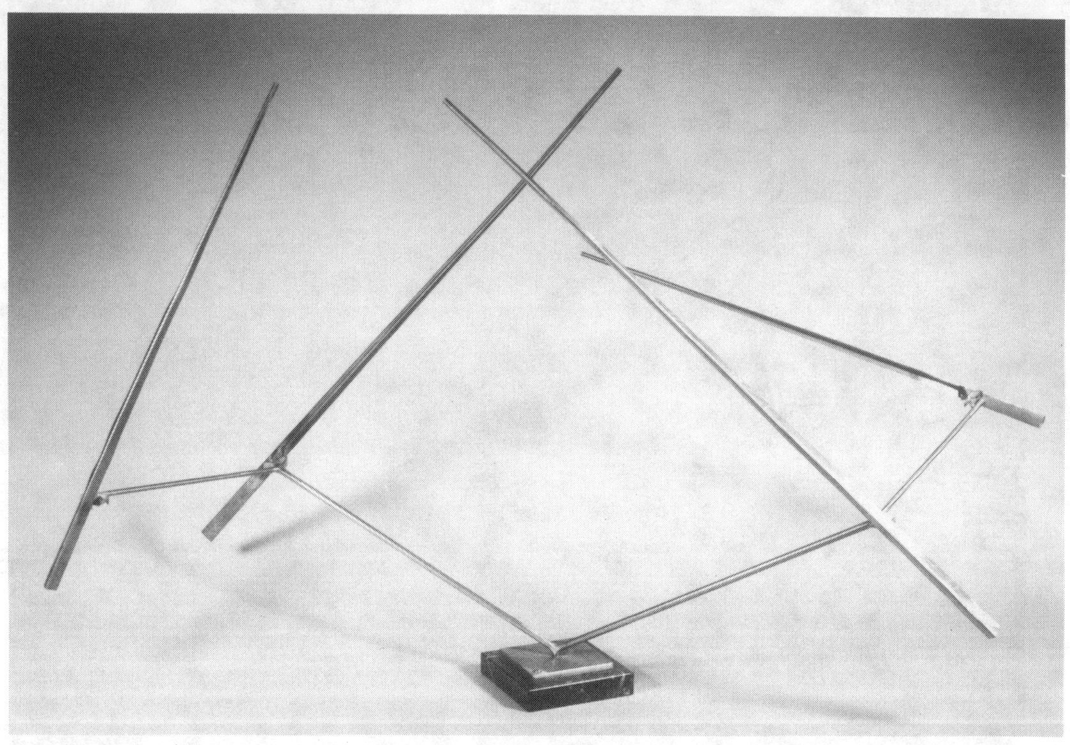

Figure 4-6: *Four Lines W/Z*, George Rickey, 1975,
stainless steel, 19" x 10" x 35", Georgia Museum of Art, Athens, Georgia.

Meaning and Universality

Discovering what a work of art means and interpreting that meaning is often difficult. Interpretation is the most challenging area of critical evaluation but should not be considered as a separate activity unrelated to the overall experience of the artwork. Determining what a work means is not a matter of simply finding verbal equivalents; words are no substitute for aesthetic experience. We must experience the work, allowing it to communicate to us in its own terms.

When we reduce aesthetic experience to a search for meaning, translating images into concepts, we risk a loss of imagination. As psychologist James Hillman writes,

> *"We sin against the imagination whenever we ask an image for its meaning, requiring that images be translated into concepts. The coiled snake in the corner cannot be translated into my fear, my sexuality, and my mother-complex without killing the snake. We do not hear music, touch sculpture or read stories with meaning in mind, but for the sake of the imagination. Though art may hide a multitude of psychological ignorances, at least it does not ask images what they mean. Interpretations and even amplifications of images, including the whole analytical kit of symbolic dictionaries and ethnological parallels, too often become instruments of allegory. Rather than vivifying the imagination by connecting our conceptual intellects with the images of dreams and fantasies, they exchange the image for a commentary on it or a digest of it. And these interpretations forget too that they are themselves fantasies induced by the image, no more meaningful than the image itself."*[2]

Speculation about the meaning of images must not be a substitute for our experience of the art work. If we exchange direct perception of the image for an interpretation of it forgetting that our speculations are grounded in the image we enter a world of free form fantasy and personal whimsy.

Our initial understanding of a work may come about intuitively without conscious effort on our part. Such unconscious realizations may take place at any time, even long after we have ceased consciously thinking about the work. Sometimes a work will remind us of something we have seen before or read about, or may evoke very real sensations of touch or sound or smell. It would not be unusual for a *trompe l'oeil* painting of apples to activate our salivary glands. Such sensations can lead us to the very heart of a work's meaning. Composition and subject matter imagery contribute to interpretive meaning. Associations with life experience, both past and present, help us account for a work's impact upon our vision. Our understanding of a work's impact grows as we are able to give general form to our specific perceptions.

Sometimes the easiest way to give general form to our perceptions is through formulation of hypotheses about the artwork. We test a hypothesis by checking it against the data of perception. If a hypothesis is supported, we affirm it; if not, we abandon it. Hypotheses are usually formulated quite naturally, unintentionally and, perhaps, even subconsciously. Hypotheses may simultaneously integrate areas of critical evaluation or may be drawn from ancillary facts about the artist, literature, religion, history, science and other factors which may have influenced the artwork.

SENSE OF AESTHETIC VALUE

A sense of aesthetic value is, perhaps, the most essential and most elusive source of knowledge required for art criticism. Study of aesthetics, a field of normative philosophy, is helpful. However, normative philosophy is based in societal standards, established mores, customs and traditions, whereas art criticism is frequently required to confront avant garde works that violate accepted norms. In cases where critics were ruled by a static interpretation of aesthetics and aesthetic value, they failed to recognize the worth of innovative works. *The Salon des Refusés* (Exhibition of the Rejected in Paris, 1863) was authorized by Napoleon III only after various of the great artists of the period had been consistently condemned by the Imperial Directorate of Fine Arts.[3]

Openness and receptivity are part of a valid sense of aesthetic value and function to prevent unjustified bias. Accurately defining the artwork and recognizing the areas of critical evaluation support valid perception, but a sense of aesthetic value remains the missing link in critical discernment.

One way a sense of aesthetic value can be developed is through exposure to great art and attention to its analysis and contemplation by others. It is doubtful that a sense of aesthetic value is developed passively; its development is an active pursuit. Even given opportunity and effort, it must be admitted that a sense of aesthetic value may be dependent on an intangible ability innate in mankind.

Just as creativity, according to Dewey, involves an undefined intuitive process, aesthetic discrimination may involve a similar undefined process, perhaps a sixth sense.[4] Fortunately, it is reasonable to assume that the intuitive process requisite to creativity, in some way, parallels an analogous process requisite to aesthetic discrimination. Because all people are capable of creativity it is not unreasonable to assume they are also capable of aesthetic discrimination. Aptitude for criticism, similar to that for creativity, then becomes a matter of degree based partially on talent, but largely on education, effort and experience. Just as few artists are great, few critics are great but those who apply themselves to the pursuit may certainly become sensitive and competent appreciators of art through the exercise of critical faculties.

Confirmation of the Critical Process

The critic should resist any temptation to rush to judgement. Analyses developed under strict limitations of time and pressing circumstances are often premature and ill-considered. When journalistic critics draw conclusions they are frequently hasty in their judgement because of publication deadlines which must be met.

Like scientific research, art criticism tries to unify disparate elements into a single concept or focus. This synthesizing process requires time and reflection. Since a single viewing or experiencing of an artwork may not be sufficient to fully absorb the work's expressive content, the critic will often profit from repeated viewings of the artwork in question. The repeated viewing or confirmation viewing of an artwork engages the critic in an act of re-seeing and re-synthesizing. Re-synthesis may add new dimensions to the critic's initial viewing of the work. Each viewing of an artwork carries with it particulars of time and place. The way we feel on a given day influences what we see and what we pay attention to. The atmosphere surrounding the critic affects his concentration. From viewing to viewing our ability to see artwork varies. This variance may seem superfluous, but circumstances internal and external to the critic can decisively affect judgement. Multiple viewings of artwork which are analyzed, understood and fully appreciated help secure our conclusions.

For Discussion

1. Do you always have a response to the art you see? Are you honest with yourself concerning your responses to artwork? Why bother criticizing artwork which you do not enjoy?
2. Explain why it is important for the art critic to distinguish one kind of style or expression of art from another.
3. Cast yourself in the role of the art teacher. A professional artist has loaned a painting to your school for display. The painting consists of two large circles of color, one red and the other green. The circles overlap slightly revealing a segment of neutral gray. You want your students to respond to the work aesthetically. How will you assist the student whose only response is "I do not like the painting."?

Chapter V: Meaning: A Series of Interpretive Moments

"Criticism is properly the rod of divination: a hazel switch for the discovery of buried treasure, not a birch twig for the castigation of offenders."

—Arthur Symons (1906), *An Introduction into the Study of Browning, preface*

Examples

The following notes, or "moments," are not exhaustive demonstrations of the type of critical analysis advocated in this text. Instead, these notes are examples that emphasize one aspect of critical evaluation and one component in written criticisms: **speculating on the meaning** of the artwork. Many appreciators of art and beginning critics have difficulty with interpretation. The notes below are examples of the author's experience of meaning in several works.

An Ideal and Practical Beauty: The Willendorf Venus:

If we could transform ourselves from modern beings to paleolithic artists working deep in the recesses of a cave in France or Spain, who would we become? Intellectually, would we be simple, childlike primitives? Would we be crude, savage creatures? Or would we be individuals having the same potential for sensitivity and perceptual insights as men and women of other ages? The fragments of ancient imagery we possess tell us of a people who were frequently artistically sophisticated and observant, not crude.

Cavern walls and rock surfaces covered with painted and incised images of animals reveal an artistic hand and eye that noted details and often rendered form with surprisingly accurate proportions. Deer, horses, cattle and bison are drawn using sure, vigorous outlines filled in with subtle shading of reds, ochers and black.

Ancient image making was not confined to a few cave walls in France and Spain. Small, carved stone statuettes have been discovered at sites throughout the world. When these small figures project the image of a woman they are called "Venuses"; The *Venus of Willendorf* (Chapter 2, Figure 2-1) is an image of this type measuring less than six inches in length, small enough to be held easily in the palm of the hand.

The *Venus of Willendorf* may look, at first, like little more than a misshapen lump of stone, but it is an image of feminine beauty, defined functionally in terms of plant and animal fertility. Perhaps it served its owner and maker as a good luck charm or as a ritual object meant to bring forth a bountiful harvest or a large and healthy family.

The swollen breasts, the wide pelvis and the general corpulence of the Venus lead some scholars to see Paleolithic Venuses as symbols of life-giving and nurturing, as the mother of earth and of mankind. This heavy-bodied little figure could effortlessly carry her young through gestation to birth.

The ancient carver of the Venus would have understood, intuitively if not consciously, the significance of his creation's attributes. His understanding may have been based on experience and observation, but it must also have been based on traditionally held values and on commonly known tool use learned from his elders. Such a view is reflective of the well-documented practices of nineteenth and twentieth century tribal wood carvers such as the African bushmen and Australian aborigines.

It may seem peculiar to suggest today that the Venus represents prehistoric, tribal man's ideal of feminine beauty. Because of her corpulence the Venus hardly reflects the manikin-like proportions exemplified by contemporary feminine beauties. But, for ancient man, beauty and fertility (function) were inextricably united. The beautiful woman was the mother, the bearer of children, the giver of life. A pragmatic case can be made for the *Venus of Willendorf* being a model of perfect womanhood.

Try to imagine being in France 25,000 years ago and being a member of a nomadic family. Movement from place to place would depend upon where plants were bearing fruit and where herds of animals were grazing. A pregnant or recently pregnant female of your tribe, physically built like the *Venus of Willendorf*, would have to travel for many days on foot with perhaps very little food. All of her extra adipose tissue would provide nourishment for her and her baby when food was scarce. Given this perspective, it is not hard to understand the Venus as an ideal. Our imaginary Venus is an ideal which is both aesthetic and practical.

THE SOUL OF A DISCUS THROWER

Although Myron's lost original bronze version of *Discobolus (Discus Thrower)* (Chapter 4, Figure 4-5) is known only through carved marble copies, its harmony and formal unity is striking. The work has a rhythmic flow suggestive of rich, mellow musical tones. Despite its flowing rhythms and formal harmonies *Discobolus* remains something of a mystery. It is surely an idealization of the male body in motion, but to what end is nature idealized and beautified? I suggest, with Plato, that while obvious visual beauty may be present, the highest or best end of Man's nature is soul, and it is Plato's rational principle of soul which Myron first cast in bronze and which is preserved for us in stone.

The epic poet Homer provides support for this interpretation in his *Odyssey.* A passage from the eighth book tells how Odysseus, challenged and goaded by Phaiakian youths, picks up a discus and tosses it well beyond his nearest competitor. On the way to demonstrating his preeminence, Homer's hero also delivers a speech to the young Phaiakians concerning the nature of the true Greek concept of noble manhood. In his speech he down-plays youth and fine physique in favor of intelligence. After his speech, and after lamenting his age, pain and cramped condition, he hurls the discus an awesome distance winning both the point of his speech and the competition. Odysseus reconciles athleticism with soul in this episode.

Today's typical vision of idealized manhood inclines toward the popular culture view which extols youthful athleticism, dieting, body culture and fitness fads. The Greek god of today in the popular mind is likely to be a college-aged, muscle-bound youth, not a middle-aged discus thrower.

Homer's tale is instructive because it alters our perception of both modern and ancient ideals of manhood. Odysseus is seen by the Phaiakians as not old and, yet, not young. The reader knows that long years of imprisonment mark the hero as middle-aged when his story begins. Time and time again in the *Odyssey,* with the Goddess Athena's help, Odysseus overcomes aches, pains, enfeeblement and self-doubt to successfully meet one heroic challenge after another. No obstacle, age or physical condition stops this hero. Perhaps the most arresting qualities possessed by Odysseus are not physical but are rather qualities of character or soul, as Plato calls it.

Throughout his poem, Homer calls Odysseus, "the great tactician," "the noble and enduring man" and "man of ranging mind." It is easy to dismiss these tributes as formalities, rather than understanding them as qualities of mind and spirit, qualities of the ideal Greek. *Discobulus* speaks indirectly to us through Homer and Plato, telling us that substance is more than mere youthful, athletic energy; it is a sum greater than all the qualities which a man may display before others on any single occasion. The figures of both Odysseus and *Discobulus* stand as ideals poised and energized, a perfect balance of physical energy and spiritual substance or soul.

BLACK LINES, NO. 189

In Wassily Kandinsky's *Black Lines, No. 189,* (Colorplate 1) the eye searches for some thread of identifiable subject matter, but there is none. The viewer finds no familiar vestige of past experience, except possibly an earlier experience of another non-objective work of art or certain microscopic or technological objects which were not known in 1913. Separated from the familiar, the viewer must confront this work on its own terms. That means allowing the painting to be self-expressive through its colors, lines and forms.

My first view of the painting was of an oversized doodle generated by a probable megalomaniac possessing no sense of line and color harmony. Later, I returned to *Black Lines, No. 189* for a second look. I still did not much like the painting. I felt it was to Kandinsky's credit, judging from his title, that he did not promise much. Black lines were all that I found in the work, but, with time, there was more. It occurred to me, and I laughed at the thought, that Kandinsky had painted an allegory of my day. Here was a cacophony of color and line constituting an overlay of near disasters finally hurtling off into nothingness like so many expended balls of phosphorescent color from a Roman candle.

The oil painting is on an exactly square canvas (50-3/8" x 50-3/8"). It is a conglomerate of soft-edged, rounded shapes painted in various shades of the three primary colors plus green, violet and orange. Superimposed over the colored shapes are a variety of black lines. The placement of the black lines appears to be almost random, although some of the lines tend to follow the contours of several of the colored shapes rather closely.

Black Lines, No. 189 is a work which moves and changes constantly. Some of the colored shapes appear to advance spatially while others seem to recede. The viewer who is looking for order and systematic representation will be disappointed by this freely inventive, improvised work. The artist traces the free play of line as it strides confidently forward, hesitates, skips, leaps or grinds to a halt. A line is a mere scratch or a scrawl in one place and is a fibrous, bristling bundle in another. Line is repetitious, hard and persistent in one section of the work and wandering and virtually non-existent in another.

No pattern governs the way I see this work. My eye plays over the surface, finding here and there a momentary resting place, an invitation or a rejection. My eye never rests for very long on one spot.

I would not go so far as to say that Kandinsky's painting grows on you; it is simply there, perhaps ready for you if you are ready for it. The painting seems always different somehow—or perhaps I am different. Can a painting register barometric pressures and other things of that sort? I wonder!

THE FRIENDLY GREY COMPUTER— STAR GAUGE MODEL 54

The Friendly Grey Computer (Figure 5-1) by Edward Kienholz is, essentially, a metal chassis set on rockers with several active lights and motors forming the semblance of a face. The work plays upon a latent fear people have about the super human capabilities of computers. This computer is not of the infallible variety. It supposedly has emotions and is susceptible to problems which are characteristic of the human personality. At the same time, this work may be identified as some potentially dangerous species.

Kienholz displays the following directions for operating the *Friendly Grey Computer*:

> *Flashing yellow bulb indicates positive answer. Flashing blue bulb indicates negative answer. Green jewel button doesn't*

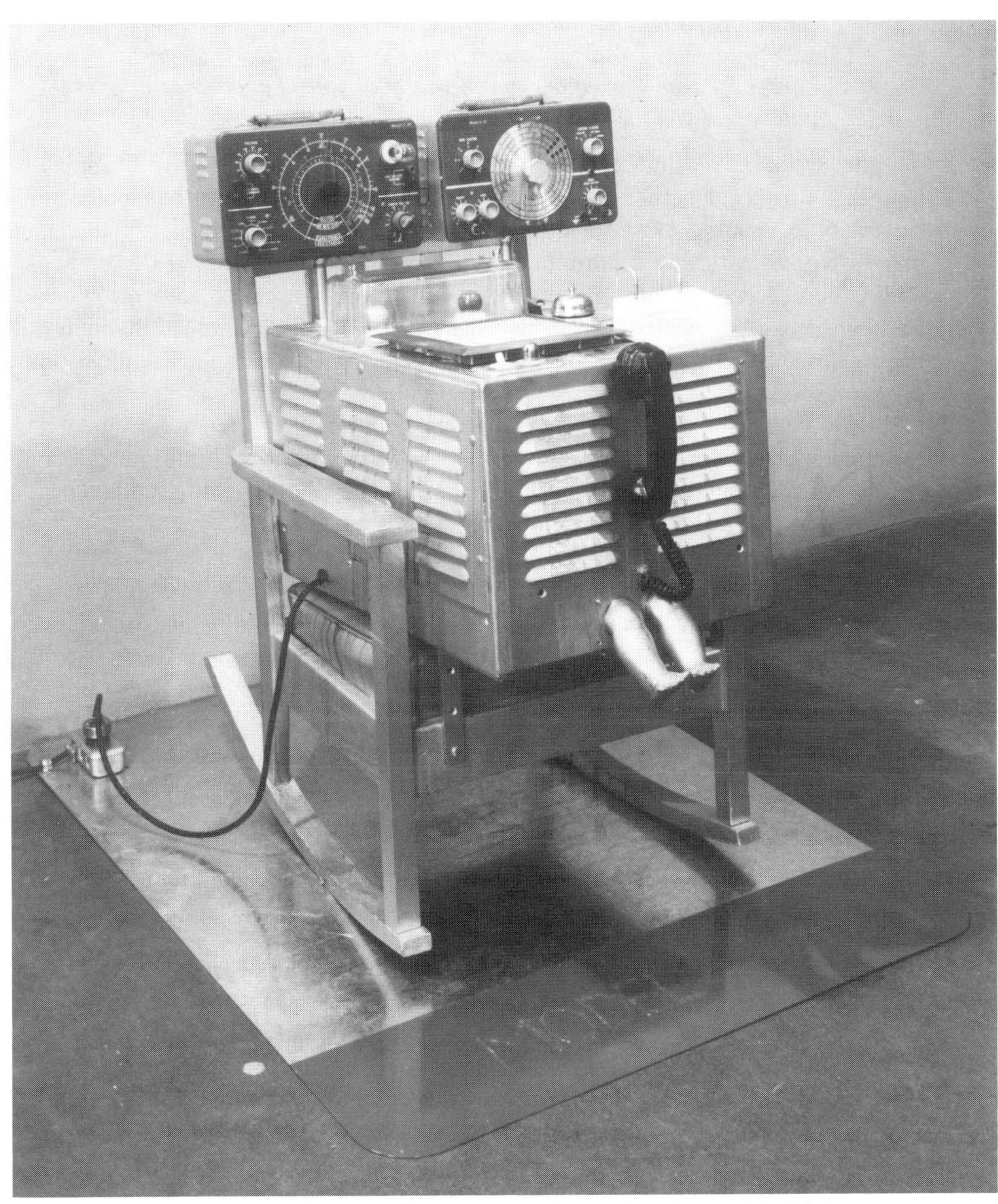

Figure 5-1: *The Friendly Grey Computer—Star Gauge Model 54,*
Edward Kienholz, 1965, 40" x 39 1/8" x 24 1/4", The Museum of Modern Art, NY.

> *light so it will not indicate anything. Computers sometimes get fatigued and have nervous breakdowns, hence the chair for it to rest in. If you know your computer well, you can tell when it's tired and sort of blue and in a funky mood. If such a condition seems imminent, turn rocker switch on for ten or twenty minutes. Your computer will love it and work all the harder for you. Remember that if you treat your computer well it will treat you well.*[1]

The work is a kind of pathetic, comic mutant, functionally complete neither as an organism nor as a machine. As a machine it has only the capability of issuing positive or negative answers to inquiries, not a very impressive showing for a computer, but perhaps a comment on binary systems. Even the yes or no answers given are pre-programmed into the work. This program is repetitive and is closed to external stimuli. Questions merely trigger a mechanism which illuminates the yellow or blue bulb. Kienholz did program the work to give more yes than no answers.

As an organism, the work is a frail and psychologically dependent incubator child, forever soliciting the sympathy, goodwill and good humor of gallery patrons. Additionally, there is an implication of psychological dependence in the work's umbilical tie to a prominently displayed electrical outlet.

The work's emotional impact upon the viewer is immediate and conflicting. You are perceptually bombarded by incongruities such as a rocking chair, doll's legs, a computer chassis crudely painted with aluminum pigment. How are these disparate elements to be ordered in the viewer's mind? It will probably suffice to consider the work's subject matter polemical in content, pointing to the dehumanization of man. Considered as a portrait, the work depicts man as the bastard son of a society preoccupied with technology and its byproducts. Man is identified as a curious, comic mixture of that which makes him sympathetically human and that which threatens to make him inhuman.

Joined in the Phenomenon of Life[2]

I had worked late at the studio; it was sometime past midnight. I was walking home when it started to rain. I was tired, had no coat, and was a little annoyed by the weather. It was not a cold rain. In fact, the weather was unseasonably warm for early spring. Oddly enough, the wetter I got the less annoyance I felt.

As I walked, for no particular reason, a picture flashed through my mind of a rusted piece of steel sculpture I had seen of David Smith's. For the sculptor, iron, air and moisture form a sometimes unhappy compound, rust. That was not the case with Smith's work. *Voltri-Bolton IV* (Figure 5-2), I remembered, seemed to tower like a rust-red sentinel where it stood. While rust may be theoretically a measure of destruction, for Smith, it had the pulsating warmth of blood; it was the sort of pre-cultural symbol of life force which Smith so often had aspired to create.

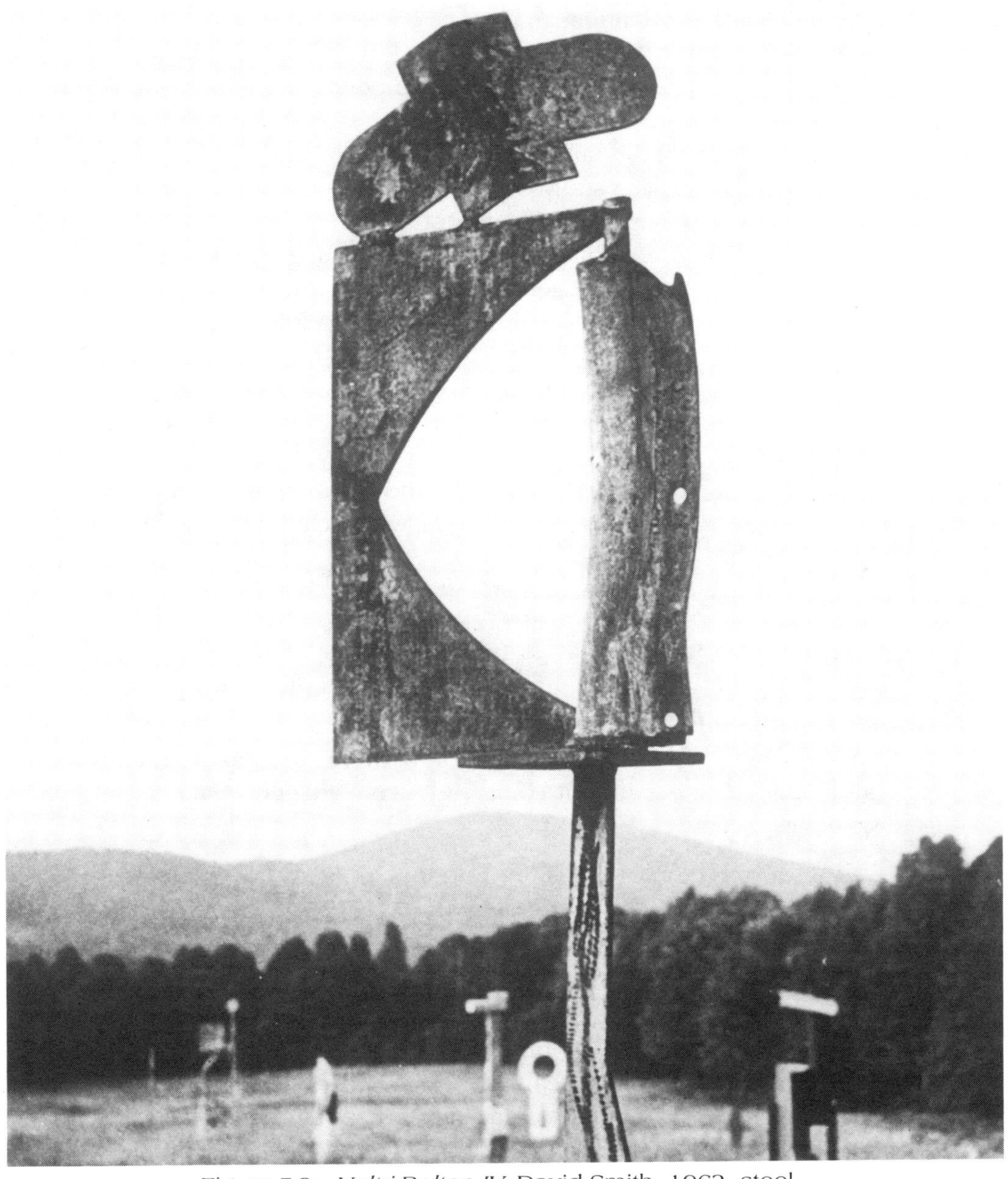

Figure 5-2: *Voltri-Bolton IV,* David Smith, 1962, steel, height 78 1/16", Collection Candida and Rebecca Smith. Courtesy Knoedler Gallery.

I had been thinking about the matter of perception as it applied to natural and constructed forms, exploring the relationship between art and perception. For every life experience there appears to be an infinite variety of ways in which that experience can be perceived or viewed. Perception is simply the way we see the world around us. The quality of one's art depends upon the sensitivity of one's perception.

I remember someone defining an artist as one who sees possibilities where everyone else sees none. Maybe that is why certain forms of art are so difficult for so many people; they have become used to perceiving things in only one way.

That night, walking in the rain, I reflected upon recent transformations my thinking had undergone. The study of art had always compelled me to adjust to alternative ways of seeing things, to accept different ways of looking at life. For instance, rather than regarding life in an unduly negative way in terms of death or decay, consider the regeneration of the earth. Despite our overwhelming technological and industrial preoccupations, this spaceship earth, as Buckminster Fuller called it, is uniquely beautiful from near and far. Too seldom, however, do we perceive it as such. We focus upon ugliness.

Natural phenomena, such as rain, evoke negative associations, despite a lack of any inherently negative qualities. In our society, frequently, a rainy day is identified as a bad day. Rain, air, raw iron and the uninterrupted passage of time results in rust. Rust seems synonymous with deterioration, impairment, inactivity and death.

Steel is an obstinate, intractable metal. It defies all but a strong arm's most determined exertion. Unlike clay which yields and absorbs impact, steel fights back. *Voltri-Bolton IV* contradicts associations of steel with defiance and rust with decay. A light drizzle, steel, air and the sculptor's hand form a union in this work; rust and steel together become a fertile measure of growth and life. Art and nature are joined in the phenomenon of life. David Smith said this in a poem, and I think I understood it completely, convincingly, walking through this rainy night.

CYSP 17

CYSP 17 (Figure 5-3) is Nicolas Schoffer's abbreviated title for his "cybernetic-spatiodynamic construction."[3] This robot-like work is a linear, aluminum assemblage with rotating blades. It is mobile and reacts to changes in light and sound intensity. Its rounded platform base houses four sets of wheels. Unlike many light- and sound-sensitive sculptures, *CYSP 17* is animated by darkness and silence rather than by brightness and noise. Low intensity lights cause the blades to turn slowly, while lights of high intensity directed onto the work cause its blades to remain stationary.

One could envision *CYSP 17* in a horror "flick," bearing down upon a terrified art patron trapped in a dim gallery of an art museum. In such a movie the art patron would probably be crushed dramatically against a Henry Moore sculpture by the advancing *CYSP 17*. In actuality the same scenario would be

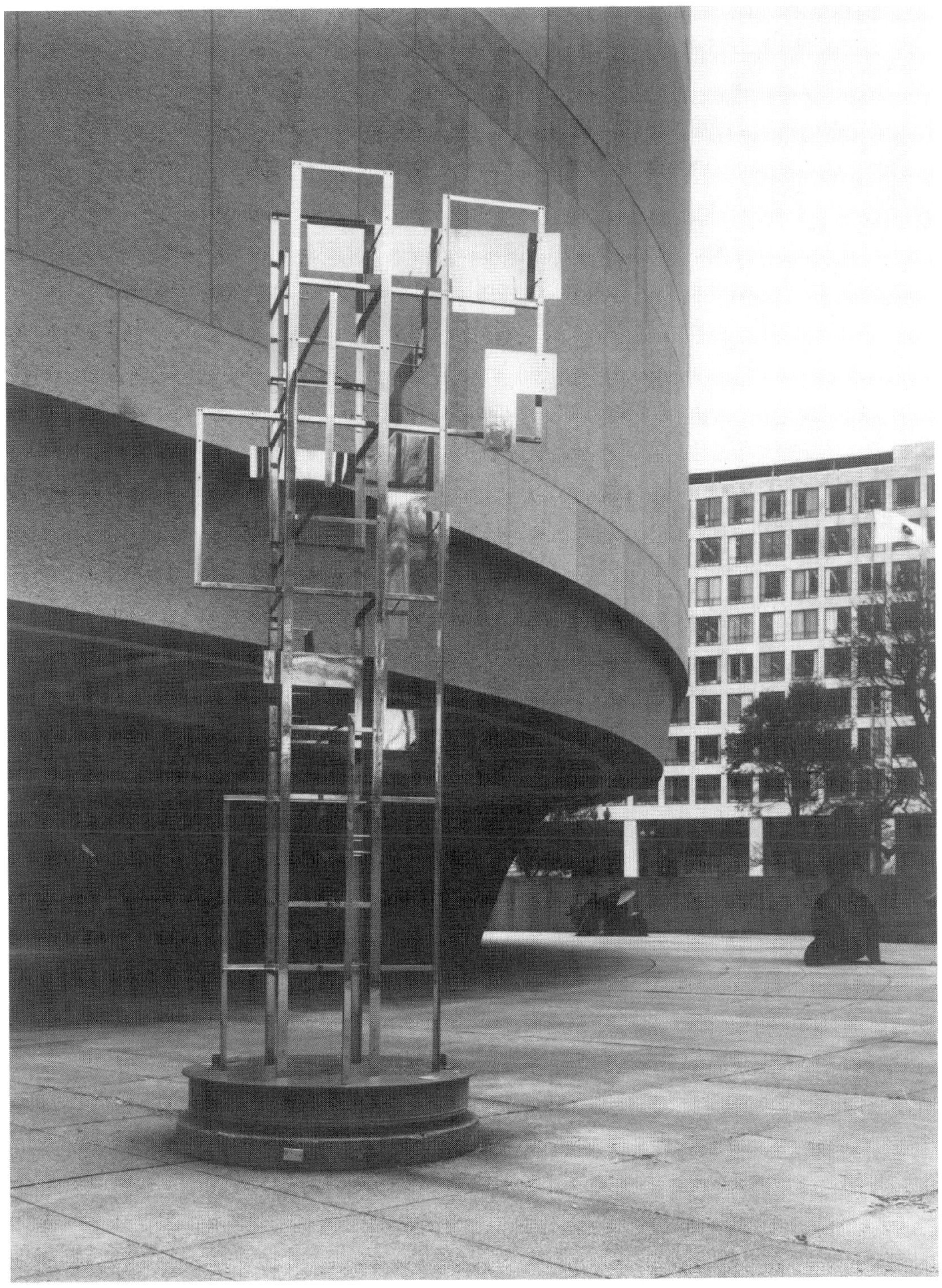

Figure 5-3: *Spatiodynamique #17,* Nicolas Schoffer, 1968, Hirshhorn Museum and Sculpture Garden, Smithsonian Institution, (72.259) Gift of Joseph H. Hirshhorn, 1972. Photograph by Lee Stalsworth.

played out quite differently; the threatened patron would emit a desperate scream at the last possible second, thus averting certain death by tripping an automatic audio-relay and shutting off the mobile structure's forward drive motors. The point of all this is not that *CYSP 17* is a mechanical ogre. On the contrary, Schoffer's work is an electromechanically responsive system programmed to behave in concert with certain environmental stimuli. Any psychological uneasiness which the viewer may feel about the sculpture's "intelligent" behavior is irrelevant to the work's aesthetic function.

If the work is not a threat or a menace of some sort then how is it to be viewed? The simple geometric conformation of *CYSP 17* makes it reminiscent of Piet Mondrian and of Neo-plasticism generally. Is the work a Van Doesburg on wheels? The obvious analogy here is probably a necessary result of Schoffer's having been compelled to use the materials and technology available to him in the late fifties. The stylistic similarities of the work to Neo-plastic constructions is a minor point. Perceptually, *CYSP 17* invades the gallery space in a totally unique fashion. It is neither floor-bound nor wall-bound; it is a free-moving, intelligent system. In an instance when a viewer finds himself face to face with *CYSP 17,* both the sculpture and the viewer function as subsystems within the confines of the gallery space. This mutuality renders useless any established rules of "art viewing" which are based on the concept of floor and wall-bound art.

A viewer's negative reactions to a mobile robotic artwork are easy enough to imagine. Positive reactions, on the other hand, are less fantastic but more instructive. *CYSP 17* must be enjoyed as a highly mobile, responsive system perceived in relation to the space which it may occupy at any given moment in time.

Chapter VI: Rational Criticism and Censorship

"A man must serve his time to every trade
Save censure—critics all are ready-made."

—Lord Byron (1809) *English Bard and Scotch Reviewers*

Rationality, Judgement and Criticism

Criticism is judgement. Ideally, critical judgement in art is an intelligent act "performed upon the matter of direct perception in the interest of a more adequate perception."[1] Judgement should be rational and enlightened; it should elucidate the form and substance of aesthetic experience. Its methods should be flexible so they may be applied in a variety of aesthetic contexts or situations. As an act of intelligence, the methods employed by critics for making judgments should be decisive; that is they should allow the critic to determine good, bad, better and worse. Also, critical judgement should not be based on rule-guided procedures that purport to be infallible. An infallible method is right by definition which means that aesthetic experience has no necessary bearing on the outcome of judgement. Instead, a method for making critical judgements should always be based upon direct perception of the form and substance of aesthetic experience.

When we fail to evaluate, to engage in rational criticism of our culture and its products, we invite censorship. Censorship seeks to supervise and control the free flow of information and ideas in a culture. Books, periodicals, plays, films, television and every form of artistic expression is subject to examination for objectionable subject matter which a censoring body or individual censor may find immoral, obscene, heretical, treasonable or a threat to national security. Other people believe all art to be a form of free speech protected by the constitution of the United States.

Censors claim to be protecting and upholding the values of the family, the church and the state. Censorship is defined by a wide range of diverse and complex issues associated with it. These issues sometimes involve mothers who want to protect, or shelter, their children from "bad" influences, citizens who feel responsible for a community and wish to preserve its traditional values or moral leaders who wish to save the easily misled from destructive temptations. Though usually well intentioned, the censor may not be constrained by rationality or fairness. Censorship is functionally arbitrary and often abruptly repressive. When art critical judgement is arbitrary it is censorial. Even an art museum may effectively censor artwork when its director removes "questionable" works from its galleries.

Censorship in History

The history of censorship illustrates the dangers and results of failed rationality in critical processes. The dialogues of Plato tell how Socrates sacrificed his life rather than have his teachings censored. He was charged with corrupting his students' morals and worshipping strange gods. He defended free and open discussion of all ideas as a service to the public and to the state.

It is ironic that Plato, in *The Republic*, advocated the subservience of art to morality, suggesting that any art which fails to promote moral principles should be banned. At one point Plato specifically recommended that mothers and other child care givers who told evil stories to children should be censored as criminals. It is untrue, however, to suggest that the Athenian democracy was rife with censorship and persecution; typically the right to speak freely in public and in private was protected.

The Roman Empire, consisting as it did of many diverse constituencies was at times tolerant of the religious and cultural practices of its peoples. However, a political recognition of the emperor's imperial, divine right of rule was required of every Roman citizen. Jews and early Christians did not support the divinity of the emperor, considering such recognition to be a form of idolatry. They made themselves, therefore, targets for persecution. Free speech among the Roman citizenry did not extend beyond the privileged classes or those in authority. Even senators were not always allowed to speak freely.

The Roman Catholic Church, under the leadership of Pope Gelasius, in 496 published the first catalog of forbidden books. Authors of books and sermons which were theologically variant were punished. An Index of Forbidden Books was issued in 1559 by Pope Paul IV and was periodically updated by Paul's successors. The last Index was published by the Catholic Church in 1948. Pope Gregory IX founded the Inquisition in 1233, and for nearly 500 years the Inquisition carried out the Catholic Church's work of religious censorship. In fairness it should be pointed out that protestant censorship was a fact from the days of the founding fathers of the Protestant Reformation. Leaders such as John Calvin, John Knox and Martin Luther were intolerant of artistic and literary deviation from their own brands of religious orthodoxy.

More recently, in 1989, the Iranian Moslem leader Ayatullah Khomeini issued what amounted to a murder contract for British author Salman Rushdie.

Rushdie authored a novel, *The Satanic Verses*, which Moslems considered heretical. For his heresy Rushdie was threatened with death.

An example of the imposition of politically-based external values is the party-line art criticism practiced by the Russian leadership. Almost from the time of the Bolshevik revolution (1917) state aesthetic doctrine has favored socialist realism in painting. Official intolerance of nonconformist abstraction reached violent proportions on September 15, 1974, in Moscow when Soviet authorities, using bulldozers and water-spraying trucks, broke up an outdoor exhibition of art. Paintings were destroyed, and artists and reporters were beaten and jailed by undercover police. Unofficial art exhibits in Moscow had been closed previously without violence in 1967, 1969 and in 1971. Systematic attempts to officially control artists' use of representation and political messages have been generally a fact of artistic life in the Soviet Union for much of the twentieth century..[2]

In 1937 at the dedication ceremony for his new "temple of German art" (the Munich Museum), Adolph Hitler denounced the Expressionists, Dadaists and Surrealists as degenerates and art criminals. He announced his intention to clean house. Hitler's declaration of war on modern art drove many artists, architects and other intellectuals out of Germany. Thousands of artworks were confiscated by the Nazis; German museums were divested of their modernist holdings, and a new style of official, patriotic, representational art was instituted.[3]

CENSORSHIP IN DEMOCRACY

If Hitler's assault on modern art and artists seems extreme, it will seem less so when you read the pontifications of U.S. Congressman G.A. Dondero from the House of Representatives in August, 1949.[4]

> *Cubism aims to destroy by designed disorder. Futurism aims to destroy by the machine myth. Dadaism aims to destroy by ridicule. Expressionism aims to destroy by aping the primitive and insane. Abstractionism aims to destroy by the creation of brainstorms.*
>
> *During that same speech the Congressman asked, . . . who has brought down this curse upon us; who has let into our homeland this horde of germ-carrying art vermin? What are these "isms" that are the very foundation of so-called modern art? . . . I call the roll of infamy without claim that my list is all-inclusive: dadaism, futurism, constructivism, suprematism, cubism, expressionism, surrealism and abstractionism. All these isms are of foreign origin, and truly should have no place in American art. . . . All are instruments and weapons of destruction.*[5]

If G.A. Dondero's words could be simply shrugged off as an aberration, or a pandering gesture to public fears of Communism, then we might forget it, but attacks still resonate through the hallowed halls of Congress.

In 1990, from the floor of the U.S. Senate, Jesse Helms called for elimination of federal funding for the arts through the National Endowment for the Arts. Citing misuse of public grant monies to foster obscene artwork, Helms proposed an amendment to NEA appropriations guidelines which would specifically prohibit the funding of "homoerotic" artwork.

There is a general misconception that censorship is practiced in totalitarian states but not in democratic societies. In the twentieth century, as in all previous history, freedom from censorship has been the exception in the world. Censorship occurs in free as well as autocratic societies; only the circumstances and nature of censorship seem to vary from place to place. As members of a democratic culture we tend to scoff at what we see as flagrant, crude methods of censorship employed by non-democratic and usually non-western societies. At the same time we ignore or are unaware of our own forms of censure.

Certain critics appear to negatively critique an artist's work because of the critic's commitment to some particular political, religious, ethical or other objective. These ends are external to the art itself and beyond the artist's creative control. Unless the artist consciously advocates these external, instrumental values through his work, his work will suffer unfavorable judgement.

Capitalistic free-enterprise practiced through advertising imposes external values on art. Advertisers (corporations) intend to sell a product or idea. Art and art history is used to peddle that product (Figure 6-1). Advertising art may be impressive in its own right, but its effectiveness is a matter of how well it sells a product.

Political, religious, ethical and other factors are frequently instrumental in artwork. Certainly, the frescos of Diego Rivera (see Figure 3-4, page 24) were heavily vested by the artist in political content. One fresco Rivera executed for Rockefeller Center in New York City was ordered destroyed by Nelson Rockefeller because of the artist's refusal to remove a portrait of Vladimir Lenin from the composition. The potential problem for the critic posed by political and religious art is critique skewed by the imposition of extrinsic value structures.

The democratic forms of censorship have especially afflicted expatriate artists arriving in America from non-western societies. These artists have typically had their works suppressed by government edict for years. They arrive in the West filled with the expectation that their works will be freely distributed, widely read or seen and perhaps understood and accepted. That expectation is at times abruptly disappointed.

Exiled Soviet artist Mihail Chemiakin painted a portrait of Mickey Mouse which incurred the legal wrath of Walt Disney Corporation. This picture was on display at an art gallery in Beverly Hills, California, when the Disney Corporation discovered its presence. Oddly, it was the artist who alerted the corporation to the painting's existence. Chemiakin wrote a letter to a Disney executive inviting him to see the work. What the artist received from Disney for his invitation was a threatening, legal response claiming copyright infringe-

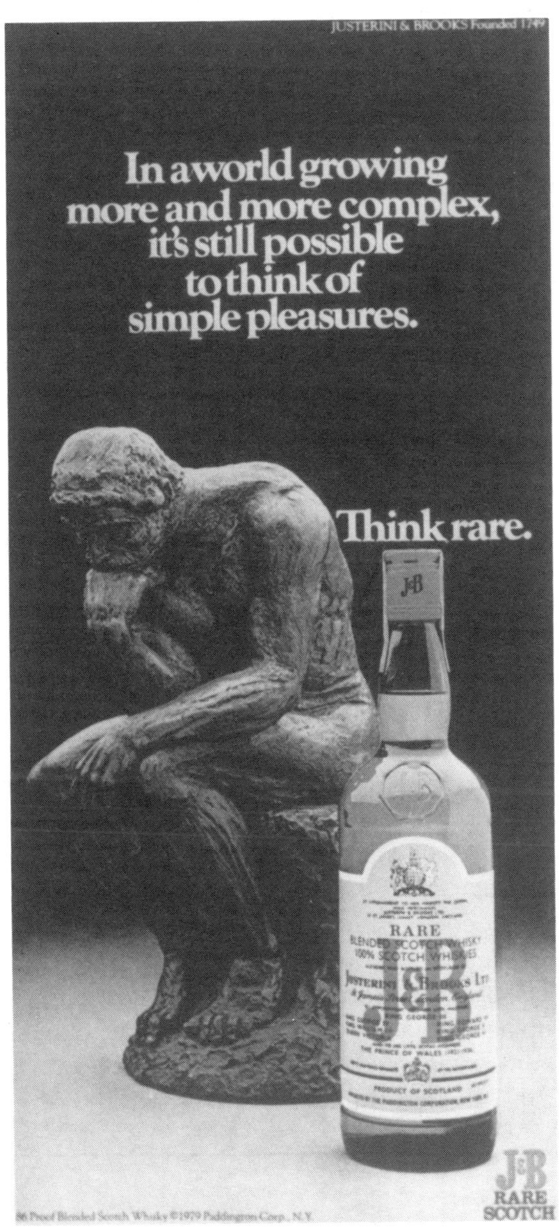

Figure 6-1: The Paddington Corporation's 1979 advertisement for J&B Scotch Whiskey, "In a world growing more and more complex, it's still possible to think of simple pleasures. Think rare."©1979 Paddington Corp. N.Y. Reprinted with permission.

ment. The artist removed his work from the gallery. An owner of the gallery summed up the episode saying, "It is sad and ironic that an artist who was forced out of the Soviet Union because of censorship of his artwork would come into the West . . . and be hit by censorship here."[6]

These exiled artists find that despite a free press their work enters the free market and has to fight for a market share against all comers regardless of inherent value or worth. Great art is sometimes lost in the fickle commercial shuffle of capitalistic culture. A smaller and smaller number of these controversial works manage to penetrate the insensitive and hardened skin of a society glutted with a dazzling array of products.

Who are the censors? No portrait can be drawn of a "typical" censor or censoring body. A censor may be a head of state, a senator's wife, a town council, a school board, a church group or a librarian. The principle, shared characteristic of the censor is an instrumental commitment which overrides every other concern. The agent of censorship usually has a moral, religious or patriotic agenda to impose on human experience. The censor is often moved to act out of some form of self-righteous indignation.

Perhaps the greatest censor is public ignorance. Widespread ignorance of art and of aesthetic concerns cultivates a close-mindedness and intolerance that is not easily arrested. Aesthetic education has the monumental and unenviable task of teaching visual literacy to an often recalcitrant and insensible populous.

We may all agree on things we would like to change simply by waving a magic wand. After all, what could be wrong with upgrading the moral climate of our community or promoting good taste in advertising or literature? The problem is with the origins of change. Advocates of censorship have no inherent difficulties with change and imposing it on society. Opponents of censorship contend that change and choice must originate from within the individual conscience. Given the testimony of history, public opinion with regard to art does not change much. An educated, enlightened and artistically tolerant public appears to be only an ideal aspiration. Reality suggests only occasional pockets of public enlightenment with no real hope of broadly-based public illumination at the end of the cultural tunnel. This is not to say the public is always wrong regarding aesthetics; even in artistic matters the greatest good for the greatest number is sometimes the best we can expect.

For Discussion

1. Echoing a question asked in Chapter VI, how should a community upgrade its moral/aesthetic climate and promote good taste? Which neighbors can a community afford to offend?

2. Assuming that literary art, especially fiction, engages the reader's imagination, inviting the reader to actively fill in details and give reality to the material, the reader becomes a literary collaborator. If pornography is

somewhat abstract and vague, leaving the consumer to imagine the details, is the pornography actually art because its consumer becomes a collaborator?

3. Read accounts of controversies involving artistic freedom of expression. Write a brief synopsis of each account clearly stating each side of the controversy. Suggest possible outcomes and affects of the controversy upon artistic practice in the future.

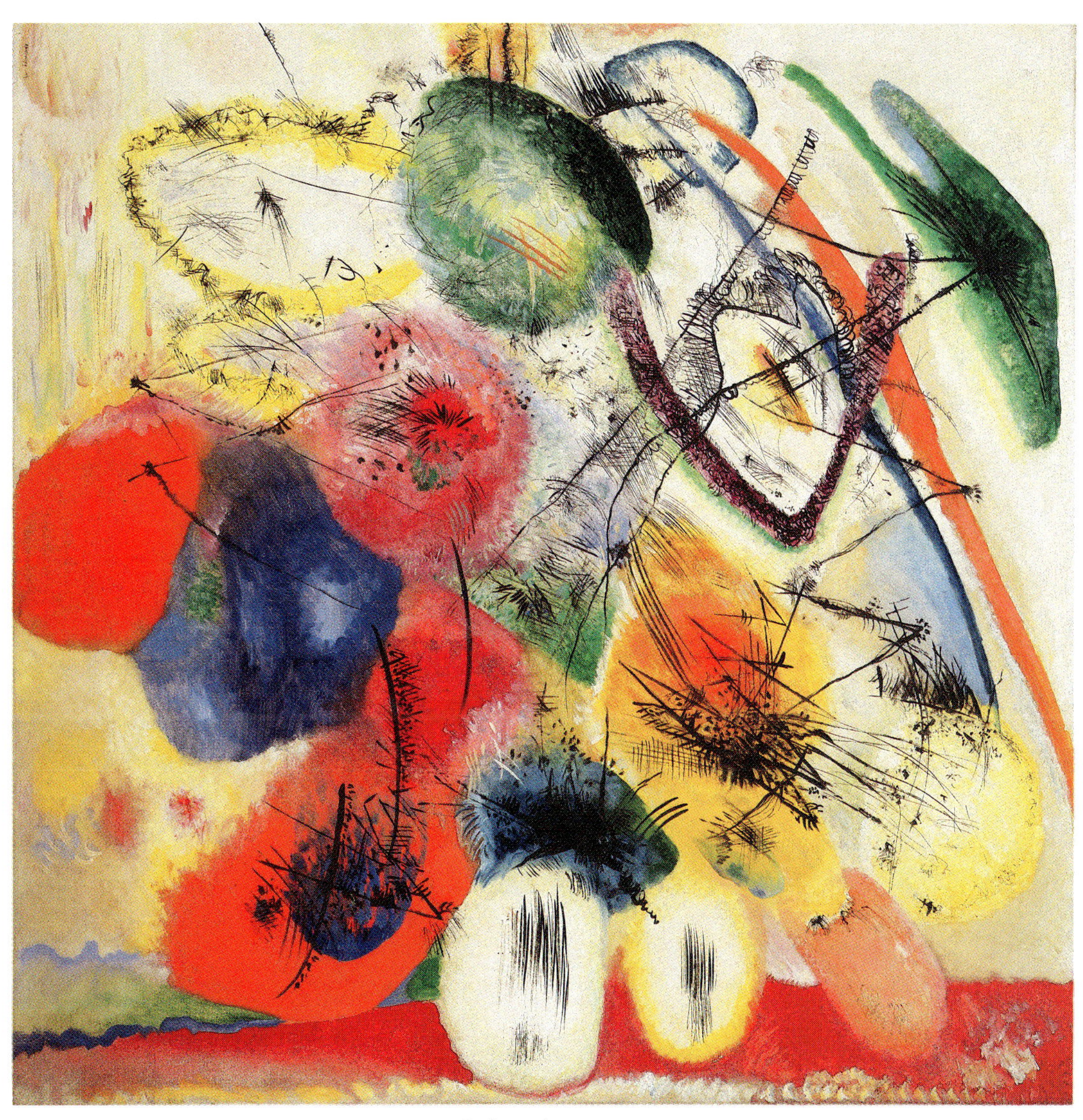

Color plate 1:
Black Lines, No. 189, Wassily Kandinsky, 1913, oil on canvas, 51" x 51 5/8". Solomon R. Guggenheim Museum, New York, Gift, Solomon R. Guggenheim, 1937.

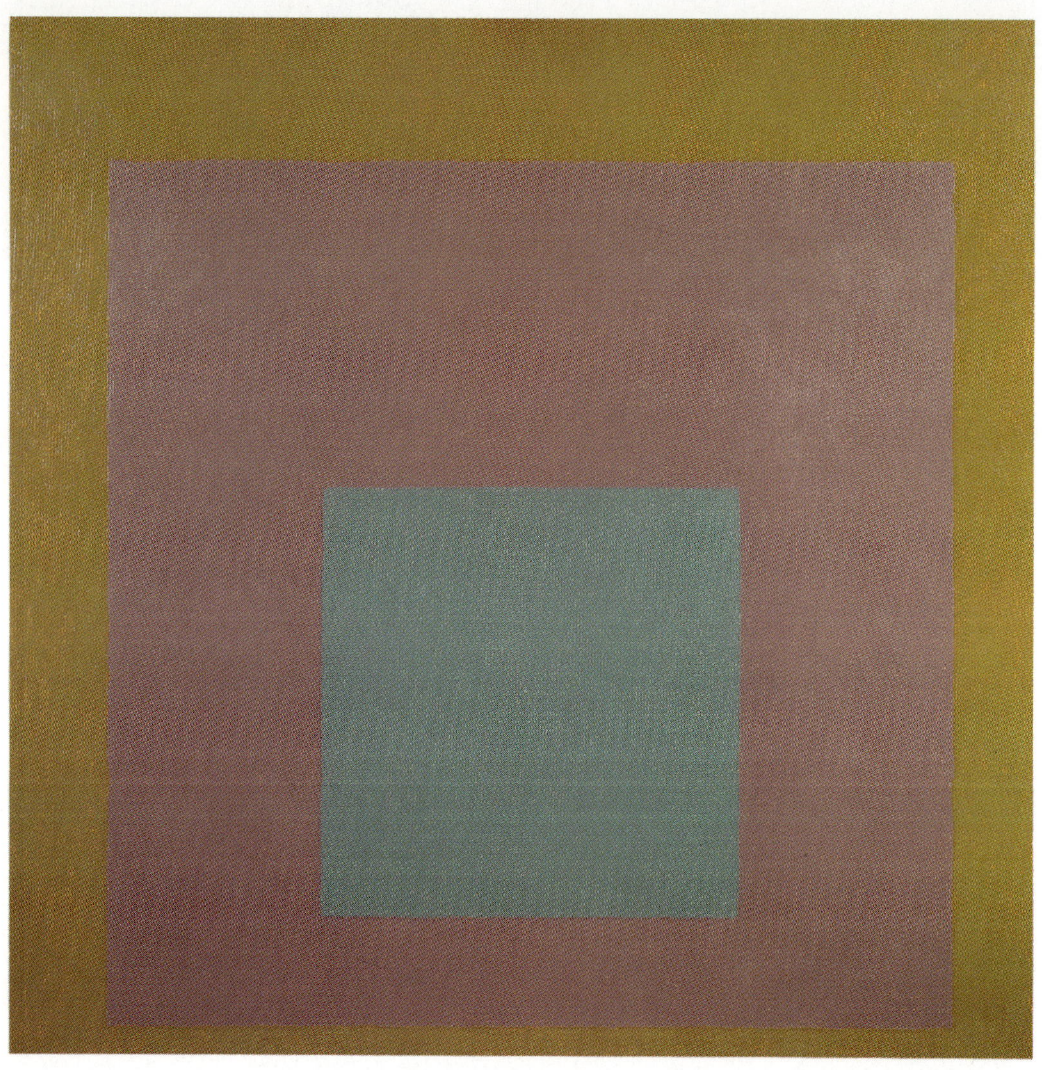

Color plate 2:
Homage to the Square: Blue Secret, Josef Albers, 1960, oil on composition board, 24" x 24", Collection, High Museum of Art, Atlanta; Purchase, 66.9.

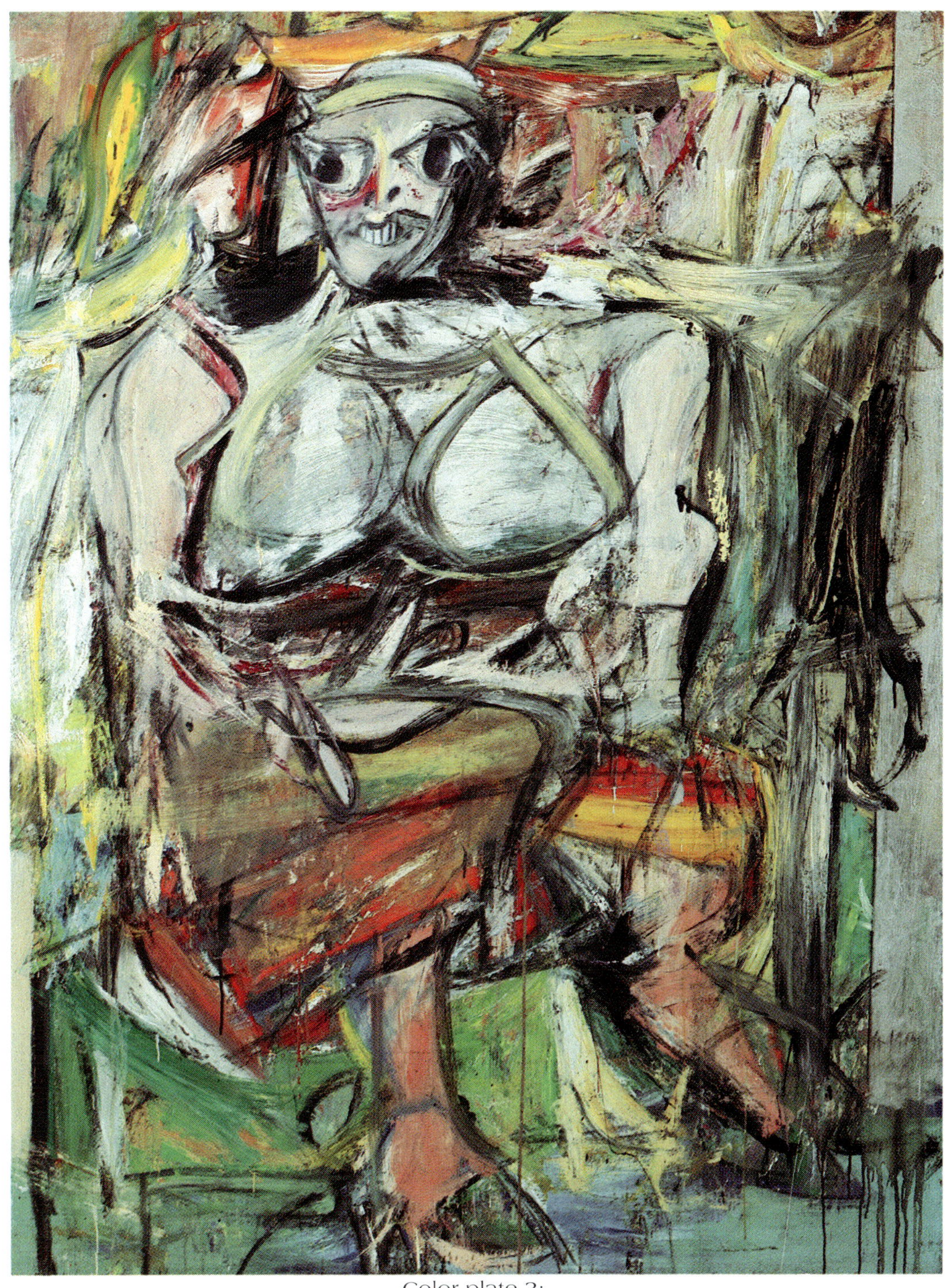

Color plate 3:
Woman, 1, Willem de Kooning, (1950–52), oil on canvas, 6' 3 7/8" x 58",
Collection, The Museum of Modern Art, New York. Purchase.

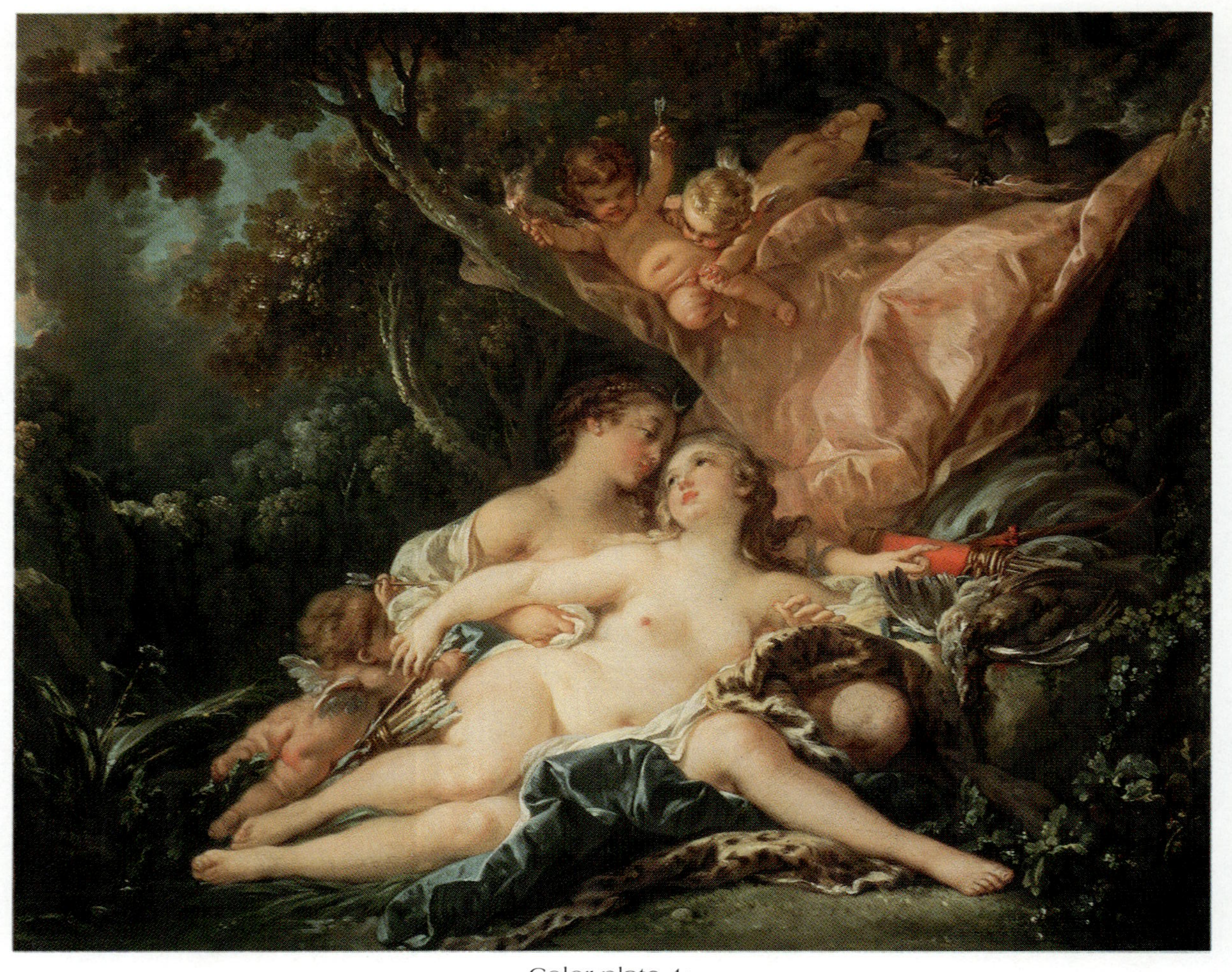

Color plate 4:
Jupiter in the Guise of Diana and the Nymph Callisto, Francois Boucher, 1760, oil on canvas, 22 3/4" x 27 1/2". The Nelson-Atkins Museum of Art, Kansas City, Missouri (Nelson Fund) 32-29.

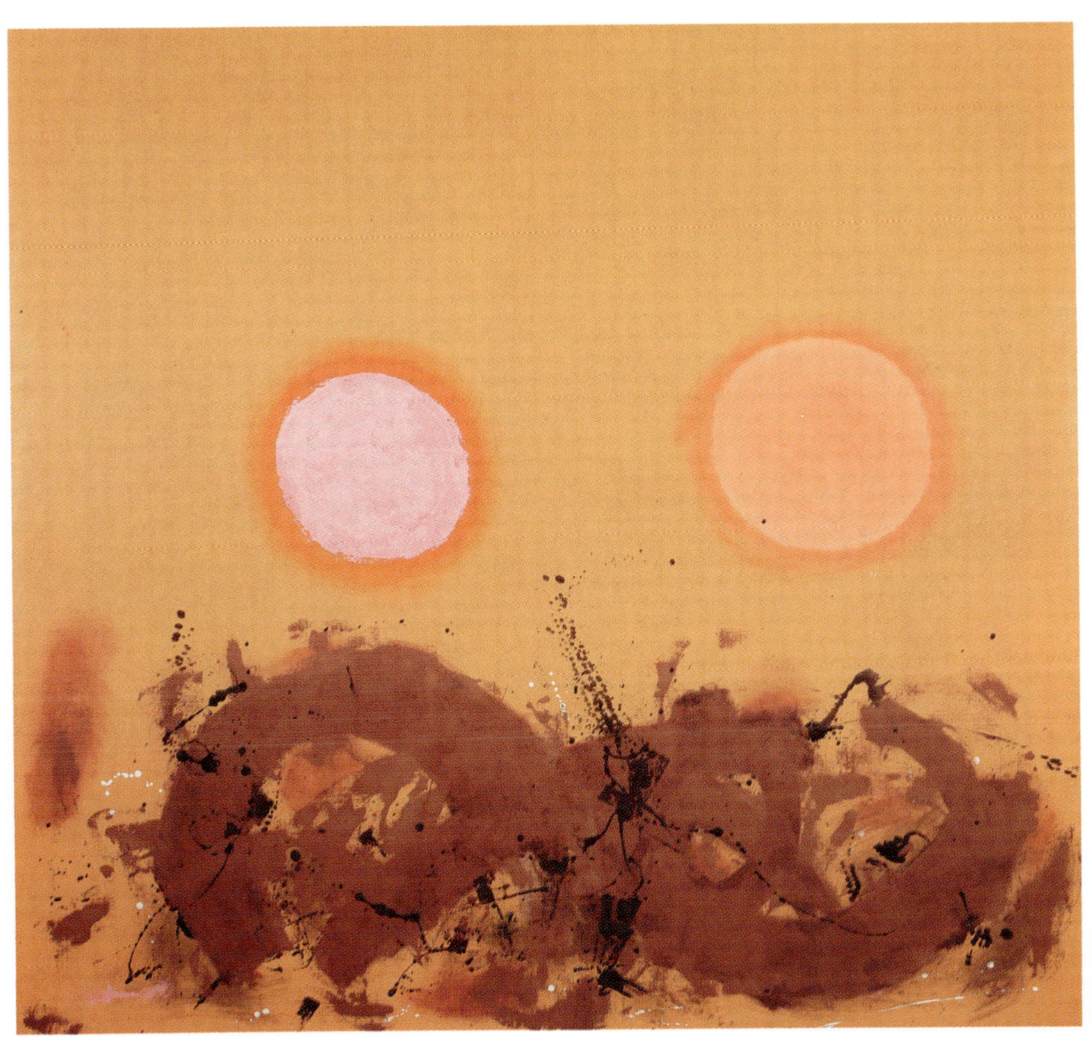

Color plate 5:
Duet, Adolph Gottlieb, 1962, oil on canvas, 84" x 90", Collection, High Museum of Art, Atlanta; Gift of Nelson A. Rockefeller, 63.2.

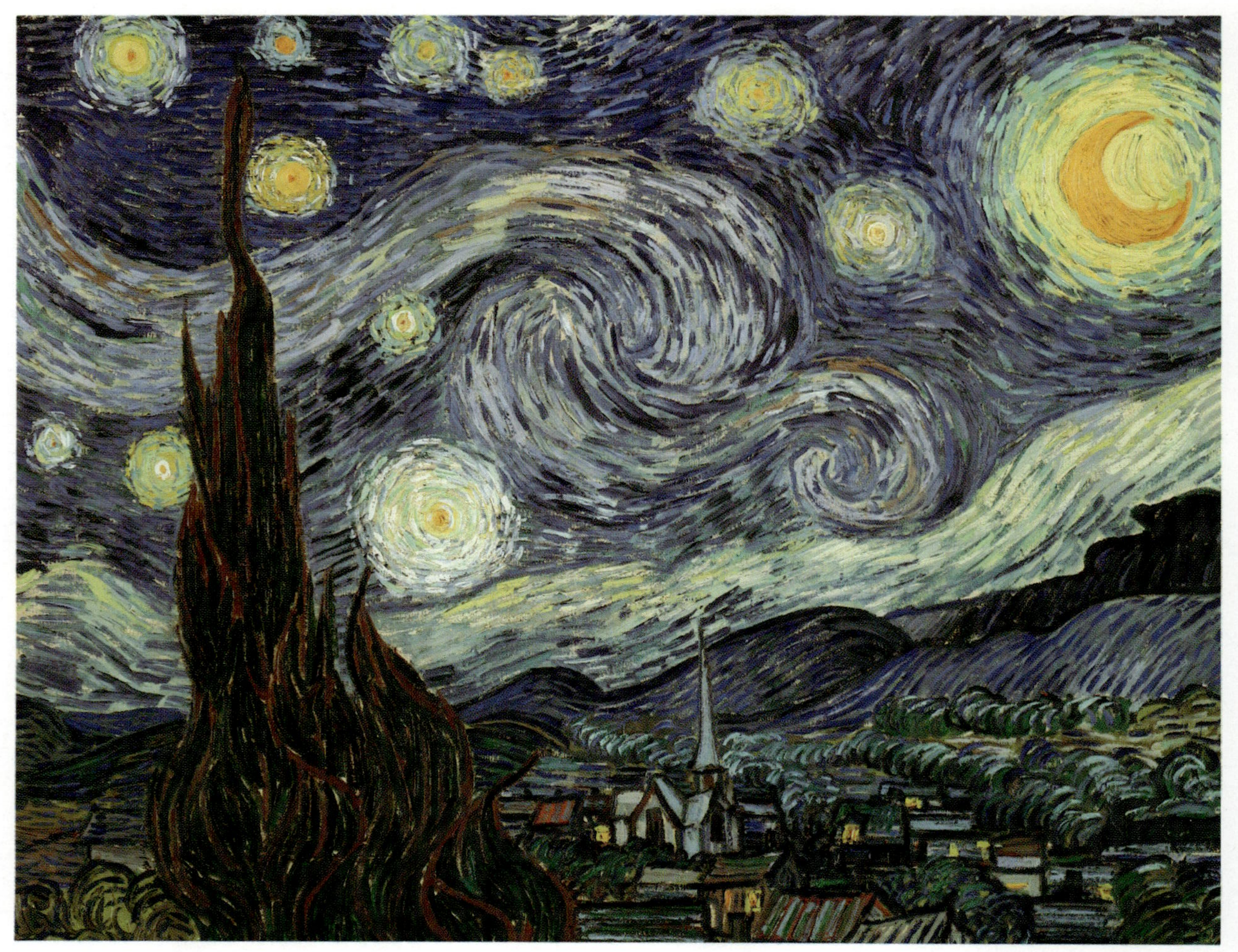

Color plate 6:
The Starry Night, Vincent van Gogh, 1889, oil on canvas, 29" x 36 1/4". Collection, The Museum of Modern Art, New York. Acquired through the Lillie P. Bliss Bequest.

Chapter VII: The Elements of Art and Composition

"The language of vision determines, perhaps even more subtly and thoroughly than verbal language, the structure of our consciousness."

—S. I. Hayakawa, *The Language of Vision* (Introduction)

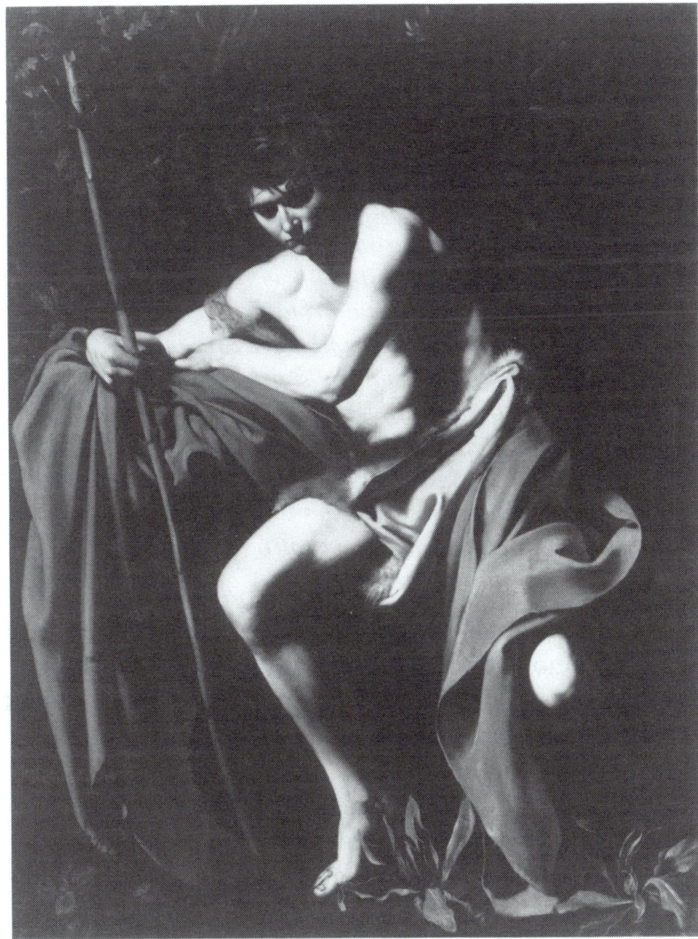

Figure 7-1: *St. John the Baptist,* Michelangelo Merisi Caravaggio, 1604, oil on canvas, 68" x 52", The Nelson-Atkins Museum of Art, Kansas City, Missouri, (Nelson Fund) 52–25.

WHAT ARE ART ELEMENTS?

When the artist creates, the art elements (line, shape, value, color, texture and space) are used as building blocks. Let us begin to examine the actual structure of artwork by analyzing each element of that structure.

It is the structure that we pay attention to as we organize our perception of artworks. We rarely see a single element in isolation; as a matter of fact, the elements only configure or make sense when they are viewed in relation to one another. If each of the art elements were a puzzle piece, the fully assembled puzzle theoretically could be put together in an almost infinite number of ways. When viewing an artwork, we see in terms of the dominance and subordinance of elements in combination. For instance, color dominates in one place, line dominates in another; a highly textured surface visually leaps from the painted canvas; a muted blue shape recedes in space.

Knowledge of the art elements helps the appreciator to understand what is seen when looking at a particular artwork. Remember, however, that the so-called art elements are an invention, a convenient means of describing general characteristics of art. For the appreciator, discussion of an artwork in terms of the art elements helps to communicate what is seen and its particular affect. Willem De Kooning's *Woman I* (Colorplate 3), described only in terms of its obscured subject matter, would leave much unexplained. Abstract works are explicable by discussion of their elemental structure. It is essential when describing *Woman I* to point out that,

> *The surface (texture) of the painting presents a mixture of incisive slashes and liquid drippings of paint. On the right-hand side of the painting is a white rectangle, very narrow and almost as long as the side of the painting. It ends in some melting dark blue colors on a lighter blue ground. The white rectangle's inner edge is broken by streaks of blacks and blues, and the white surface itself is mottled with reds, grays, yellows, and blues. Across the top of the painting runs an undulating band of yellowish-green which loses its band-like quality as it reaches the woman's righthand side. The bottom of the painting appears as a wet bluish area which recedes into the picture plane. The quality of the surface of the painting is one of confusion and multidirected movements.*[1]

A totally non-objective work, devoid of recognizable subject matter, may take as its subject the relations among differing aspects of a single art element. It may be said that Joseph Alber's entire series of paintings generically titled *Homage to the Square* is about color and color relationships (Colorplate 2).

Even a representational work requires understanding of its use of the art elements and compositional principles. Caravaggio's *St. John the Baptist* (Figure 7-1) requires analysis of the use of color and line, as well as the techniques inherent in its artist's use of chiaroscuro and sfumato. These visual features need analytical attention that is independent of subject matter considerations.

LINE

Much of the art of the Paleolithic cave dwellers is an art of delineation or outline; so too is the art of children. Today, line remains a crucial element of art; this is even true of sculpture because three dimensional forms have boundaries, contours and edges.

For the purposes of understanding what we see, line and edge may be considered synonymous concepts. Lines do not exist in nature; instead, edges are the observable quality of contoured forms or masses in the environment. If we hovered in a helicopter several thousand feet above a highway interchange, we might note a sort of calligraphic beauty in the smooth merging and diverging of the concrete roadways. Seen from the air, highways seem less utilitarian and more simply a form of design. We respond to the engineered contours as though they were linear abstractions drawn by an artist. When line is defined as the mark left by a moving point or a succession of connected points, line is being identified as an abstract concept. As the artist uses line, it is an abstraction which may vary in a number of ways. It may vary in direction, length, width and emotional or expressive properties. George Grosz's pen and ink drawing, *The Survivor,* (Figure 7-2) illustrates the emotive force of the variable direction, length and width of line. The pressure with which a line is made by the artist, and the roughness or smoothness of the drawing surface, affects line quality. As an abstract device, line may be used in a summary and schematic fashion without violating generally accepted ideas of representation. For example, various ways of drawing tree foliage, fields of grass and animal fur show just how flexible we are about accepting linear, "shorthand" representations as believable. The abbreviated marks used by Vincent Van Gogh in his pencil drawing, *Regen,* (Figure 7-3) illustrate just how believably abstract line fulfills our subject matter expectations.

Line was considered to be so essential by the artist and poet William Blake that he felt the perfection of an artwork depended upon it. His etching, *The Ancient of Days the Act of Creation,* (Figure 7-4) shows the Creator (Urizen) giving definition to the material world. One might suggest that Blake gives definition to the world through his use of line. As a painter, Blake believed painting with line was the only correct approach.[2] Line has the potential for suggesting movement. By movement we mean not only the depiction of objects in motion but pure movement or rhythm. Independent of its subject context, line may dance or flow or race across a page. Figure 7-5, a student sketch from a small bronze model, shows a wonderfully active use of line. The horse is energized and seems almost alive.

Observing linear relationships in artwork, the viewer tries to objectively identify the types of line and their location in the work. For instance, that lines are wavy, jagged, broken, textured, etc. Lines may identify contours or outline shapes.

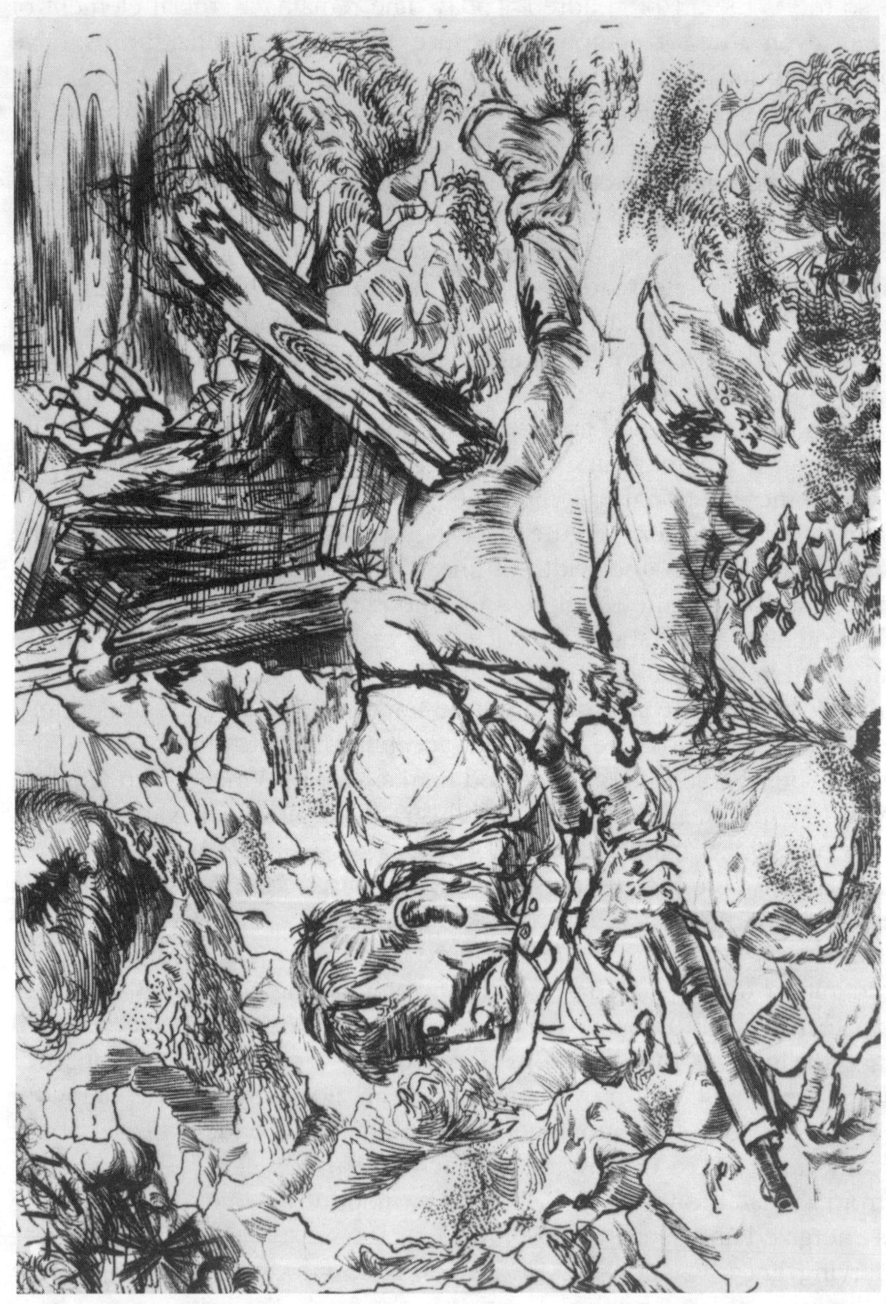

Figure 7-2: *The Survivor*, George Grosz, pen and black ink, 1936, 48.5 x 63.4 cm, The Art Institute of Chicago (Gift of the Print and Drawing Club) 1939.311.

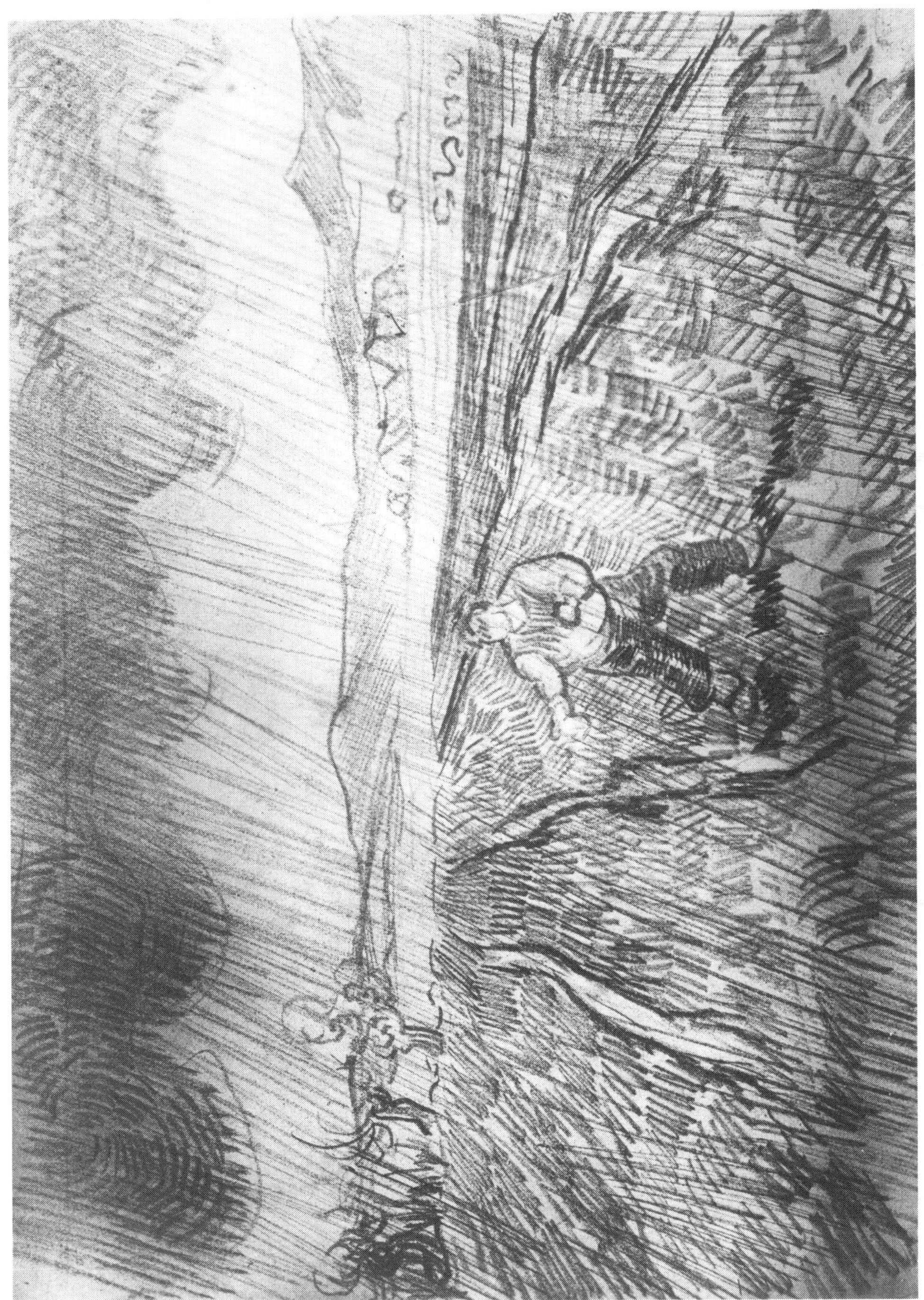

Figure 7-3: *Regen*, Vincent van Gogh, pencil drawing, Essen F. Museum (Marburg/Art Resource, NY.)

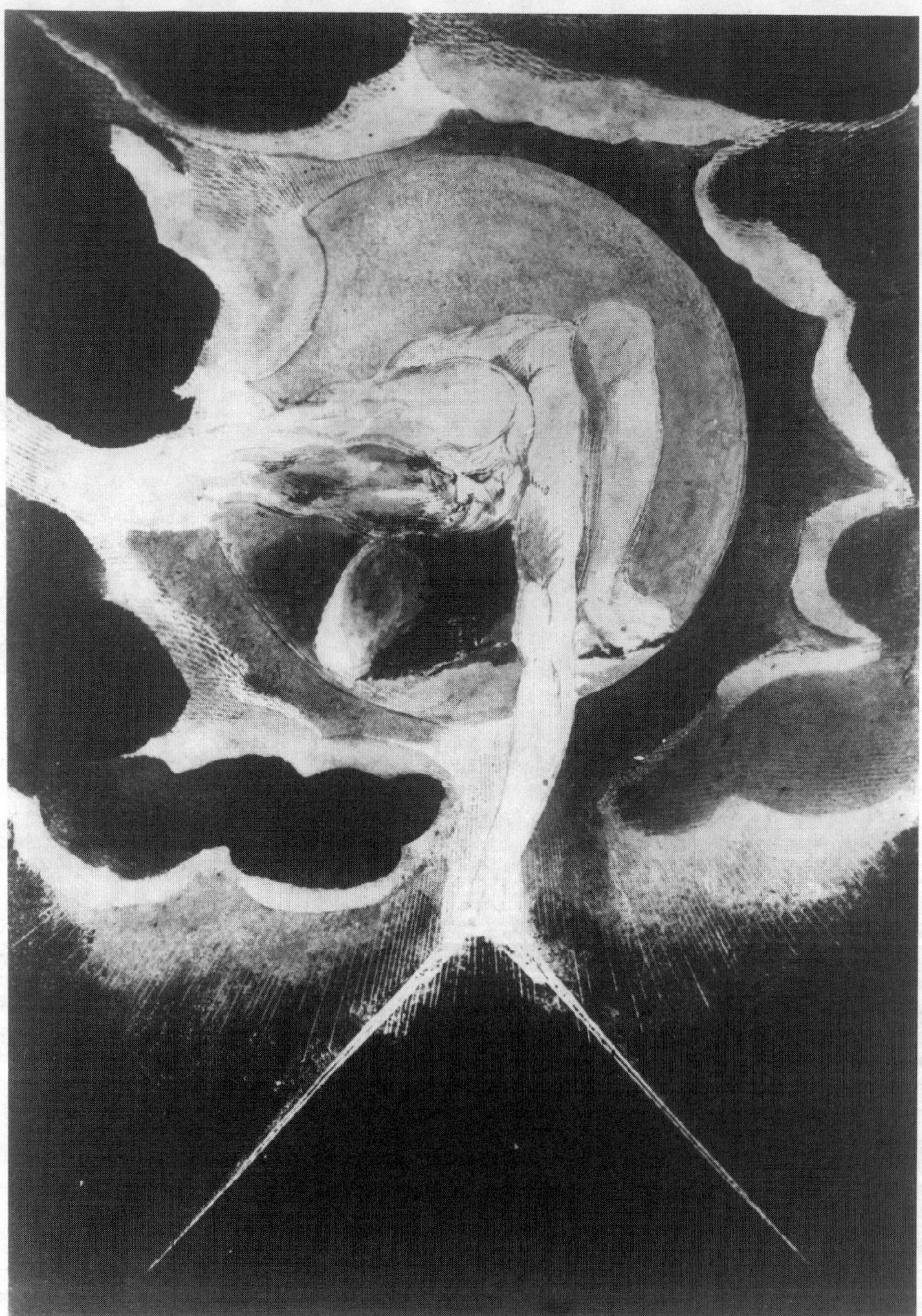

Figure 7-4: *The Ancient of Days the Act of Creation,* William Blake, frontispiece from *Europe, A Prophecy*, 1794, metal relief etching (hand-colored), the Library of Congress, Washington, D.C. (Lessing J. Rosenwald Collection, Rare Book and Special Collections Division, Library of Congress).

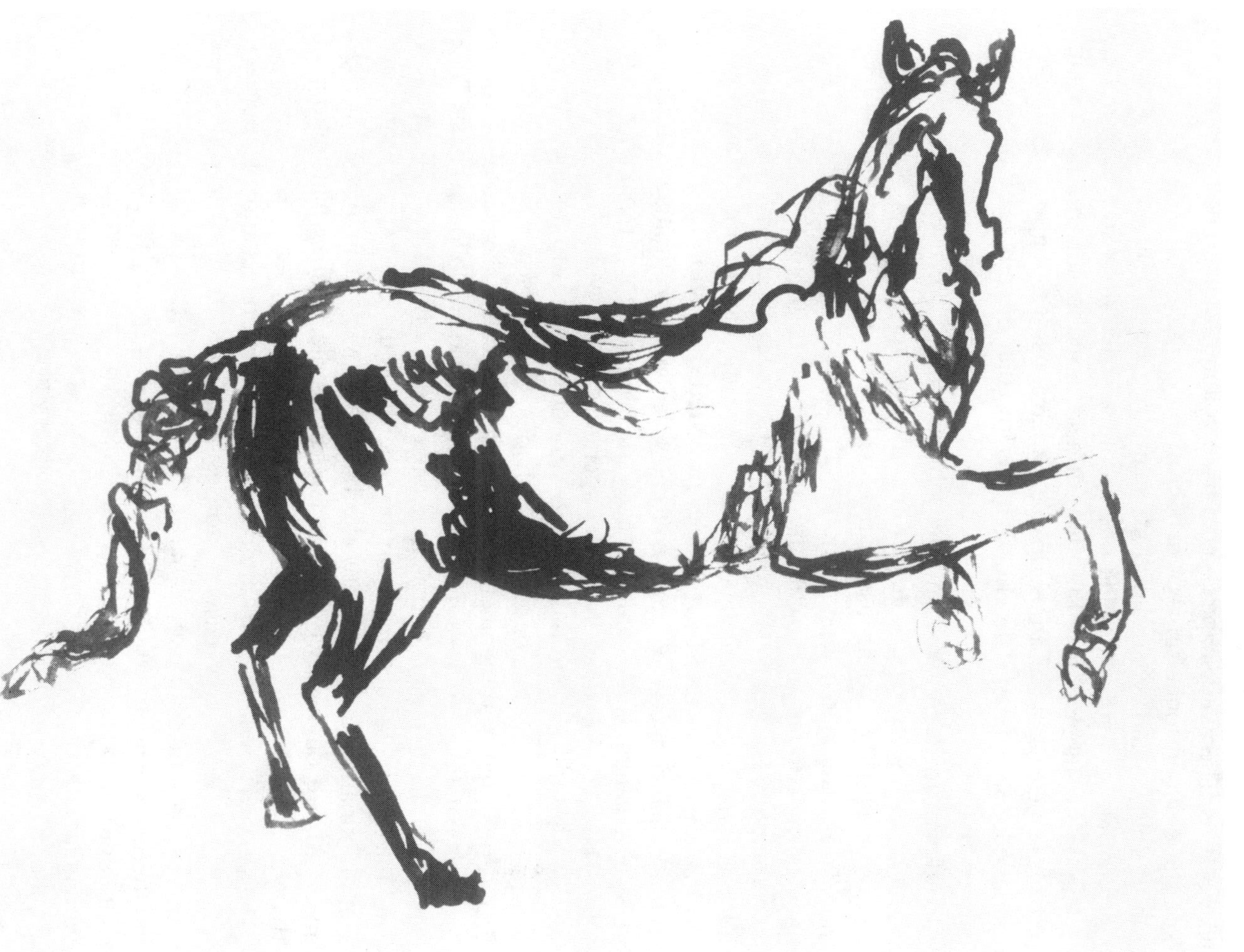

Figure 7-5: Untitled drawing of a bronze horse, Sheila Stille, 1969, India ink.

SHAPE

Shape is a word commonly used in ways which create confusion. We comment on the shape of a cloud or on the varied conformation of any number of familiar objects. The word shape is often used volumetrically to note characteristics of three-dimensional forms or masses.

On the other hand when the word shape is used in reference to a two-dimensional work of art, a drawing or a painting, it describes an area of color, tone, line or a combination of the three. It also describes an area possessing more or less measurable and describable dimensions. If a shape is regular or very simple it may be easily described; if it is irregular or complex it may resist verbal description.

One device for identifying and describing shape is the use of associative connections. When we look at a cloud and are reminded of some other familiar object, we make an association with a familiar shape and, consequently, add meaning to our perception. In the same way, an area of color in a painting or the contours of a sculpture may remind us of another object. The abstract sculptures of Henry Moore (Figure 7-6) may remind viewers of natural rock formations shaped by many centuries of weathering. Moore has acknowledged that shells, roots and river rocks provided inspiration for many of his sculptures. Such connections cause us to have feelings and thoughts which are sources of meaning and significance. A simple shape in a painting may, therefore, be a conduit to an in-depth experience of the work.

There is an unfortunate tendency to attribute attitudes to artworks which consist primarily of organic or geometric shapes. Organic shapes are characterized as emotional and geometric shapes as logical. For example, highly amorphous paintings, such as the late works of Jackson Pollock (Figure 7-7), are characteristically understood as meditatively evocative or spiritual, entrancing and filled with life substance. On the other hand the geometric abstractions of Piet Mondrian, or more recently the black and white paintings of Al Held (Figure 7-8), are often viewed as mechanical, sterile, soulless illustrations of cold logic.

These polar tendencies in art commentary are understandable because they are such temptingly easy responses, but more is necessary than the dominating presence of organic shapes in one painting and geometric shapes in another to declare a work soulful or soulless. The fact is that most artworks do not approach polar extremes in shape usage, but are a marriage of regular and irregular shapes. Whatever meanings may be inferred from shape relationships, the inference must reflect complex interactions.

VALUE

Value is a term that is sometimes meant to refer to tone, brightness or shade. Most simply, value is the relation of one part to another with respect to lightness and darkness. The lightness or darkness of any color area in a painting is controlled by the addition of black and white to paint pigments.

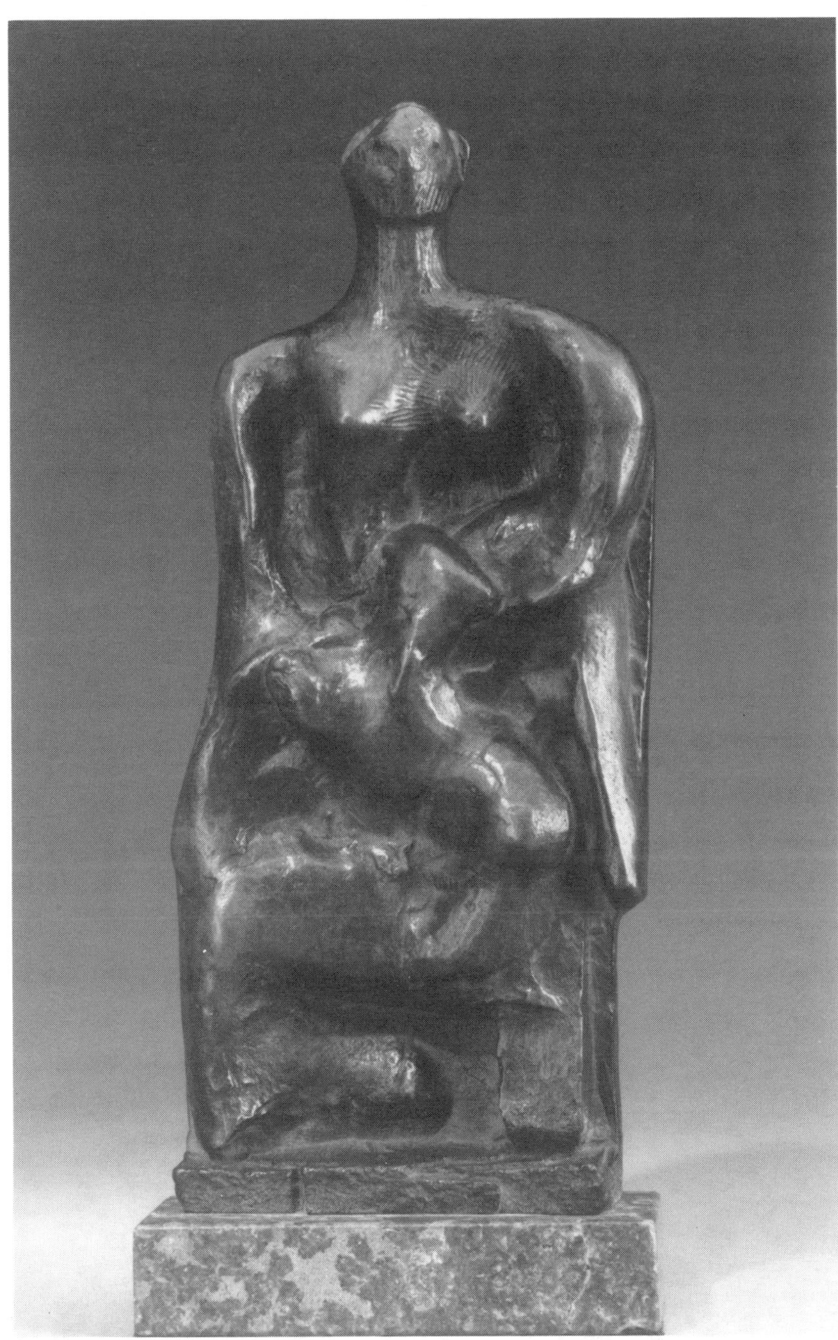

Figure 7-6: *Standing Figure Relief No. 1*, Henry Moore, 1960, bronze, 88" high, The Nelson-Atkins Museum of Art, Kansas City, Missouri (Gift of Mrs. Louis Sosland) F77-36/10.

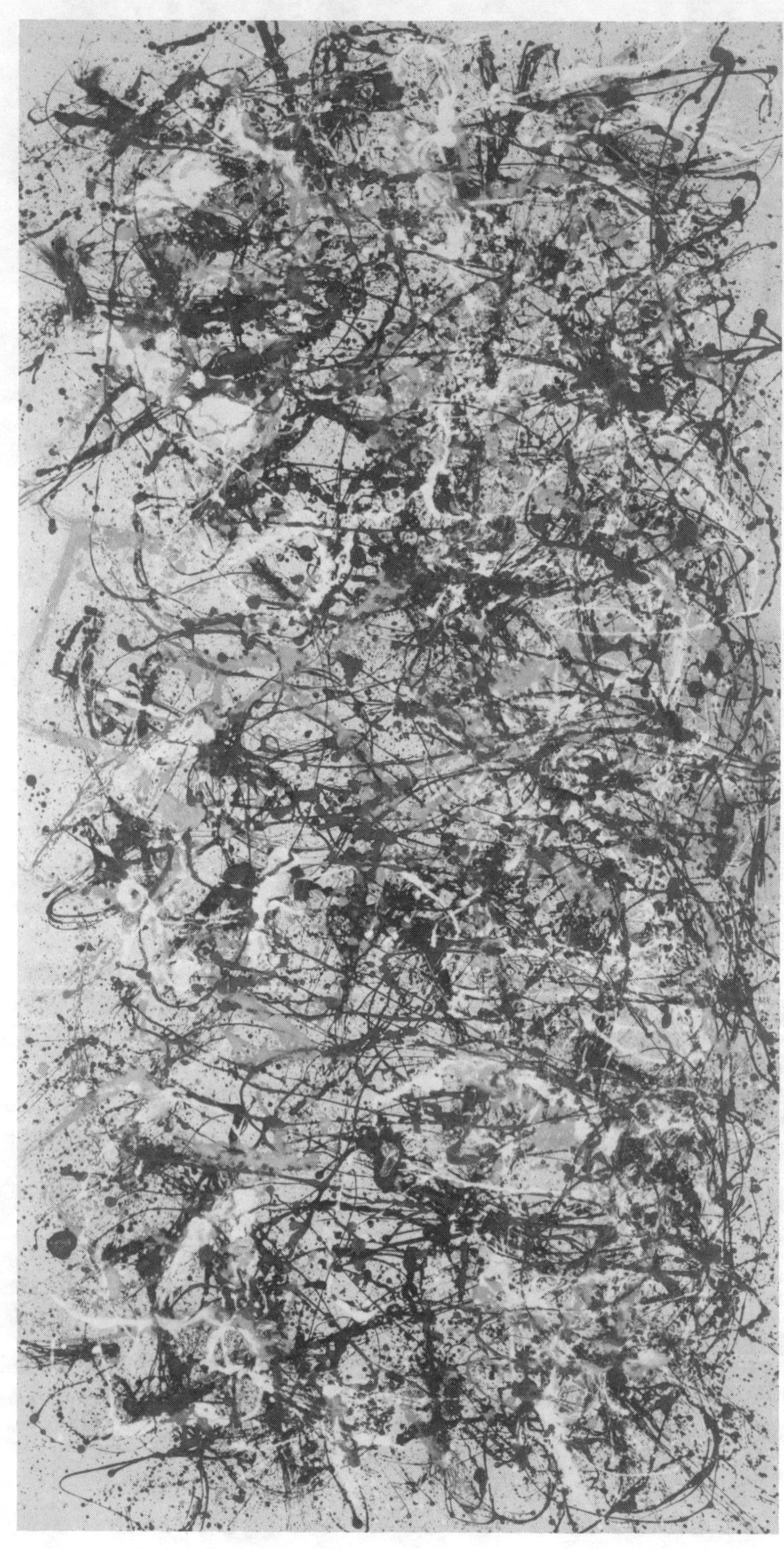

Figure 7-7: *Autumn Rhythm*, Jackson Pollock, 1950, oil on canvas, 105" x 207", The Metropolitan Museum of Art, NY.

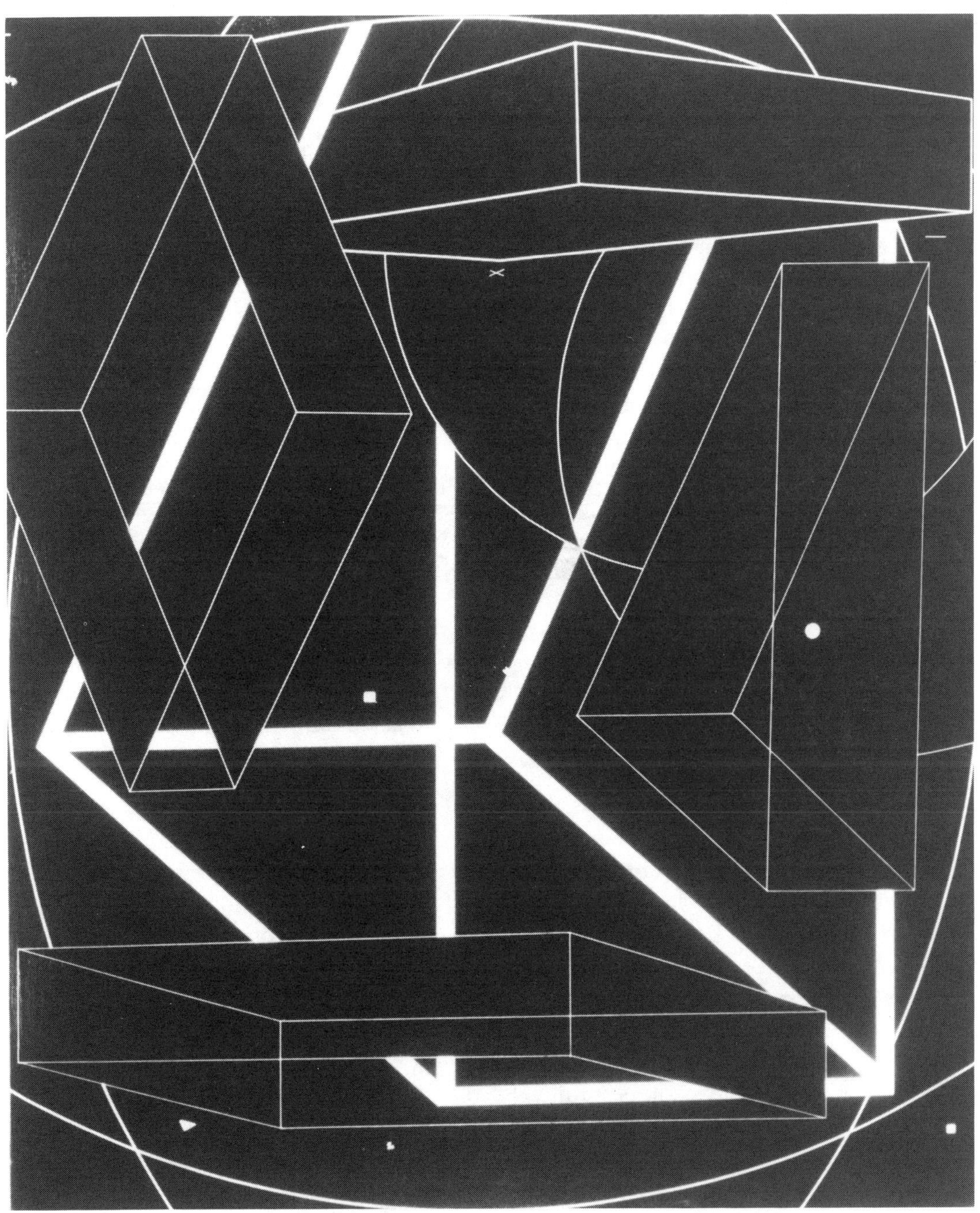

Figure 7-8: *Flemish IX*, Al Held, 1974, acrylic on canvas, 72" x 60", Collection High Museum of Art, Atlanta; purchased with funds from Edith G. and Philip A, Rhodes and the National Endowment for the Arts, 1979.134.

When white is added to any color it makes that color paler. When black is added to color it darkens it. The artist's control of the addition of black, white or gray to pigments accounts for the contrast or homogeneity of color areas within a painting.

Value is not only a property of the colored pigments used in painting. In fact, value may be best understood by reference to artworks consisting only of black, white and their combination. Graphite, charcoal and wash drawings are executed with pen or brush, water and black ink. Black and white photography and the etchings of Rembrandt are further examples of pure value studies. Much of the immediate appeal of Mary Ruth Moore's photograph, *Madonna with Peaches,* (Figure 7-9) depends upon the subtle play of light over the surfaces of the objects in her still life arrangement. Rembrandt's etching, *The Three Crosses,* (Figure 7-10) achieves a remarkable tonal range by the artist's use of lines etched into a metal plate. Darker tonalities are achieved by massing lines closely. Rembrandt's lighter areas of tone employ fewer lines etched further apart on the plate using less pressure on the etching tool.

The use of value contrasts in painting came into particular use during the sixteenth century in Italy. The Italians developed a special method for rendering the illusion of light and shade in the natural world in drawings and paintings. This technique, named *chiaroscuro,* was used by Leonardo da Vinci and has been used by subsequent generations. The technique relies on observation of the source of illumination on subject matter and the resulting variance of values. The technique was aided in early Renaissance painting by the subtle color mixing possibilities offered by oil pigments. Earlier painters of the late medieval period had used relatively inelastic tempera pigments which frustrated attempts at shading and naturalism.

COLOR

A physicist might define color as that character of a surface which is the result of the wavelengths of light it reflects. Such a definition is not of much use to either the artist or the viewer of art. The artist usually refers to the physical pigments as color. The viewer tends to consider color in terms of personal and emotional responses.

The painter uses knowledge of color mixing to create a palette of pigments which is applied to a surface. The painter's pigments serve as tools. The painter may combine colors intuitively, relying on what feels or looks right. Colors may be mixed according to some master plan, that is according to some sort of formal, structural logic. Intuitive colorists are often self-taught painters or painters lacking technical training in color mixing.

Typically, in today's professional art schools students are exposed to an introductory color design course. These courses usually teach students the fundamentals of color mixing based on some prevalent theory of color logic such as those postulated by William Ostwald (1931) or Albert Munsell (1936). Known theories of structural color logic have existed since 350 B.C. when Aristotle formulated a theory based on his belief that all colors are "blends of

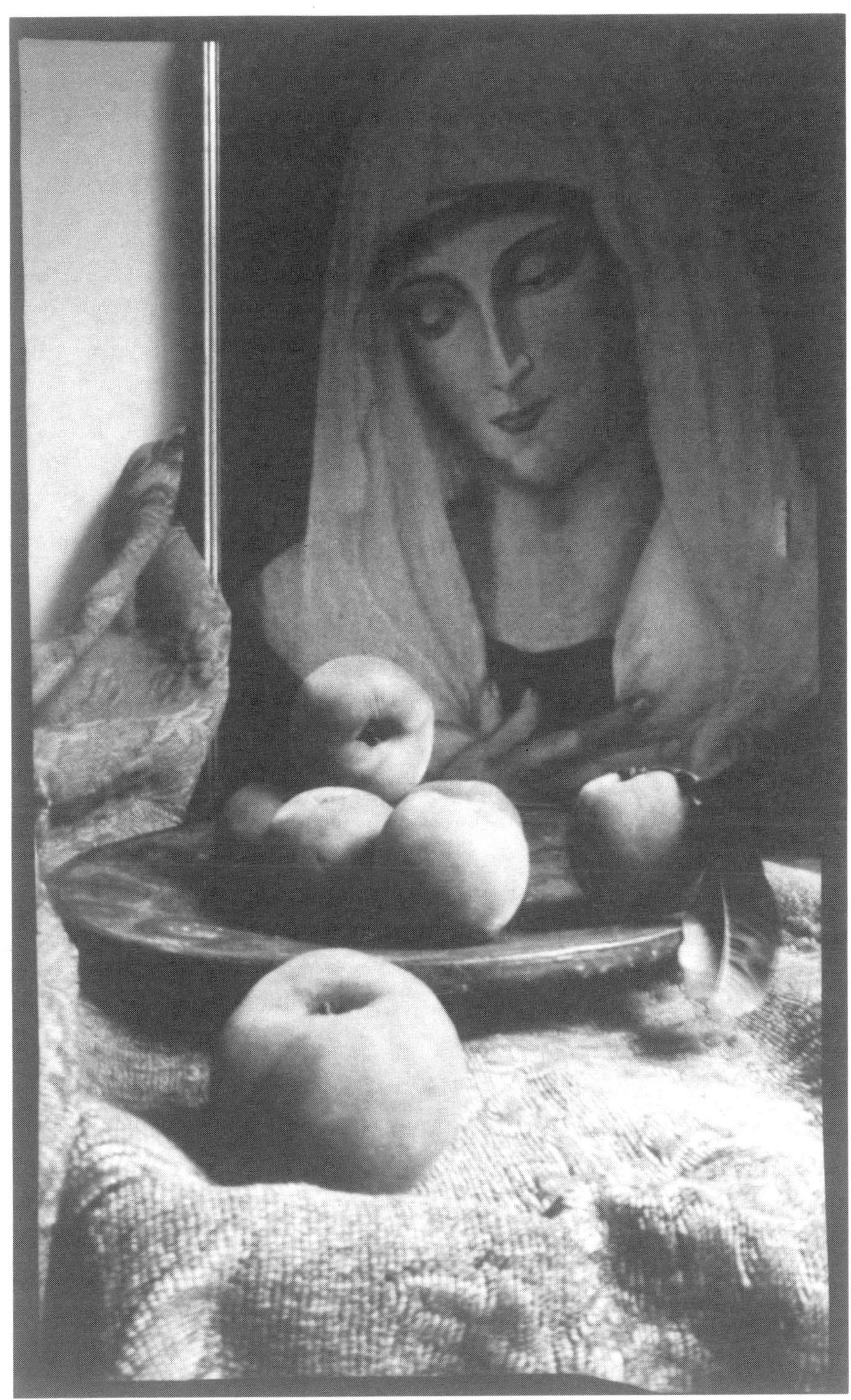

Figure 7-9: *Madonna with Peaches*, Mary Ruth Moore, photograph, 1984, Cortona, Italy.

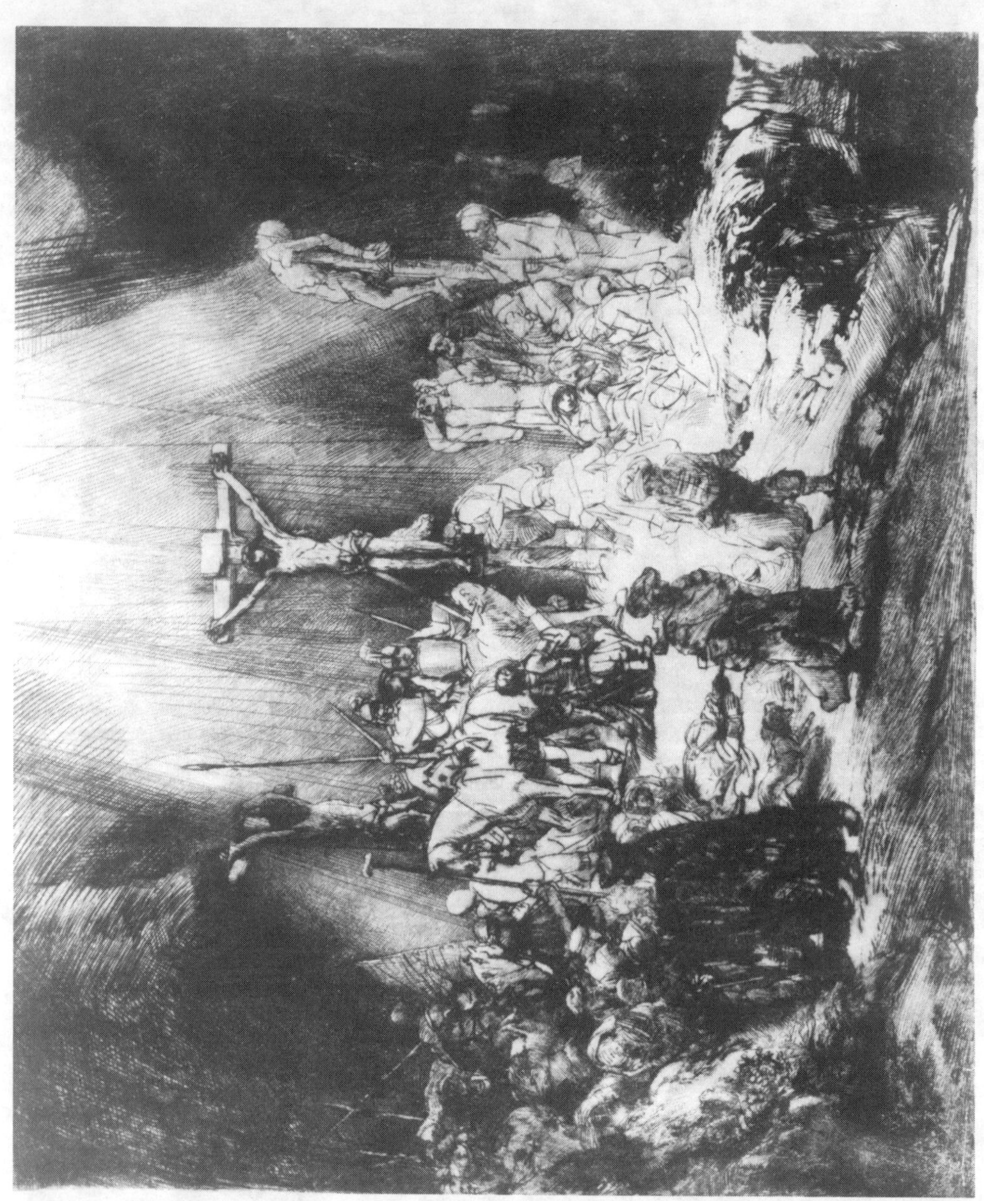

Figure 7-10: *The Three Crosses*, Rembrandt van Rijn, 1653, etching, 15 1/8" x 17 3/4", The Metropolitan Museum of Art, NY.

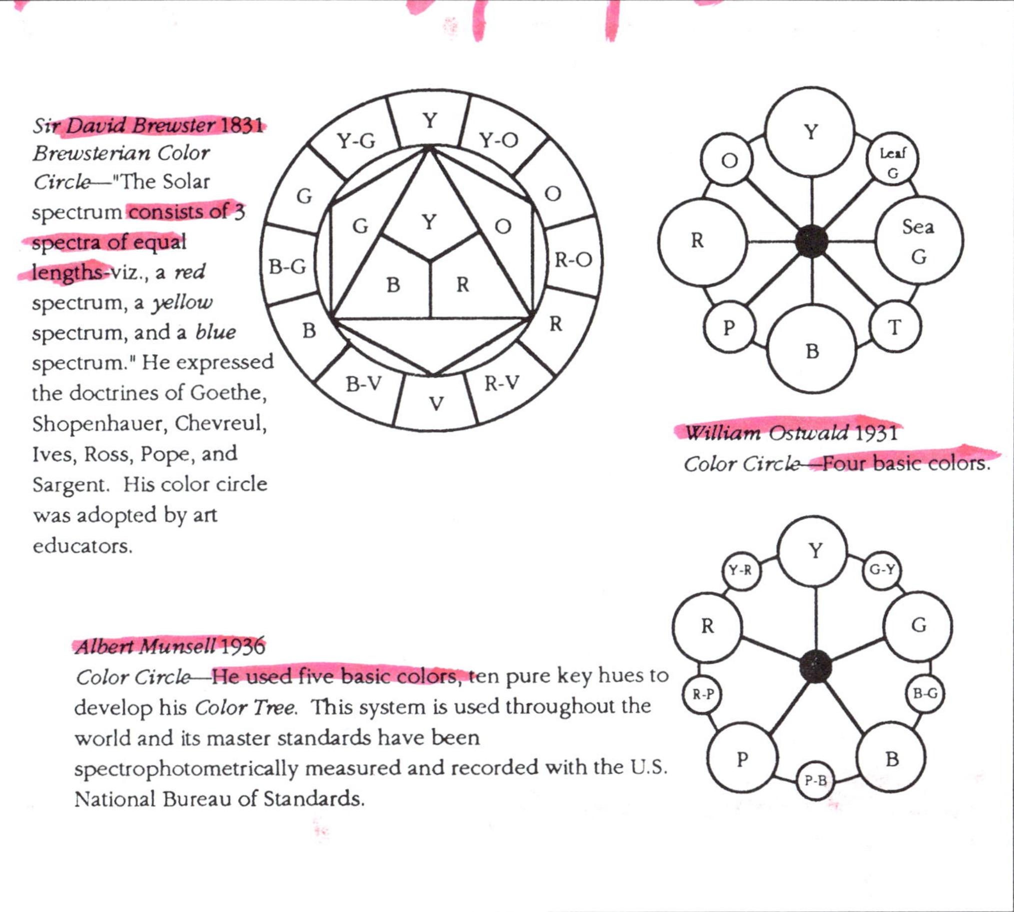

Figure 7-11: Color wheels of Brewster, Ostwald, and Munsell.

different strengths of sunlight and firelight, and of air and water."[3] Scientists and artists throughout history have schematically diagrammed color and light spectra using circles, squares, diamonds, triangles, pyramids, spheres, graphs, stars and trees. Theoretical color projections have illustrated certain common understandings about color, but they also have shown an unexpected subjective diversity. Sir David Brewster (1831) built his color circle from three basic colors, William Ostwald used four basic colors and Albert Munsell used five (Figure 7-11). Each of these theories is elegant in concept and possesses an internally coherent logic.

Painters do not usually think about color theory when painting. Appreciators and critics of painting do not typically enjoy artworks in relation to their employment of color theories. There is, however, what may be termed an ordinary language of color usage that helps both artists and appreciators to verbally communicate the perceived effects of color with accuracy. Concepts such as hue, value and intensity, and characteristics, such as monochromatic, polychromatic, analogous, complementary, primary and secondary, are basic to any descriptive discussion of color usage. A viewer needs to know enough about color to accurately identify hues and describe contrasts caused by value changes: warmth and coolness, transparency and opacity, intensity and dullness.

For most viewers, it is not the technical or physical effects of color that are most fascinating. It is the psychological effect of color that impacts most forcibly upon us. The impact or pleasure we feel from a color does not stem from our simply recognizing and classifying that color; our response to color is more open and personal. Theoretical concerns have little to do with our direct sensuous response to color.

Wassily Kandinsky wrote about a doctor who reported having a patient who insisted he tasted "blue" and saw "blue" when he ate a certain sauce.[4] All of us are subject to the fact that color elicits certain associations. The word association used in relation to color refers to any recalled objects, situations or scenes which involved color. These associations appear to be expressed, at times, through various sensory organs. We may, at times, be inclined to touch colors because we associate them with textures. We discriminate colors as warm or cool. A room painted light blue may seem large, open and refreshing. Paintings by eighteenth-century, French Rococo artists have been described as using perfumed colors (Colorplate 4).

Some color associations seem to be widely shared in Western culture.[5] Green is linked with hope, yellow with cowardice, white with purity, black with mourning, and red with blood and revolution. Non-Western cultures attribute different qualities to colors. Classic Indian philosophy associates red with ambition, desire, heroism and a striving for pleasure and material success. "Black denoted dullness, bluntness and the stupidity of the complacent self-centered person, white an illuminated repose and understanding. . . ."[6]

Beyond culturally shared associations, there are certain almost universal symbolic meanings which researchers have found relative to color. Red, more than any other color, attracts symbolic attachments. It is an "exciting and stimulating, a powerful, strong, vigorous, masterful, energetic, and impulsive color."[7] Yet red may also indicate aggression, danger and destruction. Red has been used across the centuries by rulers as a symbol of aggression and war. It has been applied to the bodies and clothing of warriors "in such different cultures as the Greek, German and Aborigine Australian."[8]

Blue has been seen as "a tender, soothing, cool and passive, secure and comfortable color which inspires calmness, confidence, responsibility, harmony and a sense of control, but it may also be slow and mildly depressing."[9] Yellow, in contrast to blue, is seen as outgoing, positive, bright and cheerful. At times, yellow may also denote treachery, domination and destruction. Green, like red, blue and yellow, expresses a set of double meanings. It is expressive of hope, nature and youthful vigor, but it may also symbolize danger and poison.

Investigators are still trying to answer the intriguing question of why so many of these described meanings are universally shared. Perhaps some undiscovered inherent genetic factors of human perception bond all of us psychologically despite cultural distinctions.

Texture

Texture, or the feel of things, is more than simply a matter of whether an object is rough or smooth. We sometimes value objects according to their tactile appeal. Commercial advertisers of body lotions, skin creams and soaps understand quite well the psychology of physical attraction as it applies to skin texture. Selecting clothes involves more than correct fit; the feel of fabric is an important criterion of choice.

Texture is either an actual tactile quality of a surface or the visual illusion of tactile qualities on a flat surface. Textural effects in a work of art can contribute greatly to our sense of richness and visual pleasure. Texture must be used carefully so that the overall continuity of the artwork remains intact. Texture is especially important in sculpture because the tactile qualities of materials have a strong impact. The sculptor relies heavily on textural effects to simulate subject matter characteristics and thereby elicit recognition from viewers.

Implied textures are completely illusionistic, and are those effects to which we respond when we look at representational paintings and other two-dimensional media such as television, cinema and photography. A genre of painting which relies on an "It looks real!" response is called *trompe l'oeil* or "fool the eye" painting. Perhaps the best known American practitioner of this approach was the nineteenth-century painter, William Harnett. Harnett's *Still Life: Helmet, Books, Trumpet, and Sheet Music* (Figure 7-12) provides a fanfare of objects each of which the viewer may visually handle and admire in terms of its apparent reality and textural believability.

Painters also use texture to create a raised surface when they apply pigments mixed to a viscous consistency. This use of thick paint is called *impasto*. Vincent Van Gogh's use of a physical buildup of paint achieved sensuous immediacy and rhythmic compositional unity. Makers of collages use physically textured elements to compose their works. The cut paper collage in Figure 7-13 makes use of both implied and actual textures.

Actual texture, as has been pointed out, is essential to sculpture. One of the chief appeals of sculpture is experiencing it through our sense of touch. Most museums frustrate our natural inclination to touch sculpture with a "hands off" policy. Some small consolation for the hands off policy of museums may be gained by remembering analogous "hands-on" experiences outside the museum.

Space and Time

Space and time are difficult concepts to visualize, unlike the other elements of art. We can see a line, shape, color, value, tone or texture, but space is emptiness, a void, the absence of something or nothing at all. We say that time

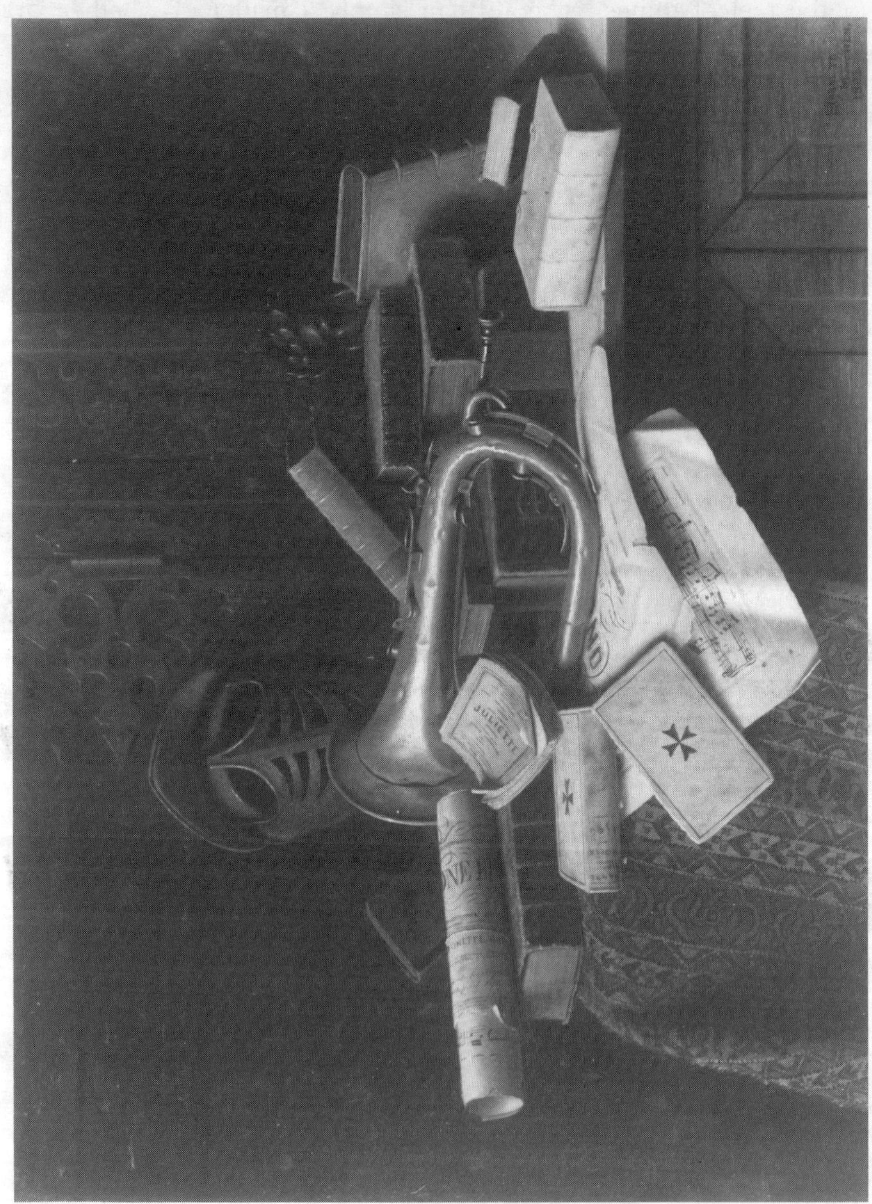

Figure 7-12: *Still Life: Helmet, Books, Trumpet, and Sheet Music*, William Harnett, 1883, oil on wood panel, 10 5/16" x 13 3/4", The High Museum of Art, Atlanta, Georgia.

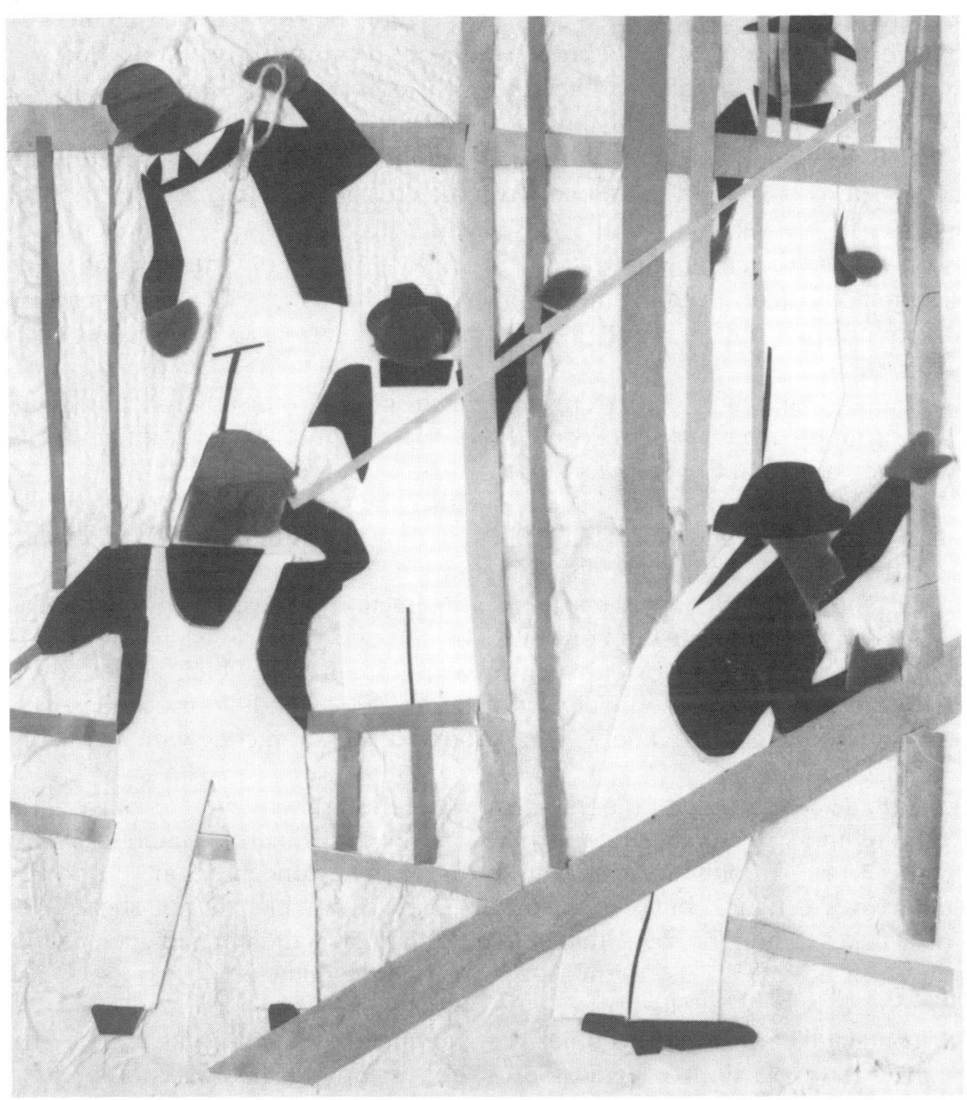

Figure 7-13: Collage, Tree Collins, student project: cut paper, fabric and fiber collage based on the tempera painting *Carpenters* by Ben Shahn, 1940–1942.

passes or that time flies, and we seem to mean that the passing of time has escaped our attention. Space and time defy description, yet both are concepts crucial to our understanding of relationships in the real world and in three-dimensional and two-dimensional artworks.

Both sculpture and architecture are three-dimensional forms or masses occupying or existing in space and time. Space serves as an environment or background for both sculpture and architecture; neither may be created or experienced without an awareness and consideration of space. When we experience sculpture and architecture as existent in space, we understand them as evolving in time. This evolution in time is an evolution of the viewer as well as the artwork. A sculpture's evolution in time may result from modifications of its form. A mobile sculpture changes as currents of air move it or when a viewer touches it. Architecture may be opened or closed to accommodate the changing weather. Over a long period of time aging changes all form and matter. Even in a few moments of time, as a viewer moves around a sculpture or through a building the viewer evolves as perceptual vantage points change.

Sculpture and architecture are set apart from each other by fundamentally differing approaches to space and time relations. Let us look at how this difference occurs in the case of sculpture first, then architecture.

A sculpture occupies space and is enclosed by space. When viewing a fully three dimensional sculpture (as opposed to a sculptural relief) you walk around it and only understand its configuration and impact after having seen it totally. The sculptor controls the work's interaction with space by manipulation of form. The viewer is controlled by the sculpture as each co-extends spatially. The sculpture extends or projects into space which surrounds it depending upon its conformation and the viewer extends himself or herself relative to the sculpture while walking around it and interacting with it tangibly and imaginatively.

A dramatic example of the interactive relationship between the viewer, the sculpture and space is illustrated by viewing Bernini's marble statue of *David* (Figure 7-14). Not only are we aware of the intense concentration and power shown by the figure, but we are intrigued by that which is not shown. As *David* flexes to hurl the stone that will fell Goliath, it is the implied giant that in some measure affects us. Bernini's *David* intensely attacks a vacant space, a space we expect to be filled by a figure of the giant. While some sculptures are self-contained, the *David* occupies a space much larger than itself. It is the capacity for projection or extension of great sculpture that conveys an ineffable, larger than life quality.

The architect has to deal not only with occupying space, but also with enclosing space. Architectural structures shape external space because they are, after all, massive sculptural forms. Buildings also shape or modify internal space. The architect has much less freedom than the sculptor because the relation of external and internal space must always be considered.

Frank Lloyd Wright's design for the Guggenheim Museum is an example of the architect's harmonious resolution of the dual demands of occupying and enclosing space. The interior of the Guggenheim reflects the outside, and the

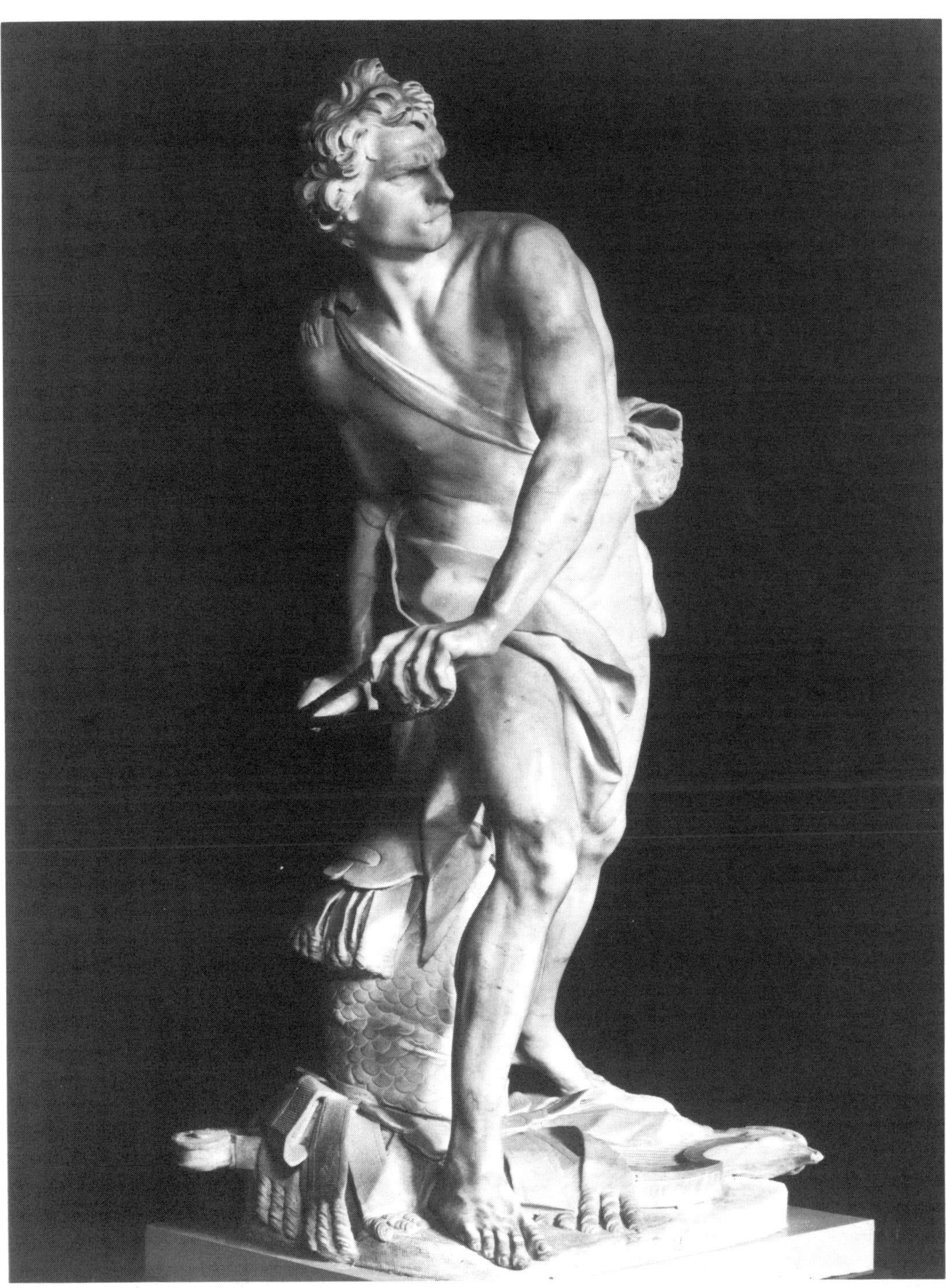

Figure 7-14: *David,* Gianlorenzo Bernini, 1623, marble, lifesize, Borghese Gallery, Rome, Alinari/Art Resource, NY.

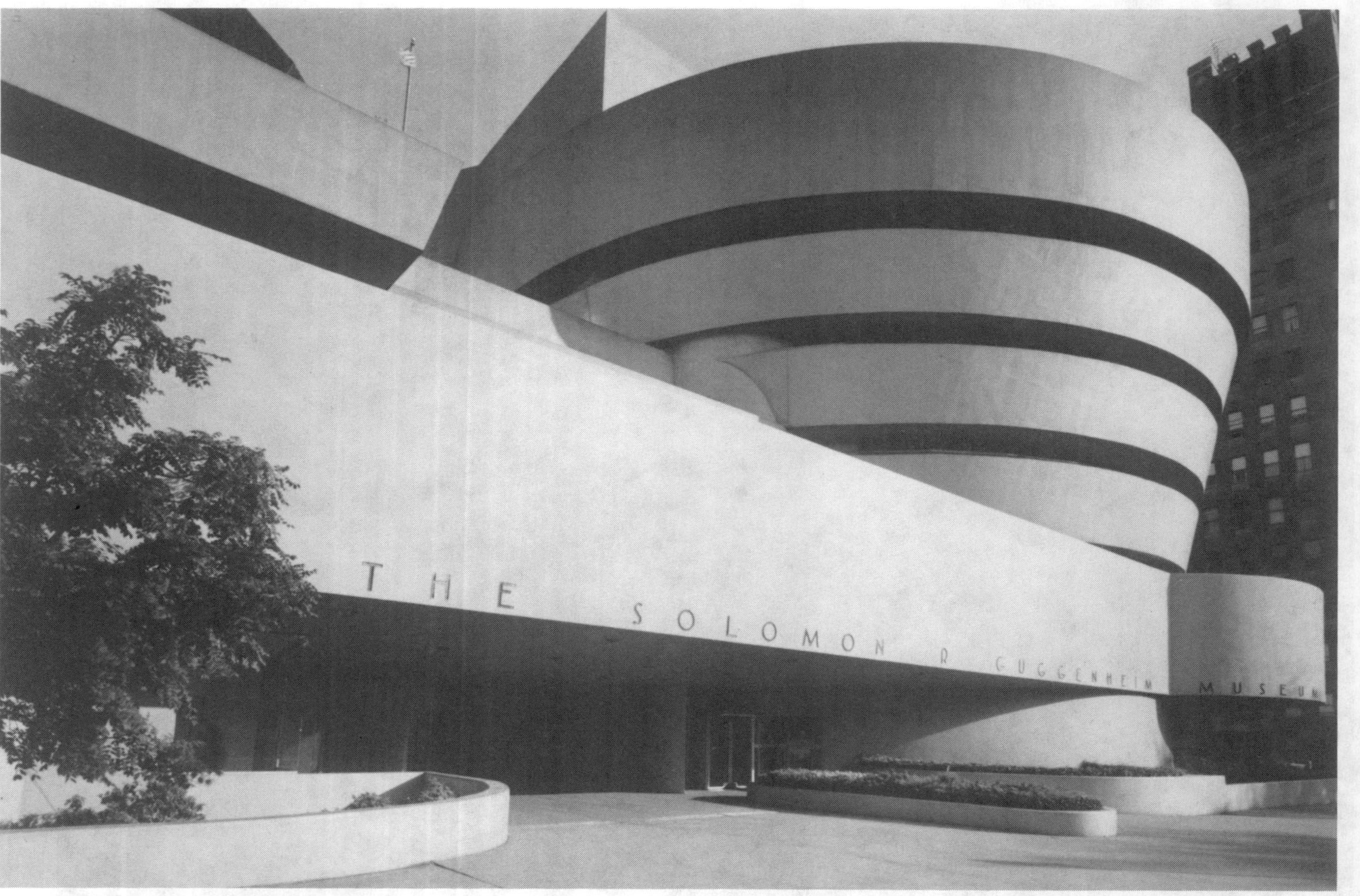

Figure 7-15: Exterior view, *The Solomon R. Guggenheim Museum*, New York, Frank Lloyd Wright, 1959, (photo: Robert E. Mates).

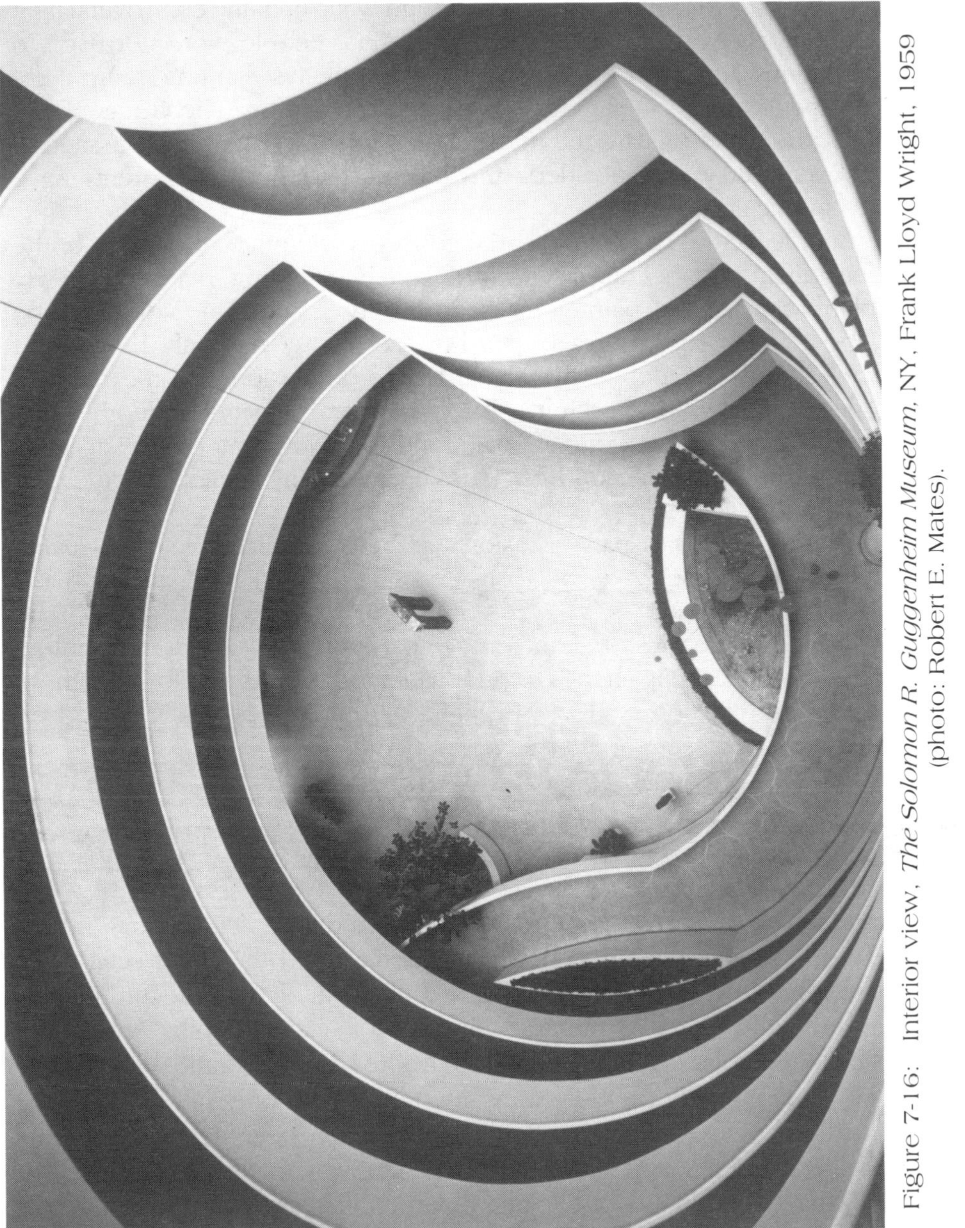

Figure 7-16: Interior view, *The Solomon R. Guggenheim Museum*, NY, Frank Lloyd Wright, 1959 (photo: Robert E. Mates).

outside reflects the inside (Figures 7-15 and 7-16). The outside consists of curves and a stack of reverse stepped, cylindrical masses, giving the appearance of a monumental, abstract sculpture shaped somewhat like an upside down wedding cake. The inside is characterized by a continuous, spiraling ramp that follows the curving, cylindrical walls from ground level to the top of the translucent-domed ceiling. Wright's design was initially controversial; it seemed to compete with the art it displayed. Also, people were not used to viewing paintings hung on curving walls. The always slanting ramp kept viewers compensating for a slightly off-balance orientation. The Guggenheim Museum is a work of art as are the masterworks it houses. With the passage of years, the controversy has subsided, and the museum and its contents have settled into public acceptance.

We cannot leave the subject of spatial concepts without a discussion of the two dimensional, pictorial application of space. Standing before a newly primed blank canvas, the painter faces an empty space. This void may be modified by a single stroke of a brush, but the painter has only height and width to work with, no depth; the space is two-dimensional. Some painters have struggled their entire working lives to create an illusion of depth while others worked to free their work of spatial illusion. No painter ever succeeds in completely eliminating illusion from painting, but many achieve a somewhat oriental quality of flatness.

For centuries, pictorial spatial illusion has been practiced by artists using one of several techniques. We will consider each briefly. First, and perhaps earliest in Western art, overlapping shapes were used to show depth. The beautiful Byzantine mosaics of sixth century Italy (Figure 7-17) demonstrate a frequent use of overlapping shapes to establish an illusion of shallow depth. In these mosaics, the illusion of depth is slight, as more emphasis is placed on decorative texture, color and pattern.

Positioning of shapes in a composition is a second technique used by artists to control the viewer's perception of pictorial depth. Subject matter which is closest to the viewer is depicted larger and lower in the composition. Distant subject matter is depicted smaller and higher in the composition. Indian and Persian art of the past consistently used this device (Figure 7-18).

Early in the fifteenth century, Italian artists mastered the art or science of perspective rendering. They learned the use of linear drawing techniques to articulate startlingly effective pictorial illusions of spatial depth. Artists like Paolo Uccello, Piero della Francesca and Andrea del Castagno based their compositions increasingly on what they saw rather than only upon what they knew. The following example is often used to teach beginning art students simple perspective. Intellectually, we know that railway tracks run parallel. We also know that wooden ties are placed perpendicular to the rails and are spaced evenly. If we draw a railroad track strictly in accordance with what we know, the resulting sketch will resemble a ladder more than a railway. If we actually stand between two rails, and look down a long, straight stretch of track, what we will see are lines receding into the distance and seeming to converge at a point on the horizon where they disappear (Figure 7-19a). Similarly, the evenly spaced cross ties appear closer and closer together until

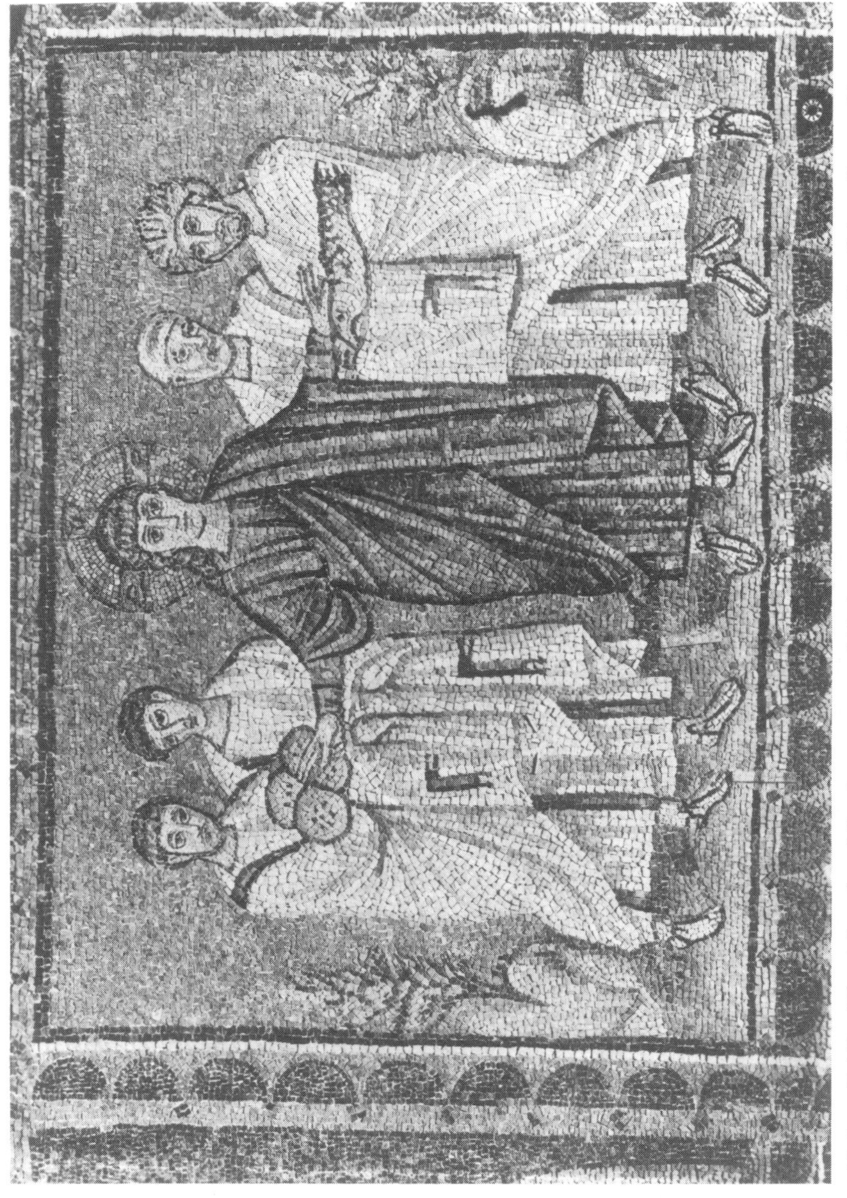

FIGURE 7-17: *The Miracle of the Loaves and Fishes*, C. A.D. 540, mosaic, Sant' Apollinare Nuovo, Ravenna, Italy, (Alinari/Art Resource, NY).

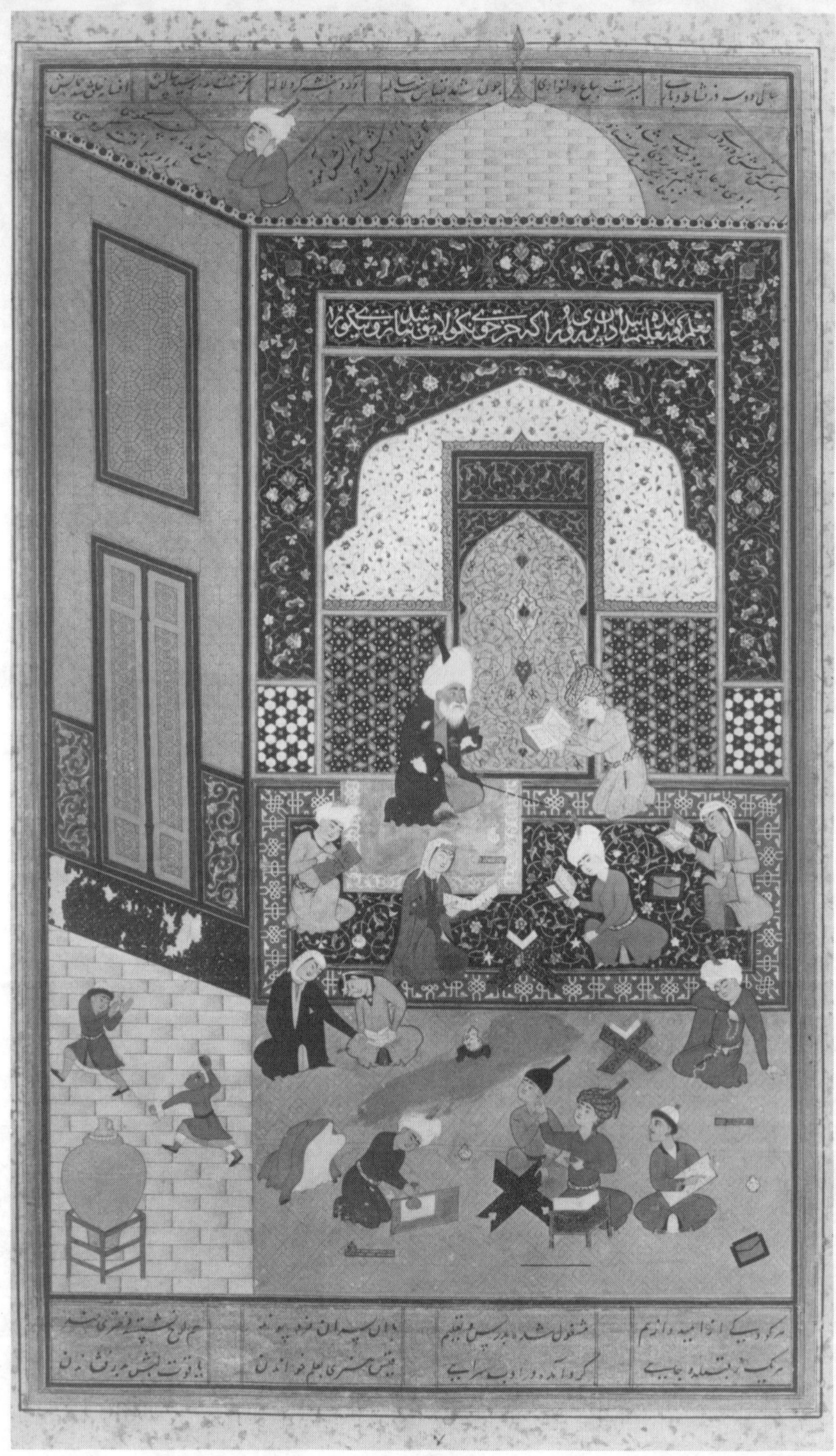

Figure 7-18: *Laila and Majnun in Love at School,* 1524–1525, miniature from a manuscript of the Khamsa of Nizami, colors and gilt on paper, Metropolitan Museum of Art, NY.

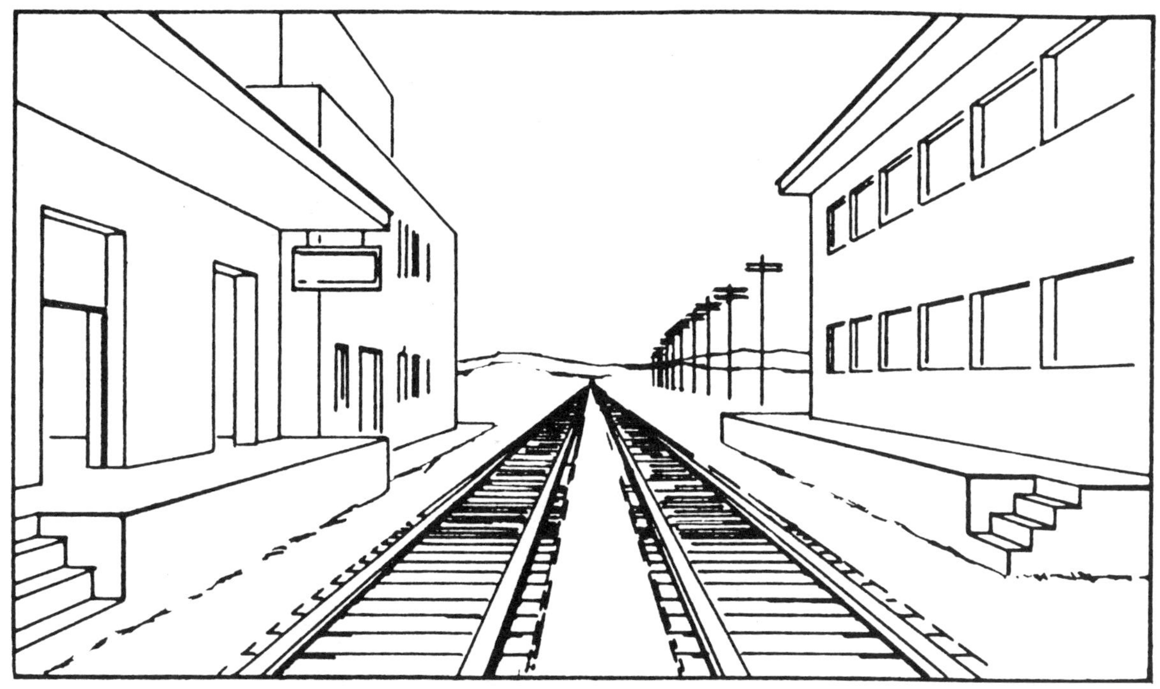

Figure 7-19a: When drawn in perspective, all parallel lines recede to a point of convergence (the "vanishing point").

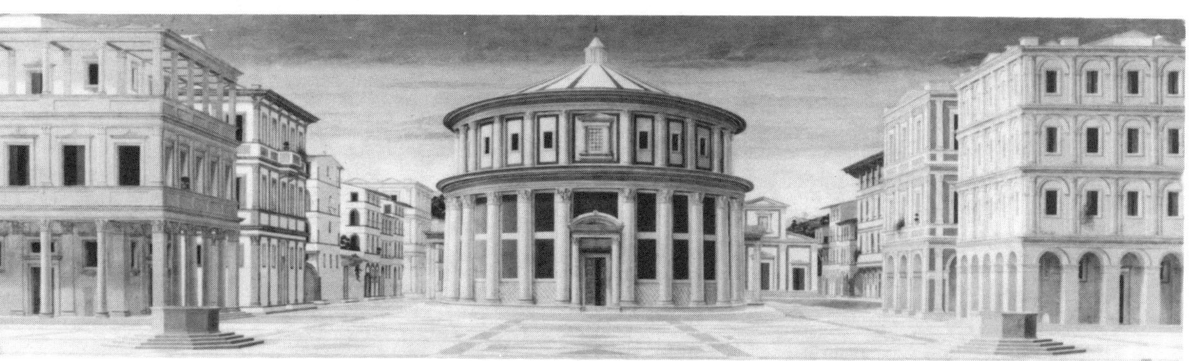

Figure 7-19b: This 15th century painting "View of an Ideal City" by Piero della Francesca and Luciano Laurana demonstrates the Italian Renaissance fascination with linear perspective.
Scala/Art Resource, NY.

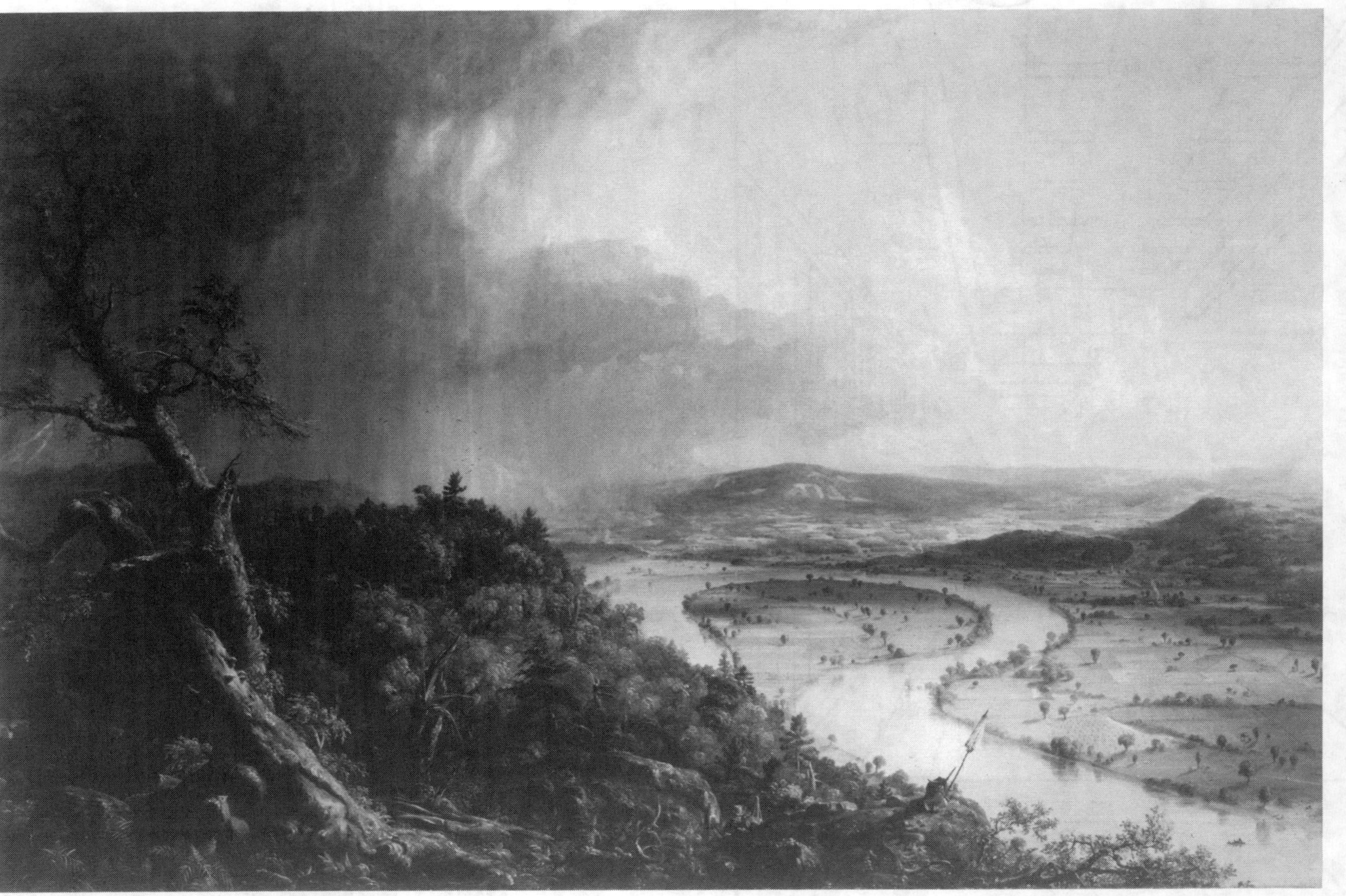

Figure 7-20: *The Oxbow (the Connecticut River Near Northampton)*, Thomas Cole, 1836, oil on canvas, 51 1/2" x 76", The Metropolitan Museum of Art, NY.

they, like the rails, merge and vanish from sight in the distance. This point of visual convergence at the horizon is called a "vanishing point." Artists during the Renaissance learned to draw using one, two and even several vanishing points in the same work. Their artwork began to reflect appearance rather than intellect alone (Figure 7-19b).

A final technique pictorial artists use to show depth is depicting distant objects as indistinct, even blurred, and near objects as clearly and cleanly drawn. Landscape painting most typically demonstrates the use of this technique (Figure 7-20).

USE OF THE ART ELEMENTS

This brief introduction to the elemental structure of art has focused on the evocative character of the elements as they guide viewing. By understanding the elements' impact upon response and perception, the appreciator's experience of art takes on richness and depth. This discussion has emphasized the inherent affective functions of line, shape, value, color, texture and space in art from the standpoint of the viewer. The viewer responds to and "reads" artwork using all available emotional and intellectual tools. The elements provide a basic vocabulary for the viewer's reading of art. The artist technically manipulates the elements with an end in mind—to produce an expressive artwork. The use of the art elements by the artist and the viewer are complementary; the artist seeks to communicate through the art elements, while the viewer "reads" them to understand that communication.

FUNCTION OF COMPOSITION

A work of art always represents a balance between some elements which are unified and others which are varied. There is no ideal combination of unified and varied elements in art. Unity or harmony may prevail in one work, while variety might outweigh harmony in another. The following discussion of compositional principles outlines the means used to relate and interrelate the parts of an artwork.

BALANCE

Balance in a work of art depends upon variables such as placement, size, spacing, proportion, and direction of shapes in the composition. Balance, as an abstract idea, is neither desirable nor undesirable. Too much balance can appear boring and static. On the other hand, a picture may not possess enough balance to configure visually. Generally, the forms which compose an artwork counterbalance one another so that a controlled tension results. This does not mean that the artist necessarily sets out consciously to balance the work; the controlled tension in an artwork may be arrived at intuitively.

The simplest type of balance is symmetrical or formal. In pure formal symmetry identical visual units are bilateral, equally distributed on either side of a vertical axis in mirror-like repetition or concentric, equally distributed relative to a central point. The result of formal symmetry is sometimes lifeless and inactive. However, through its use, unity is easily attained. Certainly unity is achieved in Giotto's strictly symmetrical placement of the figures on either side of his *Madonna Enthroned* (Figure 7-21). Giotto's repetition ensures that nothing will compete with the two central figures for the focus of attention. Perhaps more useful than a strictly formal symmetry is an "easy symmetry" in which the two sides of the artwork are varied to hold the viewer's attention but they are similar enough to be repetitious and clearly bilateral. Hans Memling's *Virgin and Child Enthroned* (Figure 7-22) illustrates this easy symmetry. The focus of the composition is clearly the mother and child, but the two figures at either side of the throne attract attention as well.

Informal, asymmetrical or intuitive balance relies upon a subjective equilibrium among parts of an artwork. This kind of balance has no dividing axis, no center point. When a work is in asymmetrical equilibrium, the viewer judges opposing forces and their tensions as balanced. This balance may be between clearly contradictory forces such as black and white, yellow and purple, or positive and negative. Such contradictory forces in balance are dynamic and prompt inquiry and interest on the part of the viewer. Contemporary, abstract art frequently relies on the dynamic balance of contrasting elements. The Abstract Expressionist painter Adolph Gottlieb intended for his images to evoke general themes such as "dualities" and "the conflict of opposites."[10] In *Duet* (Colorplate 5) we see an image that occupied Gottlieb for many years in a series of paintings called *Bursts*. The bursts here are two contrasting balls of vermillion and pink floating above a field of freely painted earthen hues and black.

Rhythm and Repetition

Rhythm is produced in a work of art by a repetition of elements in an observable sequence. Musical terms are often used to describe the concept of rhythm, because rhythm is most clearly demonstrated musically. A rhythmical sequence may flow or be punctuated by pauses or staccato beats. Rhythmical, cadenced, non-musical activities include walking, running and chopping wood, to name a few. Rhythmical sequences in visual art often occur in triads because three is the smallest number which produces a perceptible sequence. Some works of art possess a rhythmical system of "beats" and "measures." When the viewer recognizes the beat, or system of beats, in a work of art, the order in the whole work can be perceived. The perception of rhythmical unity and balance in a work is traditionally considered to be desirable.

Rhythm and repetition are inseparable. Repetition produces rhythm. Repetition is the means used in a picture or sculpture to reemphasize forms, colors and textures in keeping with some pattern. Gothic architecture makes abundant use of rhythmical repetition of columns, windows, arches and ceiling vaults to convey both grandeur and a spiritual sense of eternality (Figure 7-23).

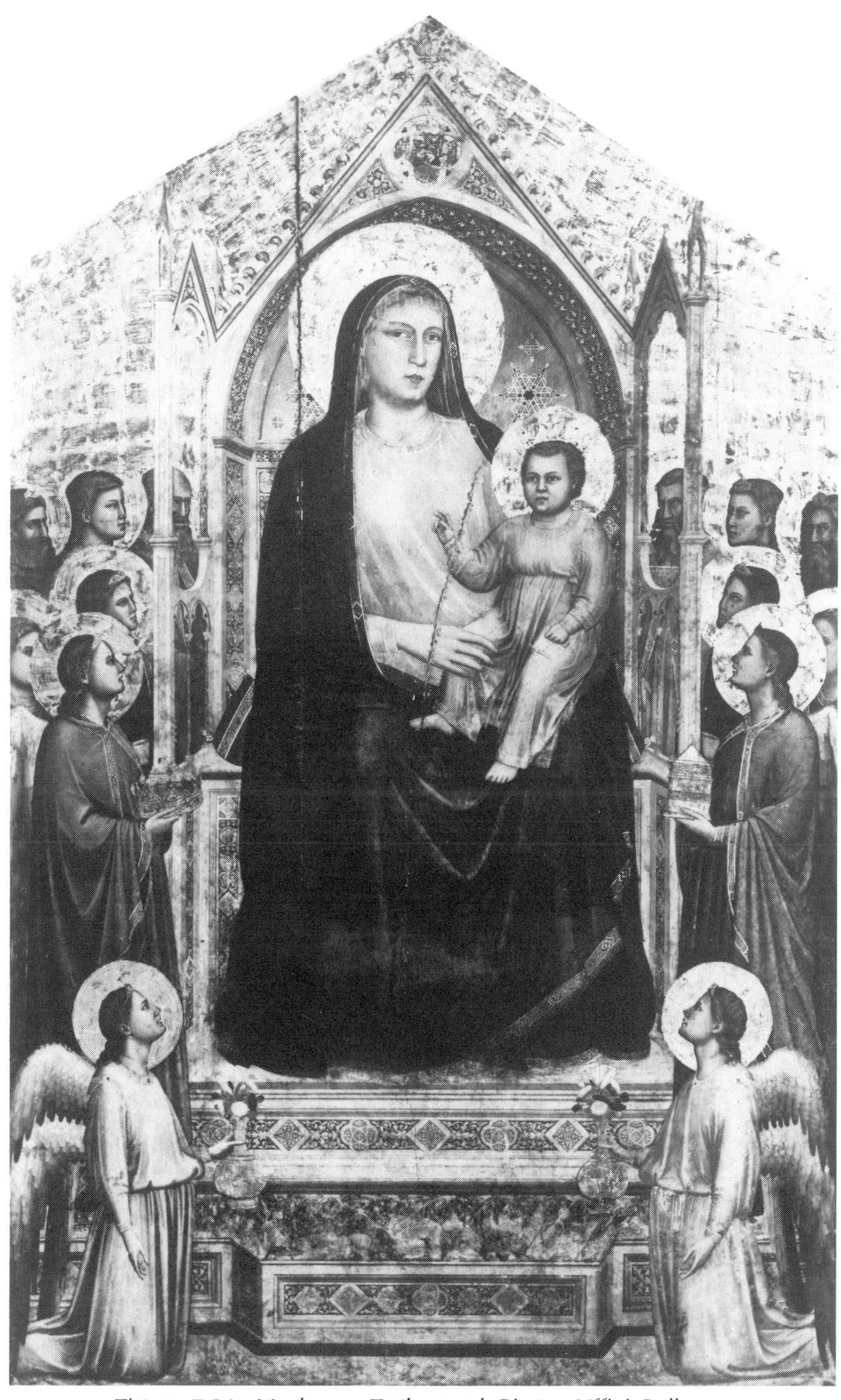

Figure 7-21: *Madonna Enthroned,* Giotto, Uffizi Gallery, Florence, Italy. (Alinari/Art Resource, NY).

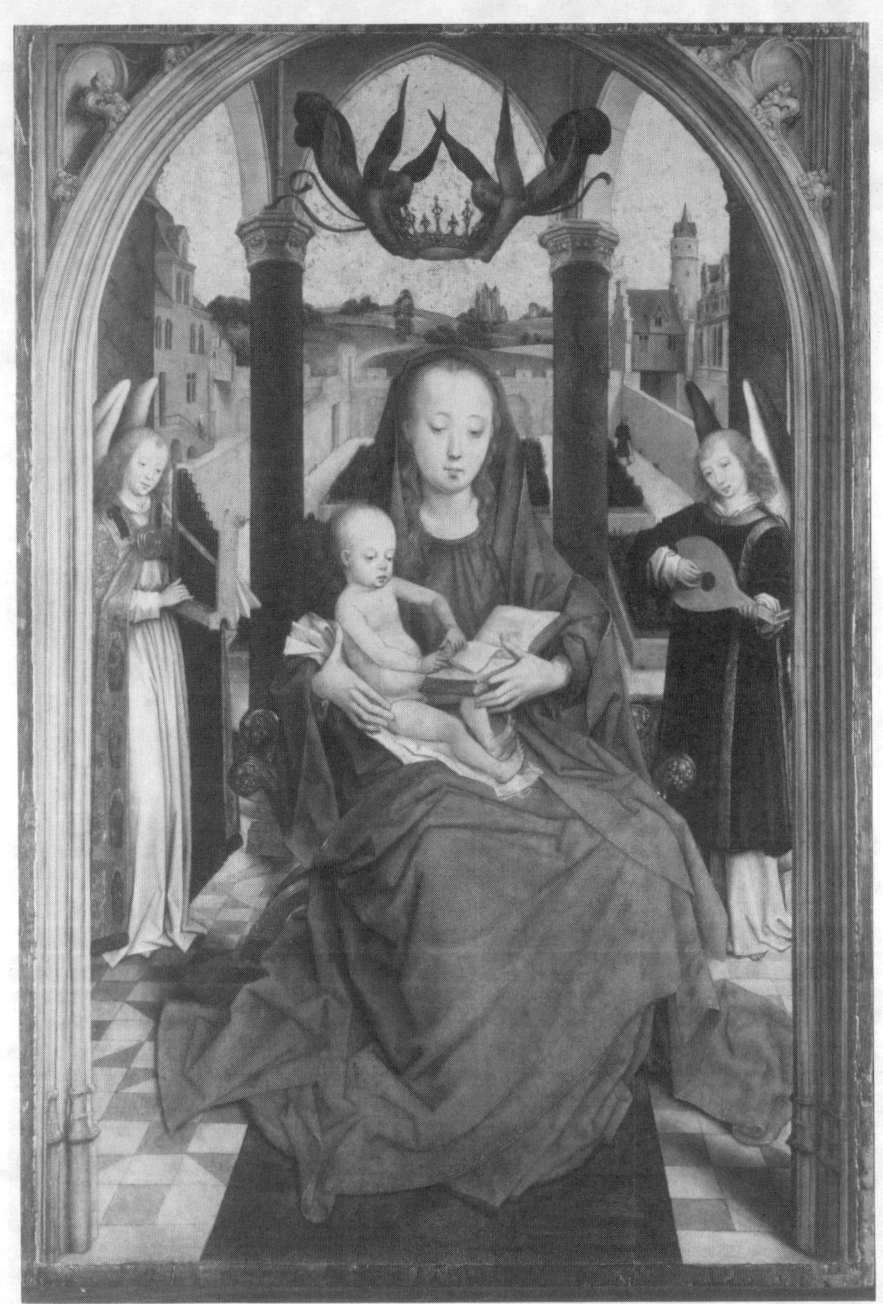

Figure 7-22: *Virgin and Child Enthroned,* c. 1470,
Hans Memling and Workshop (c. 1430/40–1494),
tempera and oil glazes on panel,28½" x 19½",
The Nelson-Atkins Museum of Art, Kansas City, Missouri
(Nelson Fund) 44-43.

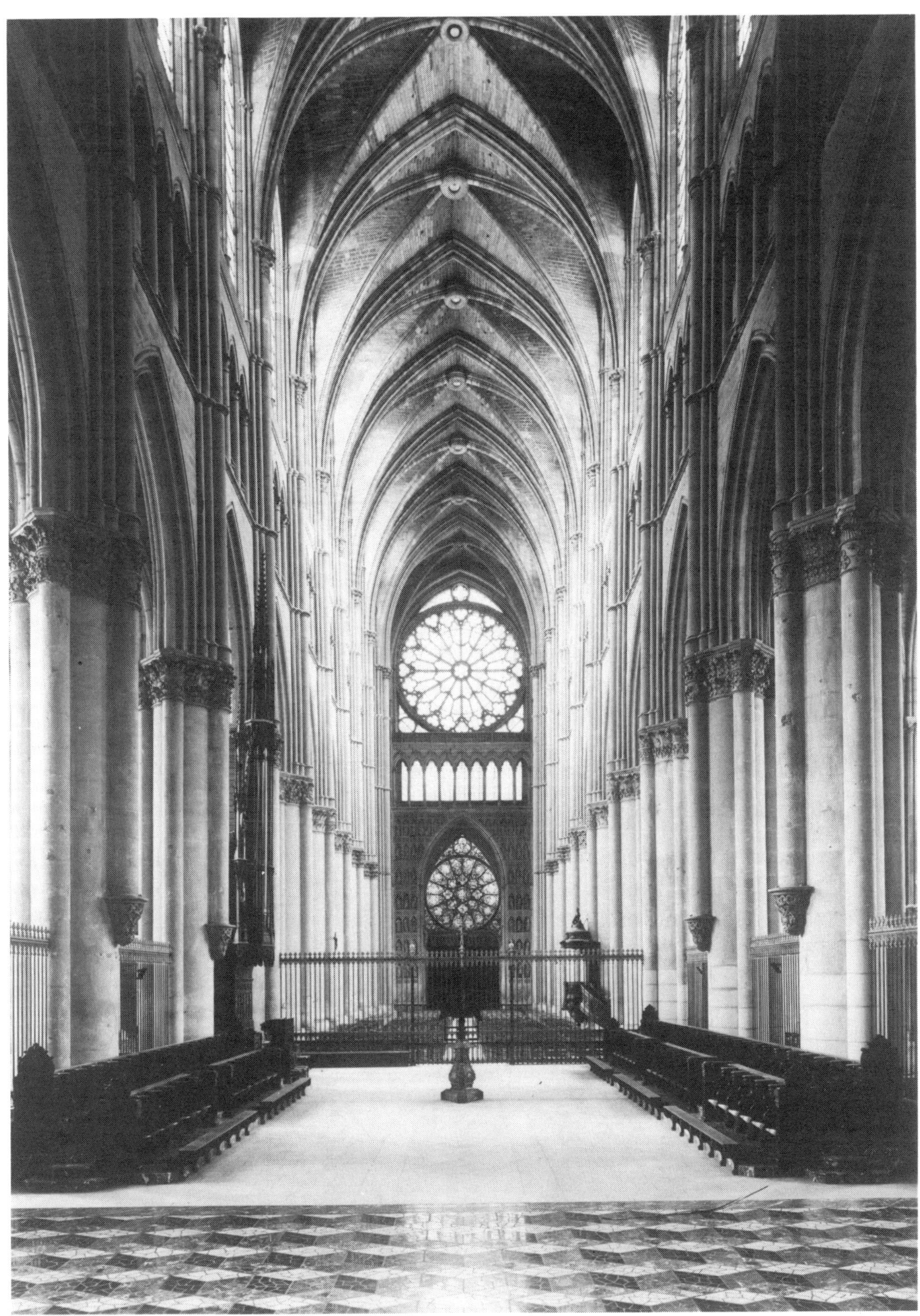

Figure 7-23: Reims Cathedral (nave looking west), 1241–85, France, (Marburg/Art Resource, NY).

DOMINANCE AND SUBORDINANCE

For one part of an artwork to dominate, that part must stand in contrast to what surrounds it. The dominant part must become a highly accentuated focal point of visual interest. Dominance in a work of art is usually a part of an overall alternating scheme in which elements are stressed and diminished repetitively. Subordinance of one part of a composition allows another part to draw attention. Failure to orchestrate emphasis invites ambiguity and indeterminate viewing of the artist's work.

In certain artworks compositionally subordinate elements provide the key to significance. For instance, in Pieter Bruegel's *Landscape with the Fall of Icarus*, a plowman dominates the foreground and center of the painting, while the tragic Icarian myth is played out in the lower right-hand corner (refer to Chapter I, Figure1-2). Bruegel's device works beautifully; the viewer is surprised to discover the legs of the fallen Icarus disappearing into the sea.

FOR DISCUSSION

1. Do the elements of art exist independently of what they describe or does their actuality depend upon what they describe?
2. If an artwork were dominated by the artist's use of only a single element, would that work be necessarily lacking? How many "elements" should be present in an artwork?
3. When is understanding of an artwork's elemental structure important?
4. How do the art elements relate to the compositional principles of art?
5. How do the art elements and compositional principles help the viewer of art understand what is seen and experienced? Choose an artwork from a local gallery, museum, or perhaps from your own home and specifically describe the function of composition in that work.

CHAPTER VIII: THE MEDIA AND METHODS OF ART

"Beyond the qualities of creativity, self-expression and communication, art is a type of work. This is what art has been from the beginning. This is what art is from childhood to old age. Through art, our students learn the meaning and joy of work—work done to the best of one's ability, for its own sake, for the satisfaction of a job well done. There is a desperate need in our society for a revival of the idea of good work. Work for personal fulfillment, work for social recognition; work for economic development. Work is one of the noblest expressions of the human spirit, and art is the visible evidence of work carried to the highest possible level."

—Dr. Edmund B. Feldman (statement of focus for the National Art Education Association, 1982)

Without a working knowledge of artistic processes, material usage, techniques and craftsmanship, the historian is limited, the critic lacks breadth, and the student sees incompletely the art attended to. For the historian of art a work of art has certain characteristics which define it, and distinguish it from another artwork or from anything else with which it might be compared. While the time of an artwork's manufacture and the place of its making are important, the manner of an artwork's making is indispensable to a defining knowledge of it.

For the critic of art, who evaluates and judges art, the goodness of a work may depend upon the quality of workmanship exercised by the artist. For instance, I might question a steel sculpture's poorly welded joints if the welds interfere with my visual enjoyment of it. It would help any critic of metal sculpture to have some familiarity with fabrication processes.

Some materials and technical processes in and of themselves are inherently beautiful and aesthetically pleasing. The potter working at his wheel, drawing clay up from a shapeless lump to form an elegant bowl, works with a process that is pleasant to behold. Other processes may not be so enjoyable to watch, but they result in products fully as beautiful as the potter's bowl. It is through study and exposure to materials and artistic processes that the student will develop a heightened sense of aesthetic value and intelligent appreciation.

ARCHITECTURE

It was once popular to call architecture "the mother of the arts," conceivably implying that the pursuit of building design and construction predates other forms of art making. This is mistaken since the origin of any of the arts remains a mystery. Architecture may with justification be called "mother" when the sustaining qualities of motherhood are metaphorically referred to. Architecture has nurtured the other arts by providing space for their exhibition and at times providing a motivation for their creation.

Customarily, the architecture most studied is that which is felt to be culturally, historically, and aesthetically meaningful. Such archetypes of culture are not the architecture most of us are familiar with. Our homes and offices are the built spaces we know best. If a house or an office building is an example of architecture, then is a prison, a barn or a fast food restaurant also architecture? Inherently, yes; all of these structures enclose and occupy space. But the qualitative question to ask of each example is how well does it enclose, and how well does it function in space? It is the arrangement of space in a structure and the use of masses and planes that gives force and credibility to the term architecture applied to a building.

Proportionate relationships among the parts of the building determine significance. Architectural proportions from the earliest times were based on geometric relationships in quantity, mass or size. These mathematical ratios were not unbiased standards, but were culturally determined, reflecting the ideals, aspirations and symbolism of an epoch and a people. Proportions in a building have always represented a balance between a building's intended function and the builder's aesthetic sensibility. The architect always weighs and balances form and function in planning.

When we describe a building as a form existing in or occupying space, we express that architecture resembles sculpture. Also, the same materials, traditionally esteemed by sculptors are those often chosen by architects. Stone, wood, clay, and metals are favored by both sculptors and architects. Contemporary ferroconcrete, (concrete combined with a reinforcing matrix of steel) works in the same way as the sculptor's armature which supports clay and plaster forms. Freestanding architectural masses such as columns, pillars, and monoliths possess a sculptural presence. It is difficult to imagine an ancient Egyptian temple without its sculptural reliefs. Early builders typically worked also as masons and sculptors.

Architecture encloses space by employing either of two basic constructive systems: (1) a solid type (sometimes called a shell), or (2) a frame type (sometimes called skeleton and skin) (Figure 8-1). Prior to the industrial revolution of the eighteenth and nineteenth century buildings were generally constructed using a solid type structural system. Since the industrial revolution and with the development of new synthetic building materials most buildings use a frame or skeletal type construction.

Solid construction relies upon a unitary self-supporting material for structural reliability of walls (inside and out) and roofs. Materials favored historically for traditional solid construction were stone, wood, or brick.

Framed construction relies upon the attachment of walls and roof to a system of skeletal support. This system functions to provide the rigidity needed for the integrity of internal and external walls (the skin) and roof.

Ancient builders used the stacking and piling of stones and other natural materials as one means of solid construction. Simple stacking of cut stone blocks in the ancient world resulted in impressive, monolithic structures, but as a means of enclosing space, stacking and piling had limitations. Other, less expensive, labor intensive ways of architecturally enclosing space had to be found.

The simplest, most efficient way to enclose space is to set a beam horizontally across two well-anchored vertical posts. England's "Stonehenge" exemplifies this building method using stone posts and horizontal stone lintels. Both the Egyptians and the Greeks exclusively used mortarless, post-and-lintel masonry construction. One of Egypt's greatest tributes to post-and-lintel construction is the "Temple of Amun-Mut-Khon-su" which was built beside the river Nile at Luxor. The temple's colonnades create a forest of closely spaced posts throughout the interior. The use of stone lintels necessitated the close placement of the interior columnar supports. Stone's weight and lack of tensile strength meant that only short lateral distances could be spanned between vertical supports. Consequently, Egyptian structures did not enclose extensive areas of open space. Huge gatherings of people were held outdoors in open areas.

The problem of spanning intervals using stone lintels was partially solved by construction employing the round arch and vault. Although the practice of arch and vault construction was known in earlier times, it was the Romans who fully realized the potential of the round arch for spanning and enclosing space. By serially building round arches one behind the other, the Romans created barrel vaults which enclosed impressively large spaces free of intrusive columns. And, by intersecting one barrel vault at right angles to another a crossed or groined vault was created which at the time enclosed the largest built spaces in human history. Also, by building round arches radially (rotating them 360 degrees), the Romans created hemispherical domes of impressive scale, such as the Pantheon (Figure 8-2).

While the arch, vault, and dome permitted builders to circumscribe great spaces, the huge quantities of masonry used created great bulk and weight. This weight was structurally absorbed by the use of very thick supporting walls and buttressing. Buttresses or abutments absorbed the lateral pressure created by the weight of arched masonry construction. Buttresses were often built into

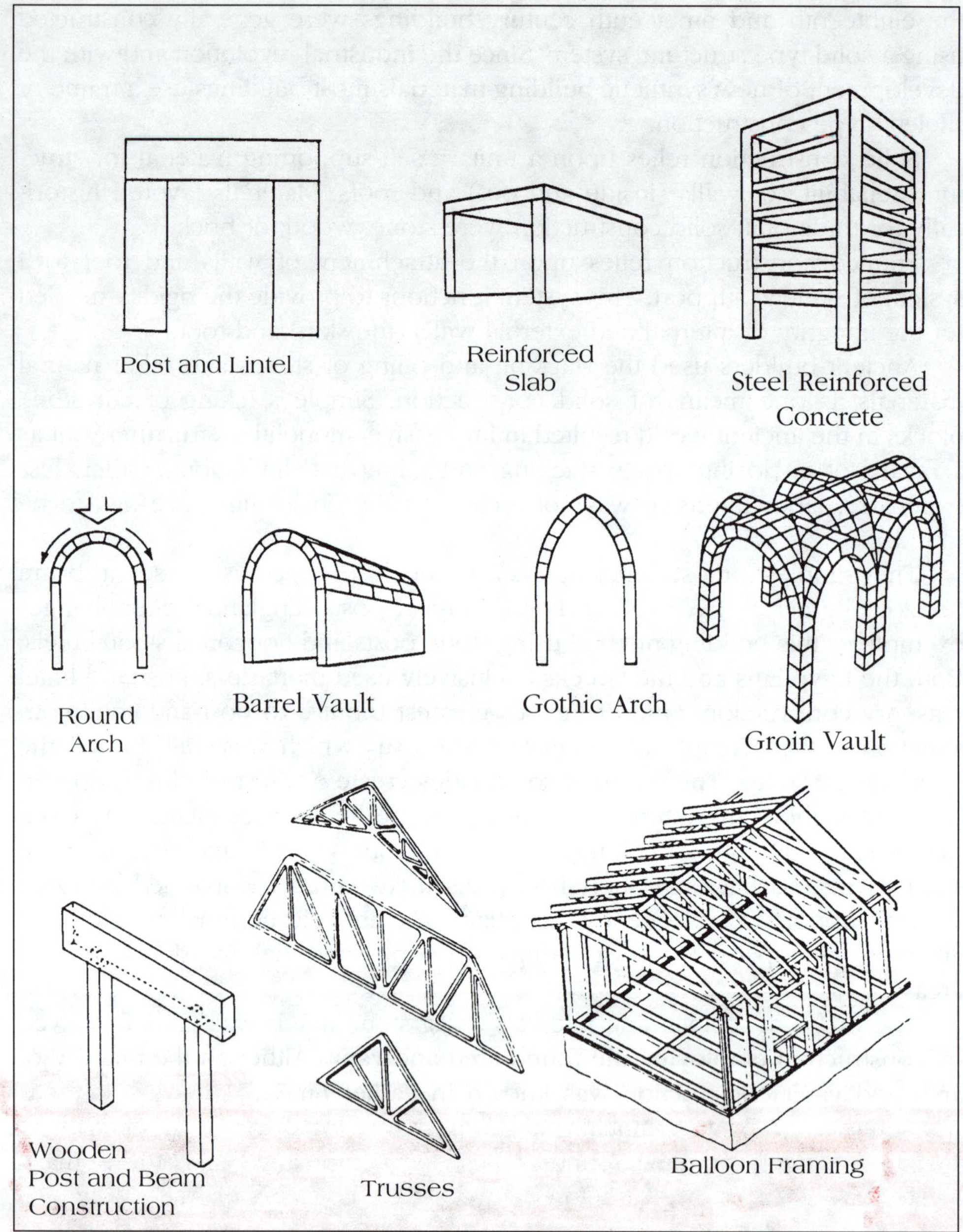

Figure 8-1: Structural Building Systems (Solid and Frame Type).

walls, and were thus hidden from view, but increasingly buttressing was made visible. In the great Gothic churches of Europe external buttresses are a harmonious part of the buildings overall design.

Some geographical regions of the world lack stone which can be quarried for building purposes. In such areas timber or the earth itself is used for building. Constructive systems using wood or earth vary considerably from masonry post and lintel and arched systems. The construction of early wood

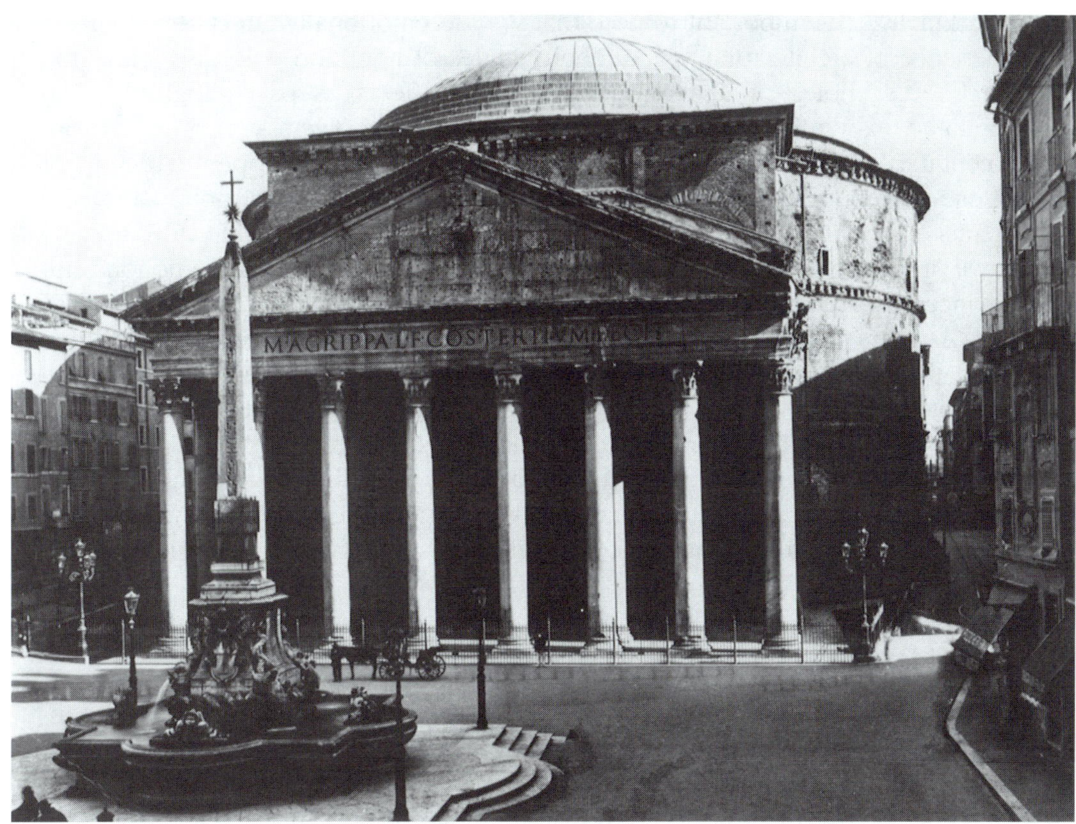

Figure 8-2: The Pantheon, Rome. Exterior.
(Alinari/Art Resource, NY)

post and beam structures predates post and lintel, and possibly provided a model for later masonry construction.

Trussing was an important early device used for bridging space with wooden beams. Relying on the use of triangulation, builders created rigid, three-sided wood frames which would span and enclose large areas. Often post-and-lintel stone walled structures were covered using wood beam, truss type roofs. Today, trusses continue to be used in most wood-frame construction.

Early in human history earthen construction consisted mainly of certain mixtures of clays and other natural materials to form bricks which were dried in the sun, then used. Later, clay bricks were baked in fire which made them much more durable. Sun-dried bricks are still used for solid wall construction in areas where wood and stone are scarce and the climate is hot and dry. Some early native American peoples used a combination of moist earth smoothed over a woven stick frame. This was called "daub and wattle" and was used for erecting permanent dwellings. Builders of early log structures used moist clay to close up chinks between the logs and to improve the insulating properties of the construction.

Finally, it is important to note that we are emotionally affected by our experience of architectural space. The qualities of light and color as well as the architect's choice of materials and textures affects us psychologically. The architect may build into a design a sense of unity or diversity. A built environment may promote relaxation or evoke tension. Spaces may open to the eye or close promoting an atmosphere of freedom or inviting claustrophobia. Occupants of certain enclosures may feel protected and secure. Architecture may be awe inspiring and humbling. A very great range of human emotions are evinced by architecture.

As users of architecture every day, we experience structured spaces in duration, that is, in time. We pass through enclosed spaces sequentially, experiencing a limited perspective from any singular vantage point. The affects on the observer of experiencing architectural space are cumulative and complex.

With the coming of the industrial revolution in the eighteenth and nineteenth centuries, architecture changed dramatically. New materials were developed which led to a Renaissance of building activity which is still in progress today.

SCULPTURE

We enjoy sculpture visually but our tactile sense also governs our apprehension of three-dimensional form. It is important to realize sculpture's reliance upon the eye controlled by the hand. Sculptor Constantin Brancusi recognized the significance of touch in his work titled "Sculpture for the Blind." The eye alone never reveals the essence of sculpture. Eye and hand work in combination to create sculpture. Eye and hand work together in the knowledgeable appreciator who understands sculpture.

In addition to its tactility, sculpture possesses mass. When sculpture is said to be "in-the-round" we not only respond to it frontally, but we are able to walk completely around it, to experience its total mass and surface qualities. Sculpture is not always created completely in-the-round. The ancient Egyptians created huge figures in relief. Relief sculpture projects from background supports. Egyptian figures carved in high-relief extended from walls or other vertical support. A relief sculpture is called "high" when more than half of the form's natural circumference projects from the supporting surface. Low-relief or (bas-relief) sculptural forms project only slightly from their background.

The first sculptors to completely break Egyptian relief sculpture's attachment to the wall were the early Greeks. Their freestanding in-the-round male and female figures invited the viewer for the first time in history to experience sculptural form in a strikingly lifelike manner.

Although naturalistic forms have inspired sculptors since the earliest times, modern sculptors have explored radical abstraction of natural forms. Abstract sculpture invites the viewer's complicity in enjoying planes, textures and inventive forms which are unpredictable and unexpected. The viewer may become a participant in a series of singular impressions which have great impact. This impact and vitality might never accompany one's experience of more orthodox figurative sculpture.

One way to understand sculptural history is to look at sculptural development as occurring along an energy continuum (Figure 8-3). This means defining sculpture in terms of motion (both potential and kinetic). At one end of this energy continuum would be sculpture expressing implied movement; while the other end of the scale would include sculpture which is operatively active. Physics' traditional distinction of potential and kinetic provides useful parameters for such a scale. The value of this approach is demonstrated when we take note of the formal incompatibility of traditional figurative and modern abstract sculpture. History's earliest figurative sculpture, as well as contemporary real time, abstractions extend rationally along an energy continuum.

At the "implied" extreme of an energy continuum would be sculpture which by its conformation suggests movement. Myron's "Discus Thrower" implies dynamic motion. In fact, most figurative statuary offers some suggestion of movement simply by its lifelike appearance.

Within the definition of "conformational" there are formal energetic distinctions. For instance, while the "Discus Thrower" implies motion but does not actually move, sculptures such as Tony Smith's contemporary, geometric, primary structures neither move nor imply movement (Figure 8-4). Also, purely conceptual "sculpture" which exists only as apriori structures of thought (plans, ideas or concepts) is further removed from any implication of motion than even Smith's stationary steel cubes.

Opposite of motionless works are sculptures which are environmentally responsive, real time constructions. These "kinetic" sculptures express some

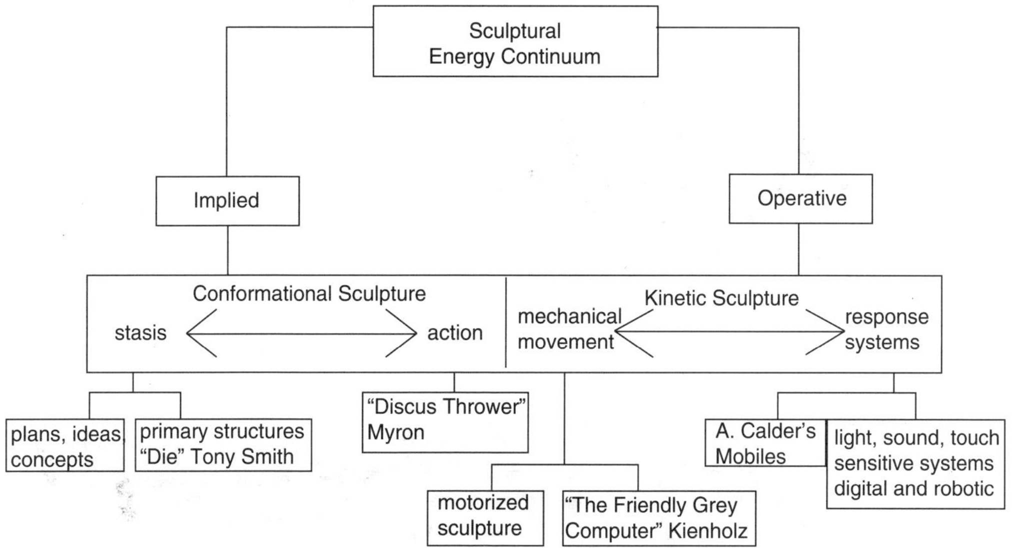

Figure 8-3: Sculptural Energy Continuum

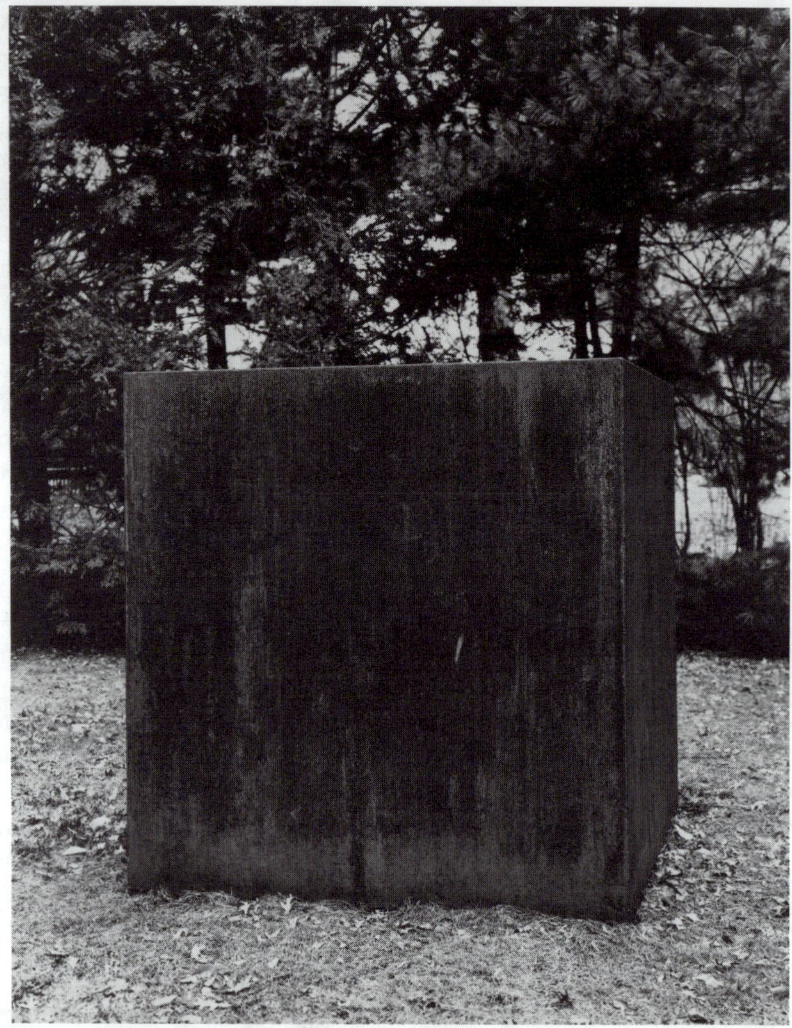

Figure 8-4: *Die,* by Tony Smith,1962. Steel, 72" x 72" x 72". Private Collection. Photo by Ivan Dalla Tana. Photograph courtesy Paula Cooper Gallery, NY.

kind of physical motion. Sculptures, such as the mobiles of Alexander Calder and George Rickey (Figure 4-6) move as shifting currents of air dictate. Other electronically advanced sculptures are touch, light and sound activated. At one extreme kinetic works operate according to strictly controlled, pre-programmed sequences of movement. Such sculptures are purely mechanical or fixed sequence constructions.

Whether or not a sculpture is figurative or abstract, whether or not it is kinetic or implies no movement at all, sculpture always has been made in one of four basic ways. It may be modeled, cast, carved or constructed. These methods may be used singly or in combination.

Examples of modeled clay objects have existed throughout human history. Most extant samples of ancient clay figures are modeled in terra cotta. Terra cotta is reddened clay which has been baked to a brick-like hardness. Not only clay but any material possessing enough plasticity to be shaped by hand may be used for modeling form. Modeling with highly plastic materials affords the sculptor an immediate and direct means of expression. Sculptors such as August Rodin and Henry Moore began making sculptures by working directly in clay, initially creating models which were then cast into a more permanent material such as bronze.

Castings are typically made from original forms modeled in clay or wax. The casting process takes a durable material such as metal and replaces a less durable prototype made from clay or wax. This is why casting is referred to as a replacement method. During the bronze casting process a hollow, negative mold is filled with molten metal, poured from a crucible. When the metal freezes (hardens) and cools the mold is broken open revealing the newly cast sculpture which, when the process is successful, closely duplicates the prototype.

Like modeling, carving has been practiced throughout human history. Carving is the act of cutting, scraping or hewing away parts of a hard, solid, mass of material to create form. The subtractive nature of sculptural carving dictates that form is created by the removal of material from the mass. If the sculptor makes a mistake by cutting away too much material the work may be ruined. A mistake means that the sculptor must either abandon a project entirely or modify the original plan and use the error as a point of departure for a new idea.

Carving is hard work. The subtractive nature of the process makes carving more perilous than additive processes such as modeling. The modeler typically builds up form little by little. The pliable nature of clay makes it easier to work with than hard, inflexible stone. The sculptor of stone must always fear breakage or striking an unanticipated flaw in the stone. The carver of wood usually follows the grain; cutting against the grain of the wood can be nearly impossible. The sculptor may work subtractively with clay, starting with a huge mass and cutting it down. Despite its difficulties, carving in wood and stone can produce work of great delicacy and variety. Gothic wood carvings and the bone and ivory reliefs of the many anonymous artisans of the Middle Ages are unmatched achievements in the art of carving.

Constructed sculpture relies upon the fastening, joining or adhering of materials. Constructed sculpture is additive in approach. The sculptor unites materials, fastening them together using nuts and bolts, rivets, clamps, etc. Or a sculpture may be assembled using welding equipment to fuse metal elements. Yet another constructive method may consist of laminated and glued wooden parts. While historical examples of constructive sculptural techniques exist, it is in the twentieth century that technology has provided hundreds of new constructive methods and devices for innovative sculptural applications.

Drawing

Drawing may be defined as Webster's dictionary defines it, "to make lines, pictures, etc. as with a pencil." The World Book indicates that to make a drawing is "to make a picture, or likeness of with pencil, pen, chalk, crayon, etc., represent with lines . . . to mark out, to describe, to form"; such definitions tell us little that we do not already know.

To make lines, marks or smudges on a surface is to draw in a fundamental way. However, to draw is to also execute meaningful marks, lines or smudges in some more or less permanent form. It appears that drawing is a natural act whether or not talent or artistic intent is present. Children seem to draw instinctively. We draw in the sand with a stick, on frosty window panes with our fingers, and graffiti has always been a part of human culture. These are very basic and ordinary examples of our use of drawing.

Drawing may be described as a means of communication or language. The drawing marks of the artist function as much as language as do words for the writer. Also, the artist uses symbols in drawing, just as the poet uses metaphor, simile and personification. The artist and the writer use symbols, examining them, taking them apart, and putting them together again, rearranging them and playing with them.

There appear to be three important conceptual processes related to drawing. *First,* one must *see*. *Second,* one must *think* and *understand what is seen*. And *third,* one should be able to *draw from a purely conceptual base*.

To be able to draw is a matter of learning to *see* and this does not mean using the eye alone. The sort of seeing meant here is close observation that utilizes as many of the five senses as can be reached at once. The artist does not rely on the eye alone to describe an observation but rather the artist learns to employ the use of touch, taste, smell, and hearing.

Thinking about what we see and understanding it means cultivating our ability to concentrate, conceptualize and imagine. Often, we look at objects without observing details. If asked to draw an object from memory, we might have some difficulty, because of a lack of experience in drawing and the expectation of having an object in front of us. The artist learns to view an object, analyze it and commit it to memory. The role of conceptualization and imagination in drawing involves much more than knowing the shape of any given form. Conceptualizing requires something other than technical adjustments. Intuition, insight and the artist's subconscious intellect may all be involved in the mystery of conceptualizing. It may be said that a process of concept drawing is like the pleasant meeting upon a page of the inspired and the unexpected.

Traditionally, in the past drawing served as a preparation for painting. Artists would make preliminary studies or sketches which were then translated into another medium such as paint. These studies provided guides for the painter's ultimate objective, completion of painted imagery on a durable surface such as wood panel or linen stretched over wood.

Another well established use for drawing may be described as illustration. Illustration has a long and venerable history. During prehistory, rites, rituals and ceremonies were illustrated in linear drawings made on cave walls, etched in stone, or on clay tablets. Early copies of Christian Biblical text were decorated with elaborate illustrative drawing. With the invention of movable type, many kinds of books were illustrated. Today, cartoons, comic strips, and comic books all demonstrate the ubiquity of illustration in our culture.

A major current use of drawing is for personal expression. Today, drawing is employed in its own right as a unique medium of expression. It is not preliminary to anything but functions as an end in itself. Some contemporary artists draw exclusively and exhibit their drawings in major exhibitions. Through drawing, these artists express a complete vision.

One additional continuing use of drawing that should not be overlooked is the use of drawing or sketching for a kind of personal "note taking." Similar to a photographic snapshot, drawing functions for the artist as a diary of awareness, as a form of graphic shorthand, having both freshness and immediacy. This often rapid recording of perceptual information is beautiful in its spontaneity and refreshingly direct.

PAINTING

Among the earliest painted images are the cave paintings at Lascaux in France (Figure 8-5) and those in Altimira in Spain. By labeling something a "painting," what is meant? Inherently any colored surface is a painting. Since the paleolithic era people have applied color to everything that would accept it. The walls of Egyptian and Greek temples and tombs were adorned with color. Egyptian, Greek and Medieval European sculpture was painted. Early Chinese and Mexican pottery was colored; the native American Indians painted pottery also. While the painting of objects appeared before the painting of images on walls, the ancient Aegean and Greek cultures along with the Etruscans in Italy painted frescos. The fresco is the most important method of early large scale painting on walls. Usually, smaller paintings on wood boards or panels were done using either the encaustic technique of painting with colored beeswax or the egg tempera process.

The first painters seemed to share an approach to the wall or panel which consisted of drawing outlines and filling-in those outlines with areas of colored stain or pigment. In fact, line and color were typically equally emphasized. Both Medieval manuscript illuminators and panel painters worked respectively in watercolor and tempera, making linear designs then filling in areas of color. Examples of drawing outlines first and filling-in continue to be evident into the modern era.

At times the term "pure" painting is used to describe a composition built up entirely of colored pigments without boundaries or patterns of lines. Pure painting depends upon a knowledge and appreciation of the intrinsic qualities of paint. Leonardo Da Vinci's use of "sfumato" to achieve muted smokelike effects reduce outline to blurred and indistinct shadows. Using Leonardo as a benchmark, it may be posited that pure painting begins with the Renaissance.

Impasto, or the thick, textured buildup of paint on a surface, is another expression of pure painting. The physical thickening of the paint surface produces a raised tactile quality that engages the viewer, drawing the viewer into the work.

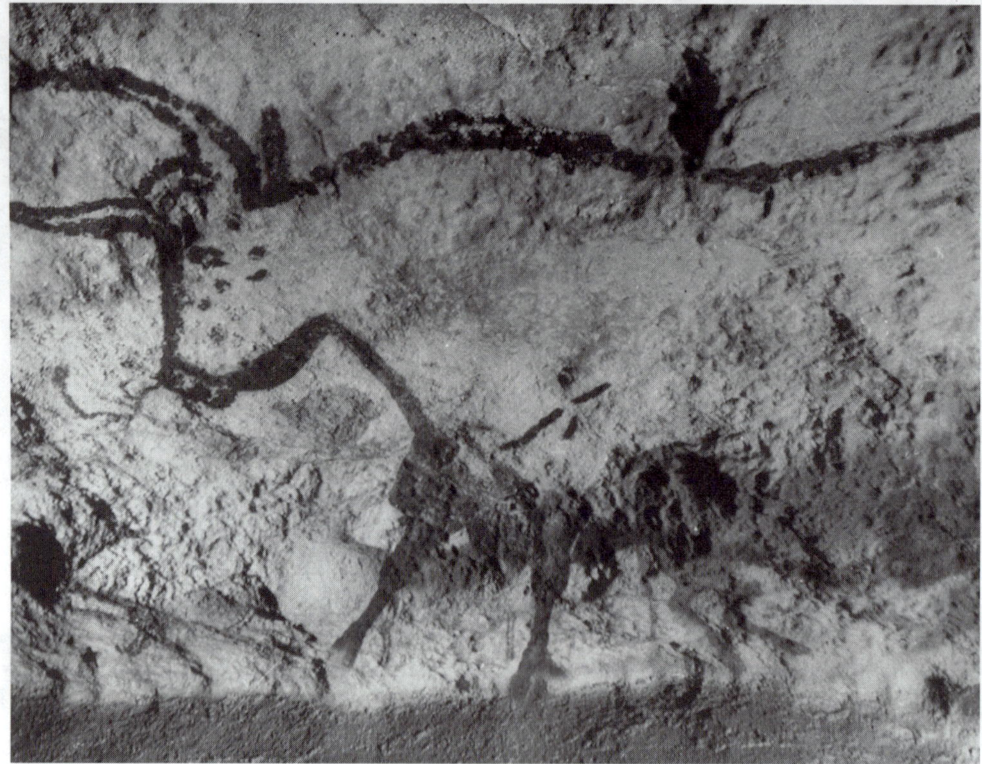

Figure 8-5: Cave painting at Lascaux: Bisons. Lascaux Caves, Perigord, Dordogne, France. (Giraudon/Art Resource, NY)

Sometimes successive layers of thin transparent colors are used by painters to achieve deep, subtle tonalities. This layering of color helps the painter to gradually bring the work into "focus" and into full, rich resonance.

In vivid contrast to architecture and sculpture, painting has a kind of intangibility about it. The painter's pigments are tangible enough but illusory qualities dominate most painting. Painterly illusion has the same potential power for expression as the poet's use of metaphor. Like a reflection in a mirror, a painting can cause us to examine and see reality in unique ways. A painting may be unreal in the way that a reflection in a mirror is unreal, but both a painting and a mirror have the capacity to heighten our perception of reality and truth.

Printmaking

A print is a result of a technical process that produces multiple images. An original print may be one of a series or edition, but it is always firsthand. In no sense is an original print a copy or a reproduction of something else. Each impression produced by the printing process is itself original. According to Carl Zigrosser writing for the American Print Council, "The print is created through contact with an inked or uninked plate, stone, block, or screen that has been worked on directly by the artist alone or with others." There are four varieties of printmaking: Relief, Intaglio, Planographic and Stencil. Prints are often created using more than one of these processes.

The total number of multiples generated of an original print comprise what is called an edition. Each print in the edition is numbered, titled, and signed by the artist. If the numbering system used by the artist employs two numbers arranged fractionally (i.e. 1/10) the top number refers to that actual print while the bottom number refers to the total number of prints in the edition. This numbering practice was not used until the twentieth century. Many serigraphers (screen printers) do not number by fractions, but rather state the total number in the edition as ED25. Customarily, AP or Artists Proof refers to an additional 10% above the total edition which the artist is permitted to keep from a commission or sale to a publisher. However, today an artist may use "Artists Proof" to denote a few prints that vary from the edition.

When an artist chooses to add color to a print through the application of watercolor, pastel, or colored pencils, those prints are designated as 'hand colored' and are not numbered as part of an edition unless the entire edition has been treated in this manner.

Fine printing may have evolved out of the early practice of hand-stamping patterns on fabric and pottery. Such stamping techniques are described by Cennino Cennini in a treatise written in the early fifteenth century. Woodcut and engraving seem to be the earliest completely mastered printing methods. German artists throughout the fifteenth century and after excelled at relief and intaglio printing.

The earliest European printmakers favored imagery that was primarily religious and based on compositions drawn from earlier paintings. Many of the secular prints done in the fifteenth century were satirical in nature, or of mythological subjects. Prints were inexpensive and their appeal to the buying public dictated to some extent the artist's choice of subject matter. The development of the printing press made widespread distribution of prints relatively simple. To this day, public taste and technical innovations govern much of the printmaker's art.

CRAFTS

At times the crafts unjustly have been considered "minor" arts. Artists of the past made no distinctions among the arts such as "major" and "minor." Every craft area has been considered at some time by some group as appropriate for expressing the noblest and most beautiful aesthetic ideals.

The crafts relate to sculpture in several ways. Like sculpture, the crafts are three-dimensional; they often employ the same materials and processes. The traditional craft media are clay, glass, fiber, metal and wood; sculptors also use these same materials. A clay vase may differ only from a terra cotta statuette in that it has a functional element. The hilt of a sword, a candle holder, and a bracelet are all sculptural. Cabinets, chests and cupboards may all relate to architecture in the ways they enclose space. Wallpaper, weaving and needlework are often reminiscent of drawing and painting.

These connections suggest that the crafts do not belong in a separate category from architecture, sculpture or painting. The segregation of crafts from the other arts by labeling crafts applied arts and painting, sculpture, etc.; fine or pure arts is a byproduct of the industrial revolution in nineteenth century Europe when the crafts experienced a period of decline. Renaissance artists of the fifteenth and sixteenth centuries such as Leonardo, Dürer, Verrocchio and Cellini made no distinctions among the arts such as fine, pure and applied. These artists designed objects of all varieties and apparently thought it natural and appropriate to do so.

Today, the fact that an object is functional in no way excludes or reduces its potential value as a beautiful work of art. It is a defining quality of the crafts that the relation of function to form is crucial when valuing craft objects. What is most important about a craft object is that (1) it may be both beautiful to look at and efficiently useful, and (2) it's function may be an outgrowth of its form or vice versa. Therefore, a cup and saucer as well as an oil painting may each be in the same measure functional.

Beauty and function should augment one another. An object's decorative detail and beauty should heighten the visual impact of that object. Those same decorative qualities should also give meaning to the object. This interaction of form and decoration is readily evident in the selections we make regarding personal adornment and cosmetics. A necklace does not merely adorn or decorate; it encircles the neck, it emphasizes the undulating curves of the upper body, it marks the distinction of head and body. Cosmetic makeup, body painting and tattooing (well done) harmonizes with a person's anatomical structure.

All of these factors and others are considered in the design of everyday objects. And when an object's function guides the designer's approach, the resulting design solution will be harmonious to the extent that a balance of function and form enlightens every consideration.

Graphic Design

Graphic design until recently was called "advertising design" or "commercial art." The designation "graphic design" characterizes best what artists working in this field actually do. While graphic designers create visual imagery intended to cause people to buy products or services, they also augment communication. All successful art communicates, but graphic design targets its communicative efforts with great specificity. Graphic artists design books develop logos and visual symbols, and create advertising. The tools of the graphic artists are type, photography and illustration. These design tools or implements must effectively convey a message. Effective communication in a modern society requires that a message be clearly, quickly and, if possible, permanently impressed upon the consciousness of a focus audience.

We live with graphic design day in and out through constant exposure to advertising. The cumulative psychological effect of all the myriad images that assail us through mass media is unknown. While advertising may be visually lovely, stimulating and funny, there is a downside. Any underlying or ambient meanings conveyed through graphic design are often less important to advertisers than sales of a product. For instance, an advertisement may effectively sell a cigarette, but at what "cost" to the consumer? A question increasingly asked of advertisers is one of ethical responsibility.

An historical overview of the field indicates that there are three primary factors that have driven the growth of graphic design: 1) Johan Gutenburg's invention of the printing press (fifteenth century), 2) the industrial revolution, and 3) the twentieth century revolution in electronic technology.

Gutenburg's press made possible the widespread production of prints and books, rendering obsolete the scriptoria (copy houses) of Europe. The industrial revolution developed mechanization and eventually the production line so that extensive quantities of goods could be produced. Graphic artists were enlisted by manufacturers to inform the buying public of their products.

Following World War II, the computer transformed graphic design. Using ever more complex and esoteric hardware and software, designers working at computer terminals are able to manipulate typography, photography, and illustration.

Today anyone having access to a personal computer can learn to use desktop publishing software for designing everything from advertising to books. The effects of this ubiquitously available technology on art and human behavior will continue to be exciting, innovative and controversial.

PHOTOGRAPHY

Photography, like printmaking, makes images by mechanical processes. But it is not the equipment (the camera or the printing press) that make either photographs or prints works of art.

For centuries, curious people sitting in darkened rooms observed that light streaming inward from a small opening in an exterior wall would project a clear image of the outdoors, upside-down on the opposite interior wall of their shadowy interiors. Cameras work in a similar way. The development of photography is really built upon the evolution of two devices, the camera (box) and the film needed to permanently record the image. For the photographer, camera and film are the equivalent of the draftsman's pen and paper or the painter's brush and canvas.

Photographs are works of art when they transcend the mechanical processes by which they are generated. A broad range of potentially expressive effects and subtle nuances are available to the artist-photographer. As an artist the photographer must do much more than simply "point and shoot." If the result of photographic picture making is to be art, the photographer must intelligently make crucial choices. The type of camera and film selected are immediately important. Choice of subject is important. Framing and composing the subject is a decisive choice. Finally, darkroom processing and printing are critical to the resulting image.

Until the nineteenth century, early relatives of today's camera used no film. A specially constructed box called a "camera obscura" was employed to focus images, which were then observed as projections of light against an inner surface of a box. Some artists even used the camera obscura to obtain accurate, tracings of scenery. A sort of permanent "film" for recording subjects was finally invented in the mid nineteenth century when experiments revealed that a plate treated with silver solutions could indelibly fix an image. Two Frenchmen, Joseph Niepce and Louis Daguerre perfected this method of fixing images on a plate about 1837. Finally the box (camera) and the plate (film) were combined and near the end of the nineteenth century dramatic technical improvements excited public enthusiasm for photography. Cameras today have become simple to operate and inexpensive. Now, even small children make photographs and operate video cameras. Photography is taught in school art classes along with drawing and painting.

The motion picture grew out of still or single frame photography during the first quarter of the twentieth century. Improvements in film quality and rapid exposure time made it possible for Edward Muybridge to shoot objects in motion and freeze the image. The first basic motion pictures grew directly out of the still photographer's ability to shoot many single frame photographs in rapid succession and then project them onto a screen in the same way.

CHAPTER IX:

WRITING ABOUT ART

"Just in proportion as he is sentient and restless, just in proportion as he reacts and reciprocates and penetrates, is the critic a valuable instrument."

—Henry James (1893), *Criticism*

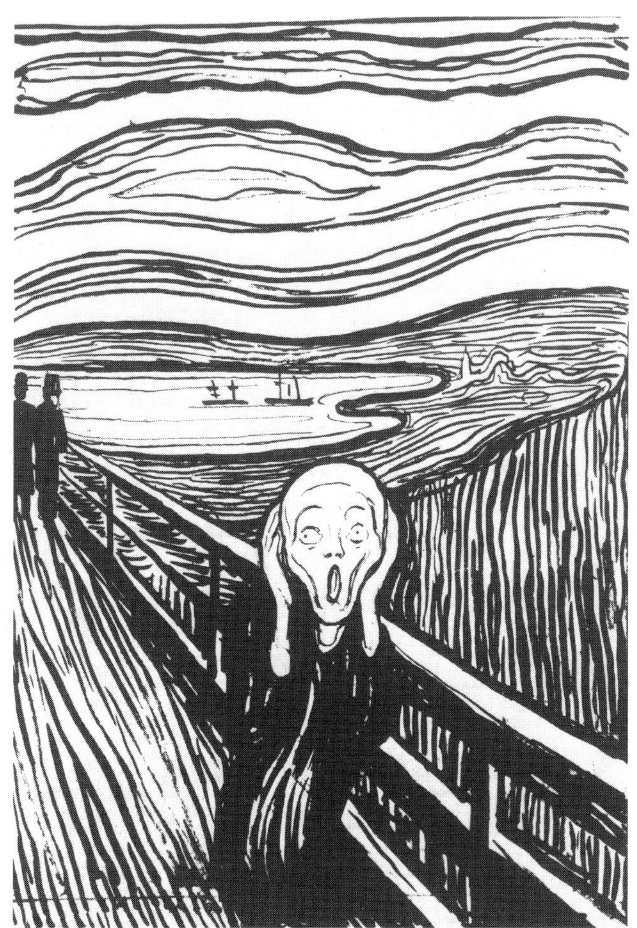

Figure 9-1: *The Scream,* Edvard Munch, 1895, National Gallery of Art, Washington, D.C., Lithograph, (Marburg/Art Resource, NY).

FROM YOUR REPSONSE TO A WRITTEN CRITICISM

Most thorough written analyses involve several components. These components are not to be taken as prescriptive or hierarchial; they are simply a list of the pieces which are usually included in a written criticism. Each of the components is explained and illustrated below to assist students in their early attempts to draft criticisms.

When we are attempting to organize our thoughts and write a criticism of an artwork, our responses should be based upon a continuously willing attention to the aesthetic situation. Our intuitive responses may be exhilarated, troubled, agreeable or indeterminate. In a criticism of Edvard Munch's painting *The Scream* (Figure 9-1) one student wrote:

> *I could not get the painting out of my mind. I tried busying myself with chores, I played the radio loudly, but nothing helped. I decided to see the work once more to confront it and, perhaps in the process, face my own obsessiveness.*[1]

Our response may also be expressed in terms of some personal value or belief to which we are committed. Critic John Berger looked at Rembrandt's *Bathsheba* (Figure 9-2) and responded to what he took to be the artist's love for his model; he wrote,

> *Rembrandt's image of Bathsheba is that of a woman loved by the image maker. Her nakedness is, as it were, original. She is as she is, before putting her clothes on and meeting the world, before being judged by others. Her nakedness is a function of her being and it glows with the light of her being.*[2]

The character and substance of our response will be enriched and made clear as we explore the measure of the work's expressive qualities. Even as we initially respond to an artwork we already may be aware of complex relationships that will be described and analyzed in our written criticism.

REFERENCING THE ARTWORK

A written criticism is an attempt to communicate an evaluation of an artwork to the reader. For the criticism to be effective, the reader must know which artwork is being discussed, what it looks like and what the critic is seeing that affects his/her response and evaluation. Therefore, a written criticism must provide a frame of reference for the reader. Common features in the frame of reference include a broad description of the work, the formal or structural elements which compose it and the imagery which may be present.

Point out and distinguish the lines, shapes, colors, textures, spaces or masses which make up the work. Essentially, the parts which make up the whole are to be labeled for discussion. Also, if the work has identifiable subject matter, identify it. A referencing of Jacques Louis David's *Oath of the Horatii* (Figure 9-3) would note that:

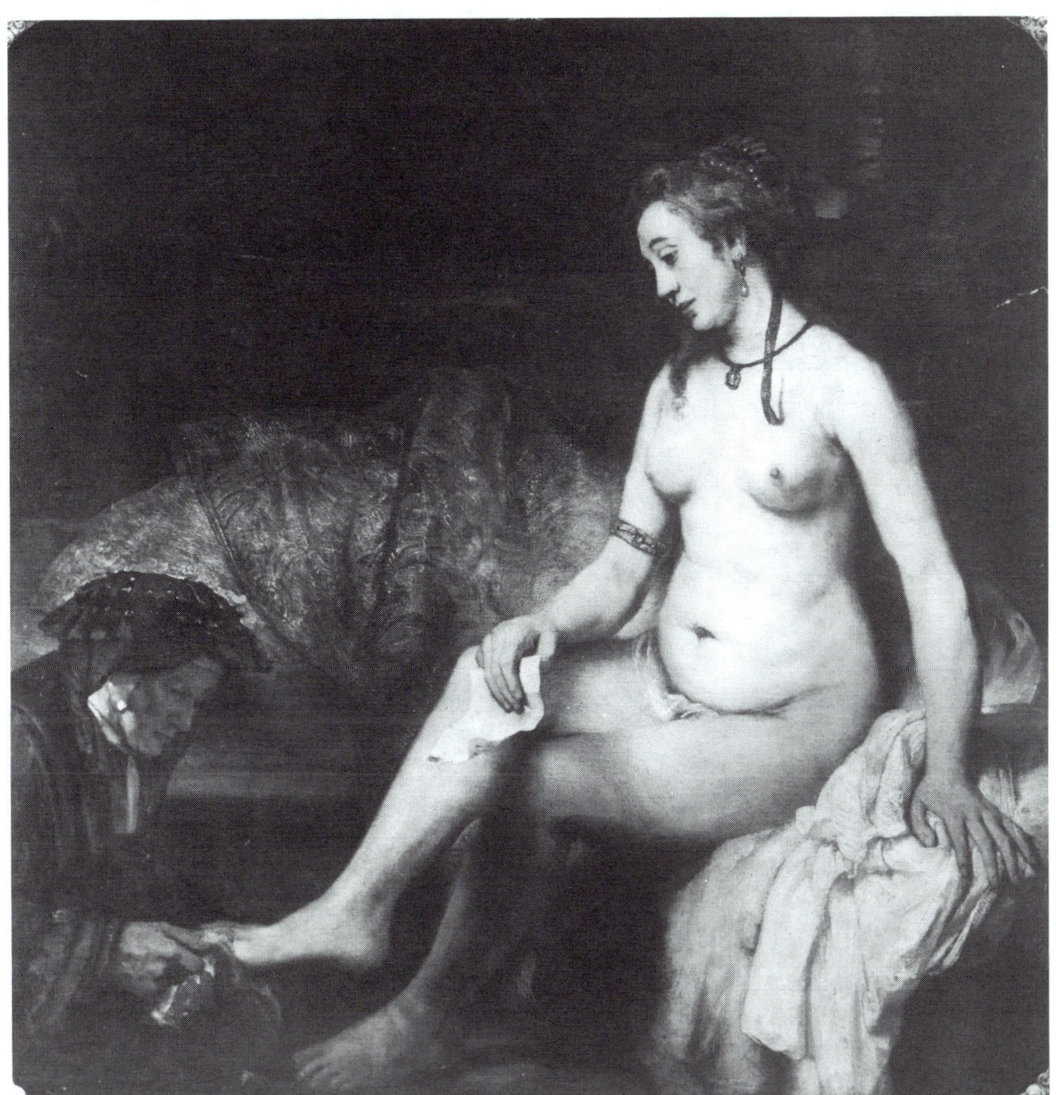

Figure 9-2: *Bathsheba,* Rembrandt van Rijn, 1654, oil on canvas, 55" x 55", Louvre, Paris, (Giraudon/Art Resource, NY).

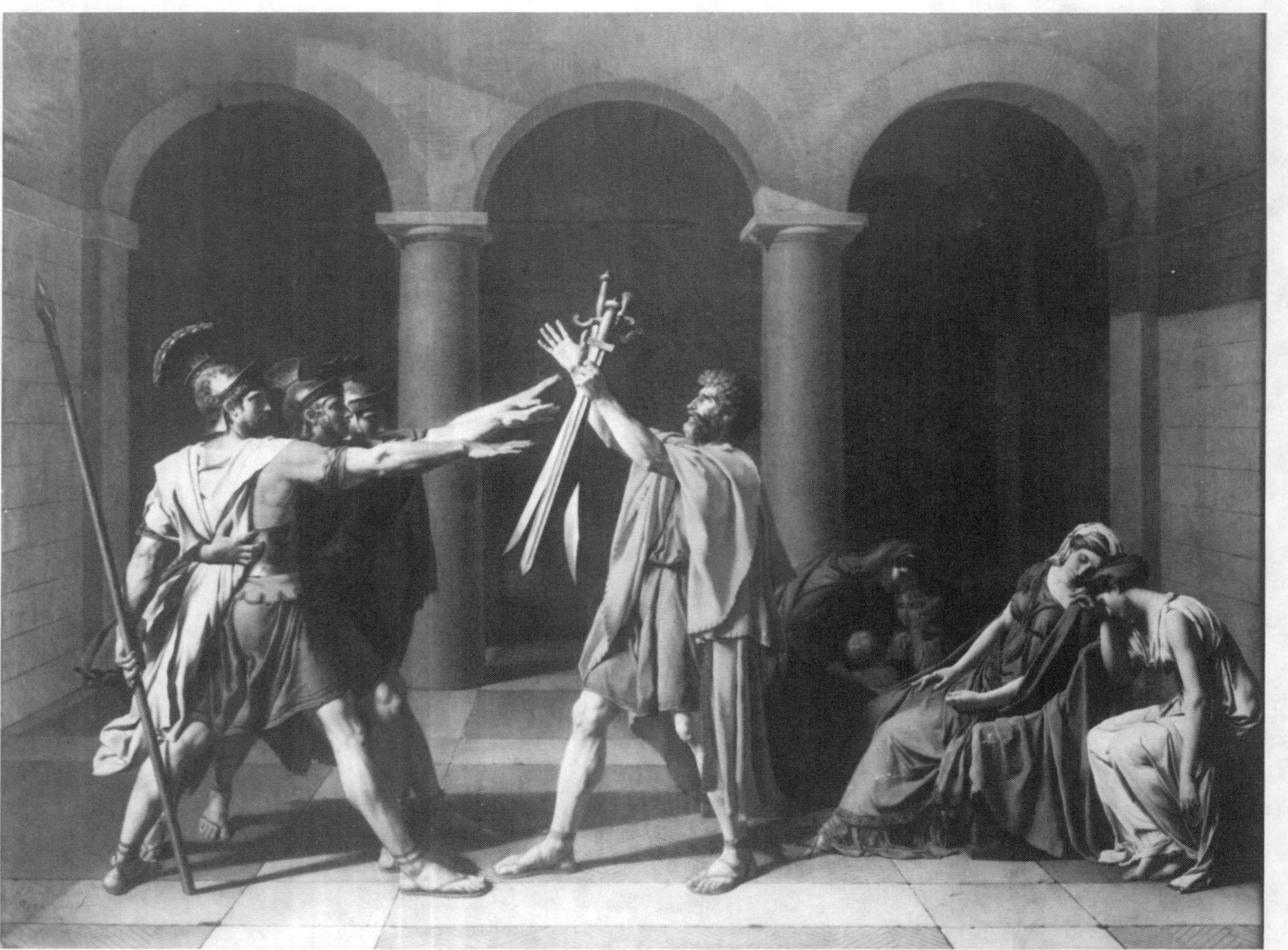

Figure 9-3: *Oath of the Horatii,* Jacques Louis David, 1784–85, oil on canvas, 14' x 11', Louvre, Paris, (Giraudon/Art Resource, NY).

Standing dead center in the lower half of the composition is the toga-wearing patriarch of the Horatius family. He holds his head in strict profile to the viewer; his feet are spread, turning his body into a slight three-quarter frontal view. . . .[3]

Referencing of Vincent van Gogh's *The Starry Night* (Colorplate 6) would note that the work is "painted in tones of yellow, orange, green and blue."[4] A contemporary sculptural work such *Cybernetic System* by Wen Ying Tsai (Figure 9-4) may be most precisely described as consisting of:

. . . twenty-four vertical, stainless steel rods. Mounted on the tip of each rod is a small diamond-shaped plate. The rods vibrate uniformly when the work is operating. The vibrations are produced by an oscillator (motor) located in the base of the sculpture.[5]

RELATING AND INTERRELATING THE PARTS OF THE WORK

Describe any kinship discovered among the work's formal elements (i.e. color and shape). If the work has recognizable subject matter, describe relationships perceived among these representational elements. Also describe any systematic relationships which exist between the work's representational and formal elements. Relating and interrelating parts of *Oath of the Horatii,* a critic might point out that:

The number three is compositionally important, tying the work together. As I have already said, the father holds three swords. The Horatius brothers at the left, number three; there are three women at the right, and the architectural framework in the background consists of three round arches supported by two Doric columns. Also, the figures in the foreground conveniently arrange themselves into three groups.[6]

A particularly effective student analysis of Ben Shahn's *Sunday Morning* (Figure 9-5) further demonstrates the manner in which formal and representational elements are tied together.

Like apples in a bowl in a still-life painting, these four men sit on a bench located predominantly in the foreground. There is only the suggestion of some sort of empty framework in the background, suggesting aloneness while at the same time creating a sense of depth. The artist has also used value and overlapping to suggest depth; however, the depth is shallow and we are forced to inspect these four characters who are depicted with a combination of loose, painterly strokes and contour lines.[7]

The student went further with her analysis, discovering a remarkable interrelatedness in Shahn's composition. She carefully delineates the similarities and differences among the four bench-sitters.

To begin with there are seven examples of three men sharing in common a characteristic while the fourth man is different.

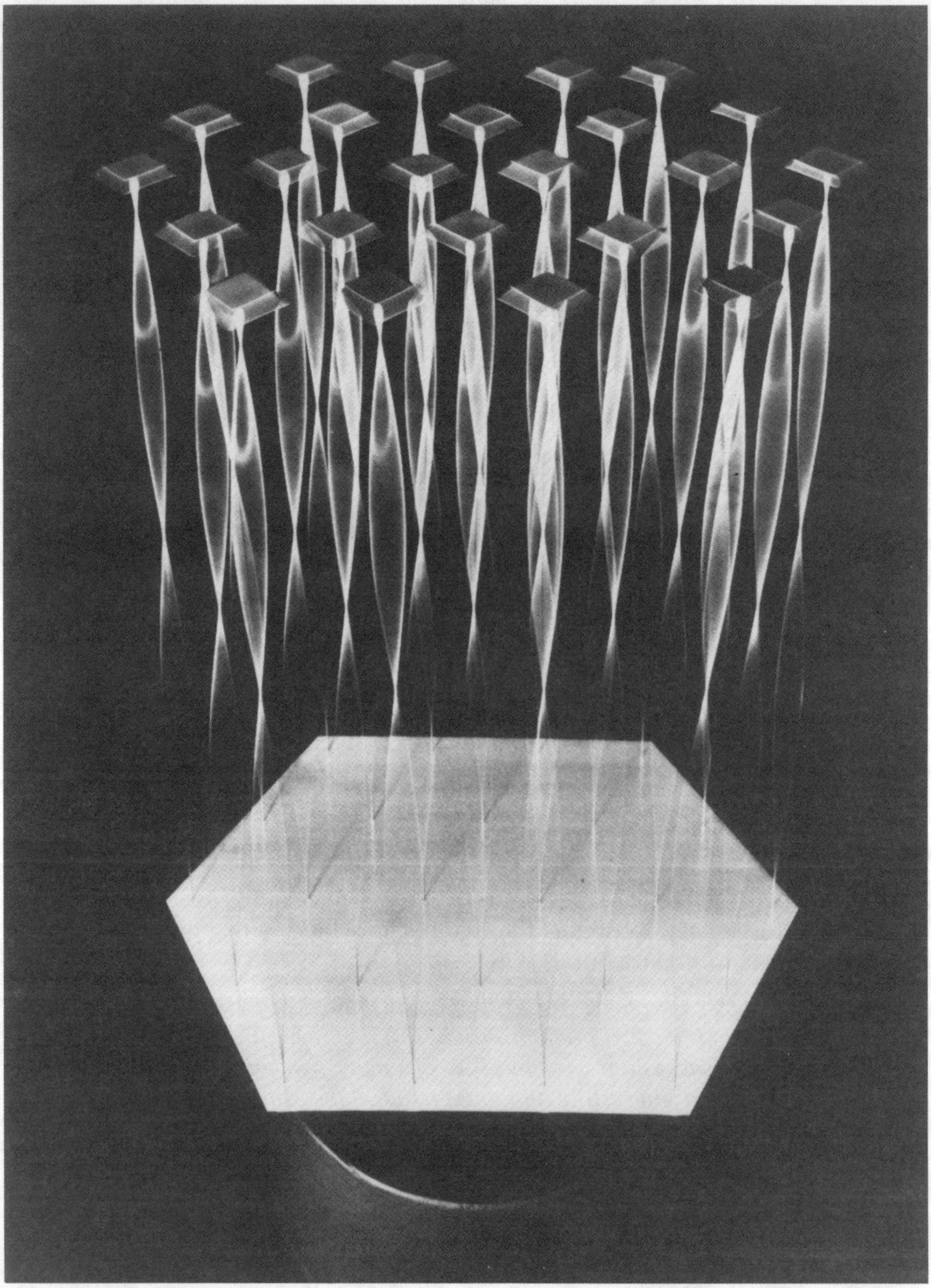

Figure 9-4: *Cybernetic System,* Wen Ying Tsai, 1969, mixed media, © Addison Gallery of American Art, Phillips Academy, Andover, Massachusetts 1969.33.

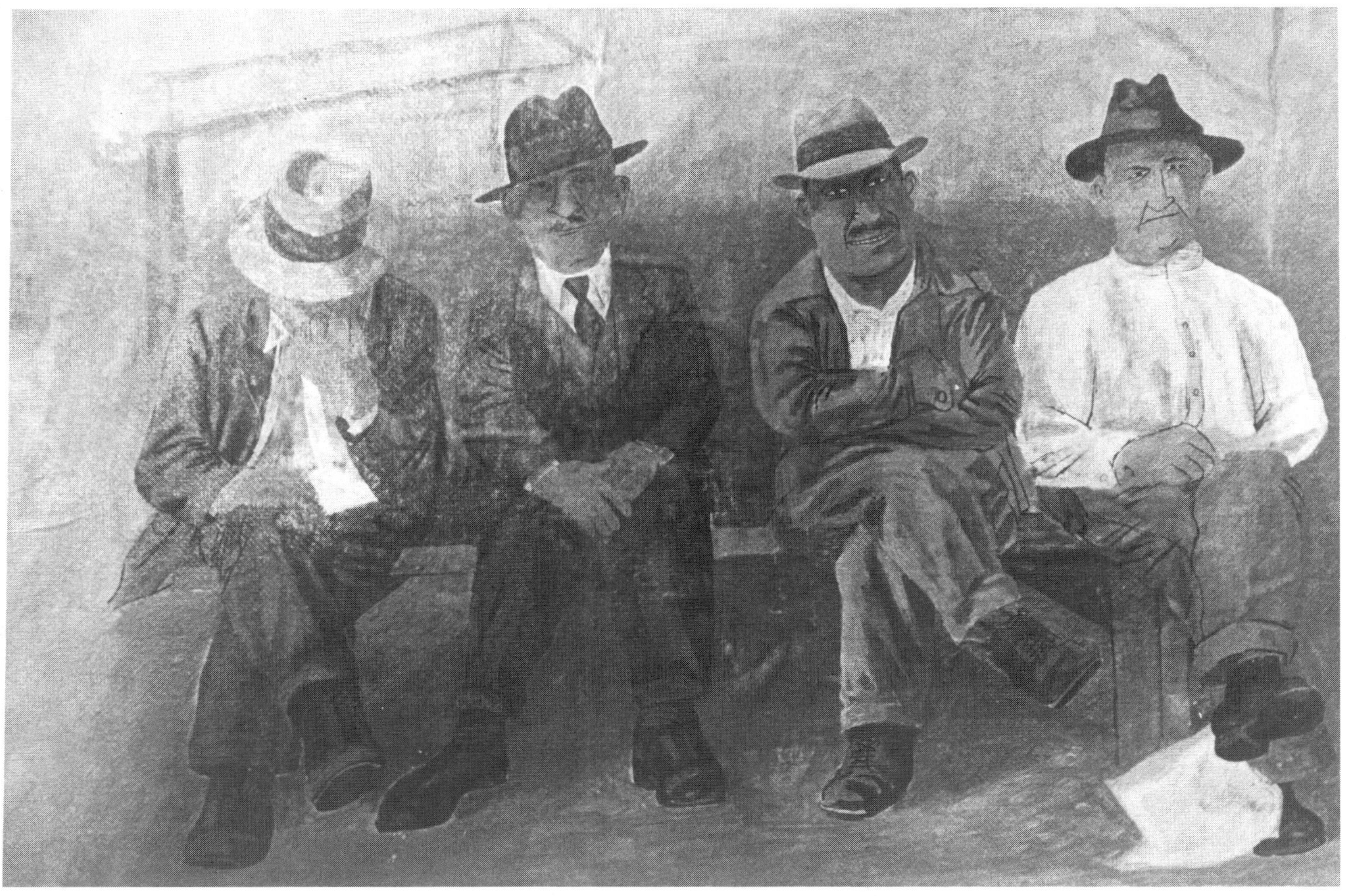

Figure 9-5: *Sunday Morning,* Ben Shahn, 1938 or 1943, tempera on paper, 15 3/4" x 23 3/4", Georgia Museum of Art, Athens, Georgia.

Three men have crossed their legs and one has not. Three man have crossed arms or hands and one does not. Three men have on a coat or jacket while one has dressed only in his crisp white shirt. His shirt is collarless while the other three have on shirts with collars. Three are without ties and wear working shoes, while the odd man out, the only one who looks dressed for Church, wears a tie and dress shoes. Smiles and smirks appear on three faces and the fourth man looks down, absorbed in facial picking. The three frontal faces have eyes that look right at us, the viewer. We are challenged to become one of them and share their experience. The one distracted reminds us not to count on the loyalty of their undivided attention! They merely glance at us in our passing.[8]

Speculating on the Artwork's Meaning

The emphasis of analysis should be on discovery of meaning (interpretation). Meaning builds on the interrelationship of aesthetic value, structure and imagery; it encompasses the work's total expressive implications. The aesthetic situation may possess a universality (total philosophy or world view) which should become clear. An excerpt from the sample criticism at the end of this chapter illustrates how meaning and universality are understood relative to Vincent van Gogh's *The Starry Night* (Colorplate 6):

Van Gogh's painting links the viewer with the cosmic drama of reality that is continually being played out around us. The painting becomes a medium through which we catch a glimpse of immortality, an immortality perceived in the force and energy bonding the universe.[9]

In the passage which follows, the nature of synthetical meaning is clearly demonstrated by Professor William Fleming's analysis of Leonardo daVinci's *Last Supper* (Figure 9-6). Symbolism and formal relationships unite to account convincingly for several important aspects of the work's meaning.

As an underlying motif, Leonardo draws on his Florentine heritage of harmony as expressed in numbers, in this case the symbolism and properties of the number 12. The twelve apostles appear in four groups of three on either side of the lonely central figure. There are four wall hangings on each side and three windows, alluding to the four gospels and the Trinity. Twelve also refers to the passage of time—the hours of the day and months of the year—in which salvation is to be sought.[10]

In writing a criticism, clarify your perceptual responses and synthesize information discovered through analysis to express an interpretation. If a synthesis is not possible, the critic should consider starting over and re-experiencing the work. If the analytical process has made the artwork clearer, the critic should be able to express an understanding of the work.

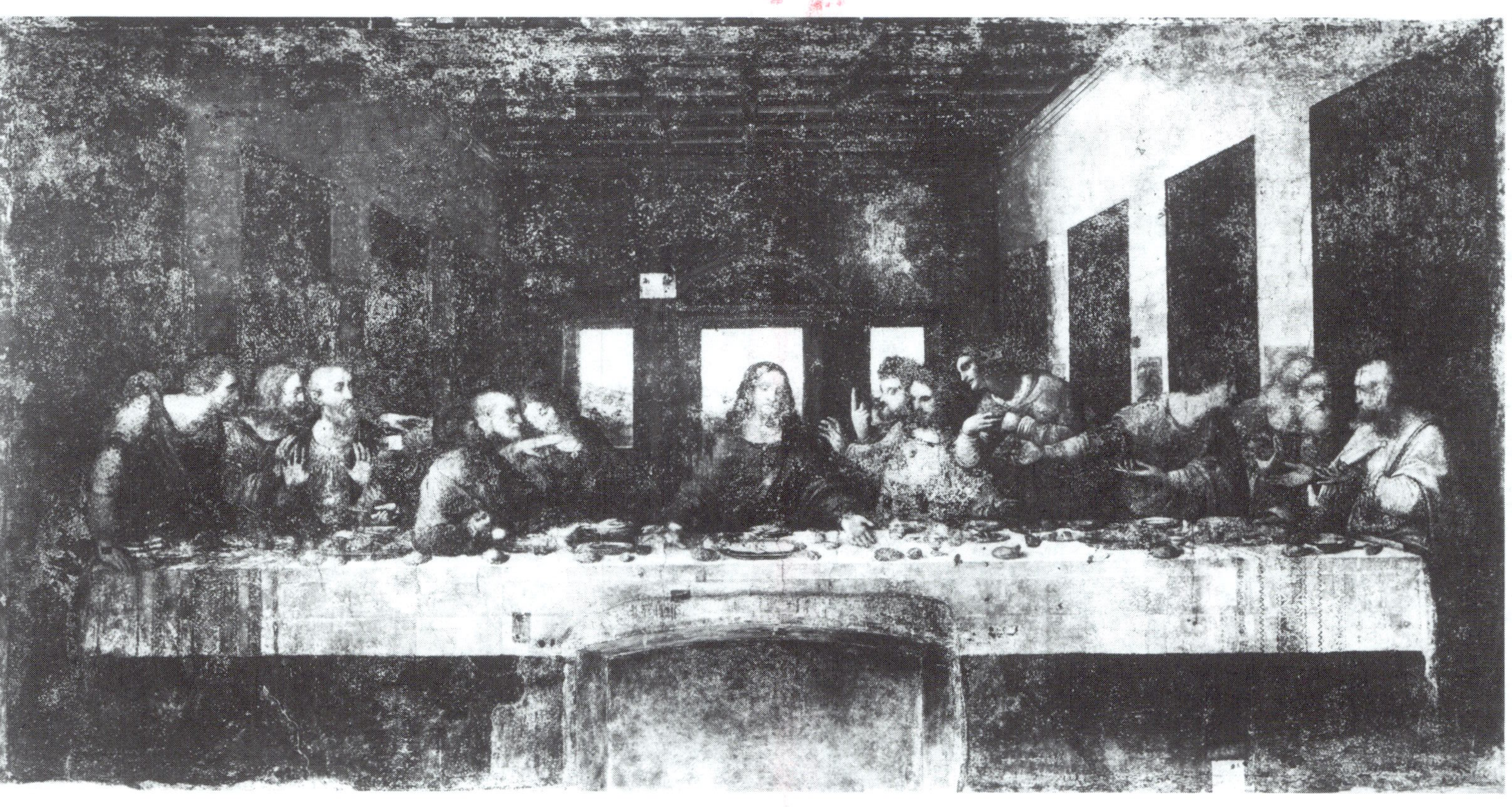

Figure 9-6: *The Last Supper,* Leonardo da Vinci, c. 1494-98, wall painting, Santa Maria delle Grazie, Milan, Italy, (Alinari/Art Resource, NY).

For some novice critics, an attempt to analyze the aesthetic situation may go no further than mechanically relating elemental structure and imagery. Their initial intuitive response is inadequate or flawed; or, perhaps, their response is not supported and accounted for by their analysis. These critics can go no further and should leave the situation and return to re-experience the work at a later time.

If response to the work is made clearer by analysis, such a realization should be expressible. Through analysis, some earlier tentative hypotheses may have been supported, or analysis may lead to proposal of an analogue or metaphor which embodies your experience of the work.

Even though responses to the aesthetic situation have been accounted for, it is desirable to **re-experience** the work if possible. **Re-experience** of the work may reinforce what you have already discovered, uncover new depths of experience or show that you were initially wrong and must start over.

SUMMARIZING AND CONCLUDING

Writing a critical analysis will have been worth the effort if you have fully accounted for your responses to the work and better understand your experience of the work. Critical analysis and evaluation are emotional and intellectual exercises which enrich and enlarge the critic's knowledge and experience. If a process of analysis has brought you to some conclusion regarding the merits of the aesthetic situation, you will have reached a level of resolution and perhaps satisfaction. However, critical reflection offers no guarantee of satisfaction.

In a review titled "Pretty Face, Decadent Soul: Art in Savannah," critic Jack Miller uneasily concluded that the extremity of the contrasts he had just experienced at an exhibit offered no satisfaction either morally or visually.

> *Returning along the stretch of lonely road back to Atlanta, I could not resolve which was the greater immorality: an art that utterly ignored present day horrors, or an art that showed nothing but horror, with no redeeming vision.*[11]

Judging the worth of a work of art is not difficult if a coherent method of evaluation has been followed. Often a verdict has been reached even before analysis is complete. We mentally note the positive and negative qualities of a work. This record is composed of the defining properties of the work compared with the areas of evaluation we have analyzed and the aesthetic values we assign.

A SAMPLE CRITICISM OF *The Starry Night* BY VINCENT VAN GOGH

Following is an example of a critical analysis in which all four components of verbal communication are employed by the writer. Responsive and speculative commentary dominate this criticism. Van Gogh's work invites a richness of response and metaphorical interpretation.

The Starry Night

Vincent van Gogh's, *The Starry Night*, is all force and energy. The force is elemental, the energy is highly charged and emotional. Although the scale of this painting is relatively small (29 x 36 1/4 inches), its impact on the viewer is large. One wonders how anything as inert as oil pigments on canvas can carry such life. But, the painting does live. Life bursts from it in an almost frenzied way. Each brush stroke has a vitality of its own, and, in concert with its neighbors, sets up a complex, rhythmic flow that welds the painting together. The artist's technique of working into a heavily pigmented surface with repeated short dashes of color animates the composition while also unifying it. *The Starry Night* depicts a moon- and star-lit village nestled in a valley between rolling hills in the background and prominent cypress trees in the foreground. The scene is bathed in a kind of marvelous celestial light painted in tones of yellow, orange, green and blue.

It is the sky that initially attracts us, and what a sky this is. The moon's light burns through darkness like a sun at midnight. The stars explode in a pyrotechnic display of pulsing radiant energy. This sky is alive with swirling forms that race across the canvas or curl in upon themselves. The bottom one-third of the painting acts as a counterpoint to the firmament above. It is quieter. The artist's brush strokes seem more methodical and the tonal harmonies are closer. Although cool blues and greens dominate the fore and middle ground of the painting, a sense of warmth and serenity pervades the little village with its church and steeple. Superficially, one is tempted to suggest that van Gogh painted *The Starry Night* in a passionate rush. But, a close look at the painting's organization reveals the care and deliberation of its making. One can not analyze or pick apart the picture's structure as though it were a Neoclassical work like David's, *Oath of the Horatii*, but there is a kind of structural integrity. For instance, the vertical cypresses interrupt the sky's lateral rush; the church steeple echoes the cypresses and interrupts the line of the hills. Instead of rushing off the canvas, the excited cosmos and rolling hills play out their drama within the painting's borders. The cypress trees, as a shape, also dominate and balance one side of the picture while the fiery moon dominates and balances the other. Try visually shifting the placement of the cypresses, the church or the moon, and you easily see the delicate balance of van Gogh's choice.

Compositional order is essential to the painting. So too, is another kind of order, universal order, defined in dynamic and real terms. We witness this order only if we are attuned to it and have the eyes to see it. Van Gogh's painting links the viewer with the cosmic drama of reality that is continually being played out around us. The painting becomes a medium through which we catch a glimpse of immortality, an immortality perceived in the force and energy bonding the universe.

The universe is active and alive, and we see our true, immortal selves reflected in this changing panoply.

Review of Criticism

Initial reading of this criticism may lead one to assume that it is written from an impressionist critical approach, but that assumption would be based on a response to writing style rather than the actual content of the essay. Careful study of the sample criticism will reveal that the defining properties of the artwork are identified, the areas of critical evaluation are analyzed and a sense of aesthetic value has been applied to the evaluation of the work.

The components are woven into the criticism in an organic, overlapping manner reflective of the work being discussed as follows:

Referencing the artwork—lines 3–5, 11–19

Relating and interrelating the parts of the work—lines 8–10, 19–37

Speculating on the artwork's meaning—lines 1–2, 38–46

PROBLEMS IN RESPONDING TO AND EXPERIENCING ARTWORK

Our response to artworks should be unimpeded and open; in reality, however, the beginning critic's emotions are often compromised by internal distortions and perceptual fallacies.[12] Naming or labeling several of these perceptual fallacies will, perhaps, help in avoiding or correcting them. If the following perceptual fallacies derived from research in psychological pathologies go uncorrected, they will inevitably lead to unresponsive and inaccurate conclusions on the part of the critic.

Categorical Response

We internally register what we see in terms of preconceived ideas or categories of thought. These preconceptions are arbitrary and exclusive. An example of this kind of thinking is a mental statement such as, "This work is too abstract; it has no basis in reality," or, "This work is no good, it's too abstract." Such statements are rarely true because they reduce perception to either/or distinctions.

Myopic Response

The viewer notices one quality of a work and fixes on that single aspect, over magnifying and over expanding its importance to the point that it distorts his perception of the whole work. Imagine a situation in which a viewer, while looking at Piero di Cosimo's *Discovery of Honey*, notices the painting's swarm of bees and is reminded of his uncle's apiary which leads to thoughts about beekeeping practices in Southern Mississippi. Carried away in this fashion, the viewer could hardly be expected to notice that the work juxtaposes Man's peaceful and warring nature, the cultured and the barbaric, to make a statement about the future of civilization.

Halo Response

Some viewers will respond negatively or positively to one aspect of a work and generalize that negative or positive aspect to represent the work as a whole. A response to one part of a work should not characterize our response to the whole work. In research, this fallacy is known as the halo effect and has been proven invalid. An artwork is usually the result of a complex interaction of qualities and our response should be measured in tonalities or shades of meaning.

Coercive Response

Some viewers of art urge themselves to respond as they think they should rather than accepting what they really feel and proceeding from there. We place needless expectations upon ourselves to respond in ways that are inconsistent with our true nature. An example of this fallacy occurred when a student was asked to analyze a painting in a local museum. The painting was mediocre, but the student, who truly felt that the painting was poor, assumed that the professor thought the painting was good. The student, therefore, forced himself to write a positive criticism that was both insincere and inaccurate.

FOR DISCUSSION

1. How does having an aesthetic experience differ from writing about an aesthetic experience?
2. Locate an artwork you enjoy and write about it. Note how the components of writing a critical analysis help unite your experience, reinforcing its wholeness and completeness.
3. You are a student who has just written an analysis of Peter Bruegel's *Landscape with the Fall of Icarus* (Figure 1–2). Your analysis was negative and explained your displeasure that Icarus, the main character of the work according to the title, is represented by the artist in a bottom corner of the painting by only his two legs disappearing into the water. You are invited to rethink and rewrite your analysis. How would you improve the analysis?

Notes

CHAPTER I: HAVING AN AESTHETIC EXPERIENCE

1 Marcel Proust, *Swann's Way* (New York: The Modern Library, 1956), 62.

2 Curt J. Ducasse, *Art, the Critics, and You*, The Library of Liberal Arts (New York: Howard W. Sams & Co., Inc., 1944), 71.

3 Ibid., 73.

4 W. H. Auden, *Selected Poetry of W. H. Auden* (New York: The Modern Library, 1970), 49.

5 John Bartlett, *Familiar Quotations* (Boston and Toronto: Little, Brown and Co.,1980), 653.

CHAPTER II: THE NATURE OF ART AND CREATIVE PROCESS

1 Albert Hofstadter and Richard Kuhns, eds., *Philosophies of Art and Beauty* (Chicago: The University of Chicago Press, 1964), 33.

2 Jeremiah 18: 1–6

3 Edmund Feldman, *The Artist* (Englewood Cliffs, NJ: Prentice Hall, 1982), 197.

4 Ducasse, *Critics, and You*, 52.

5 John Dewey, *Art as Experience* (New York: G.P. Putnam and Sons, 1958), 136.

6 Wassily Kandinsky, *Concerning the Spiritual in Art,* in *Documents of Modern Art*, vol. 5 (New York: George Wittenborn Inc., 1947), 26.

7 Laurence Binyon, *The Flight of the Dragon* (London: John Murray, 1911), 80.

8 Giorgio Vasari, *Lives of the Artists*, trans., George Bull, vol.II (Middlesex, England: Penguin Books Ltd., 1987), 107.

9 Graham Collier, *Art and the Creative Consciousness* (Englewood Cliffs, NJ: Prentice Hall, 1972), 54.

10 Brewster Ghiselin, *The Creative Process* (New York: Mentor Books, 1952), 15.

CHAPTER III: ART CRITICAL THEORY

1 Louis, Harris *Inside America* (New York, N.Y.: Vintage Books, 1987), 159.

2 David W. Ecker and Eugene F. Kaelin, "The Limits of Aesthetic Inquiry: A Guide to Educational Research", *Seventy-first Yearbook of the National Society for the Study of Education*, Part 1, Chapter XI, 1972, 258–286.

3 Dewey, *Art*, 298–325.

4 Wolfgang Kohler, *Gestalt Psychology* (New York: Mentor Books, 1947), 222.

5 Barbara Rose, *Autocritique* (New York: Weidenfeld & Nicolson, 1988), 216.

6 Edmund Burke Feldman, *Varieties of Visual Experience* (Englewood Cliffs, NJ: Prentice-Hall, 1987), 453.

7 Rita Gilbert and William McCarter, *Living With Art* (New York: Alfred A. Knopf, 1992), 33–35.

8 Peninah R.Y. Petruck, *American Art Criticism 1910–1939* (New York & London: Garland Publishing, Inc., 1981), 2.

9 Dewey, *Art*, 310.

10 Ibid., 313.

11 Feldman, *Varieties*, 471.

CHAPTER IV: TOWARDS A CRITICAL METHODOLOGY

1 Theodore Roosevelt, "A Layman's Views of an Art Exhibition," *The Outlook*, vol. 103 (March 29, 1913), 719.

2 James Hillman, *Revisioning Psychology* (New York: Harper & Row, 1975), 39.

3 John Canaday, *Mainstreams of Modern Art* (New York: Simon and Schuster, 1959), 156–157.

4 Dewey, *Art*, 73.

CHAPTER V: MEANING: A SERIES OF INTERPRETIVE MOMENTS

1 K.G. Pontus Hulten, *The Machine* (New York: The Museum of Modern Art, 1968), 190.

2 William Squires, "Joined in the Phenomenon of Life," *Apelles*, vol. 2, No. 1 (Fall 1981): 14–15.

3 Jack Burnham, *Beyond Modern Sculpture* (New York: George Braziller, 1967), 341.

CHAPTER VI: RATIONAL CRITICISM AND CENSORSHIP

1 Dewey, *Art*, 299.

2 Christopher S. Wren, "Russians Disrupt Modern Art Show With Bulldozers," *New York Times,* Col. CXXIII (September 16, 1974), 1.

3 Hitler, Adolph, speech inaugurating the "Great Exhibition of German Art 1937," Munich, translated by Ilse Falk, published in *"Der Fuhrer eroffnet die Grosse Deutsche Kunstausstellung 1937," Die Kunst in Dritten Reich* (Munich), I, 7–8 (July–Aug. 1937, 47–61) and reprinted in Chipp, Herschel B. *Theories of Modern Art*, Berkeley: University of California Press, 1968, 474.

4 Dondero, George A. "Modern Art Shackled to Communism," a speech given in the U.S. House of Representatives, 16 Aug. 1949, published in the *Congressional Record* first session, 81st Congress, Tuesday 16 Aug., 1949 and reprinted in Chipp, 497.

5 Ibid.

6 "Soviet Artist Feels Wrath of Mickey," *Athens Star,* 6 April 1988.

CHAPTER VII: THE ELEMENTS OF ART AND COMPOSITION

1 Manuel Barkan, Laura H. Chapman, and Evan J. Kern, *Guidelines*, Aesthetic Education Curriculum Program (Central Midwestern Regional Educational Laboratory, Inc., [CEMREL], 1970), 53.

2 Herbert Read, *The Meaning of Art* (London: Faber & Faber, 1972), 51.

3 Hans Kreitler and Shulamith Kreitler, *Psychology of the Arts* (Durham, NC: Duke University Press, 1972), 54–79. Material on color associations and symbolism is from Kreitler's chapter "The Meaning of Color."

4 Kandinsky, *Spiritual in Art*, 44.

5 Kreitler, *Psychology*, 60.

6 Ibid., 69.

7 Ibid., 68.

8 Ibid., 68.

9 Ibid., 68.

10 *Selected Works in the High Museum* (Atlanta, GA: High Museum of Art, 1987), 58.

CHAPTER IX: WRITING ABOUT ART

1 Buford Chance, "The Scream" (class critique, The University of Georgia, 1986).

2 John Berger, *The Sense of Sight* (New York, N.Y. Pantheon Books, 1985), 110.

3 William T. Squires, "Oath of the Horatii" (class notes on critical description, The University of Georgia, 1988).

4 Squires, "The Starry Night" (class notes, 1988).

5 William T. Squires, "Towards An Analysis of Automated Sculptural Systems" (Ph.D. diss., Florida State University, 1972), 68.

6 Squires, "Oath of the Horatii" (class notes, 1988).

7 Felicia Bush, "Sunday Morning" (Class analysis, The University of Georgia, 1990).

8 Ibid.

9 Squires, "The Starry Night" (1988).

10 William Fleming, *Arts and Ideas* (New York: Holt, Rinehart and Winston, 1986), 207.

11 Jack Miller, "Pretty Face, Decadent Soul: Art in Savannah," *Art Papers*, vol. 11, No. 4, July/August 1987, 50.

12 David D. Burns, *Feeling Good, the New Mood Therapy* (New York: William Morrow, 1980), 31–39.

Glossary

Abstract art: Art which departs to a large degree from visual reality through distortion or simplification of form. Images are based on natural appearances, but references to objects from the real world may be very slight. Works in which the representation of real objects is totally absent are often referred to as abstract, but are more correctly termed non-representational art.

Abstract Expressionism: An art style that began in the United States in the late 1940s and early 1950s and continued into the 1960s which involves the use of abstract or non-representational forms used to evoke emotion and to suggest symbolic meaning. The branch of Abstract Expressionism known as Action Painting (which included Jackson Pollock and Willem De Kooning) is characterized by disjointed and seemingly unrelated forms and bold colors or strongly contrasting values applied spontaneously using loose, gestural brush work. A less spontaneous, non-gestural branch, epitomized by the work of Mark Rothko, makes use of large areas of color to convey emotion.

Aesthetician: A philosopher of aesthetics.

Aesthetics: In general, the study of the quality and nature of sensory experience. In art, it pertains to matters of taste and appreciation and is often related to the concept of beauty, although it can refer to any sensory response to a work of art.

Analogous colors: Colors that are closely related, sharing qualities of a common hue. Analogous colors are adjacent to each other on a color wheel (for example: blue, blue-green and green).

Artifact: A human-made product; usually a simple object such as a tool or ornament.

Avante garde: French for "advance guard." Refers to radical leaders of new concepts in any field. In art, it refers to those in the vanguard—artists at the cutting edge of unconventional ideas and movements.

Bronze: A sculpture material consisting of an alloy of copper and tin (and sometimes other elements). The most common material traditionally used for casting sculpture.

Bubble-domed ceiling: A rounded roof formed by glass, plastics or other translucent materials.

Byzantine: A style of painting, design and architecture of the Byzantine Empire in eastern Europe prominent in the fifth and sixth centuries. Byzantine art was mainly religious and featured frontal poses, a lack of three-dimensional modeling and rich decoration. Its architecture was characterized by large domes, mosaics and marble veneering.

Calligraphic: Consisting of flowing, gracefully curving lines, often varying from thick to thin.

Chiaroscuro: Italian for "light-dark." The use of subtle gradations of light and dark values to achieve the illusion of three-dimensional form.

Collage: An art medium, first introduced in 1912 by Pablo Picasso and Georges Braque, consisting of materials (usually paper, fabric or photographs) glued to a flat surface. From the French for "glueing" or "sticking."

Color wheel: Relationships among hues expressed as a circular two-dimensional model.

Complementary (colors): Colors or hues that are directly opposite each other on the color wheel. They do not share any of the same hue; that is, one color is completely absent in the other. Mixing them together in a certain proportion creates a neutral gray. Examples are red and green, orange and blue and yellow and violet.

Composition: The design or make-up of a work of art, consisting of the elements of art organized to form a whole. Also, the act of composing.

Compressive strength: The ability of a material to withstand deformation from loading or being pressed together. An important principle in architecture.

Connoisseur: An individual who enjoys art and knows and understands the principles of art. Often he or she is a specialist in a particular branch of art and capable of aesthetic judgement.

Contour: A line which delineates one area from another in an object or figure (especially an irregular object or figure). This includes changes in planes within a form as well as outline. It also refers to the lines drawn to suggest these changes and to a kind of drawing using contour lines.

Cool color(s): Colors that (based on our associations with images such as ice and sky) have a cool visual temperature. They tend to recede spatially when placed next to warm colors (which tend to advance). Blue, blue-violet, blue-green and (to a lesser extent) green are cool colors.

Craftsmanship: The quality of a made or crafted object. Usually implies skill and ability in the making of an art or craft.

Cubists: Artists associated with Cubism, a style developed around 1907 in Paris by Pablo Picasso and Georges Braque which was characterized by multiple views of the same object, two-dimensionality, and geometric cube-like simplification of form. The "analytical" phase of Cubism, which lasted from 1909–1911, was characterized by ambiguous, all-over pictorial space, disintegration of form and a neutral palette. Later, beginning in 1912, the "synthetic" phase was introduced. It is distinguished by the use of collage or collage-like surfaces. It was more decorative and playful than "analytical" Cubism with fewer, more solid forms and more vivid colors.

Doodle: An aimless scribble or sketch.

Doric column: A vertical support structure from the Doric order, the earliest and simplest of the Greek architectural styles, characterized by relatively short columns (often un-fluted, i.e. without grooves) and simple square-shaped capitals.

Egg tempera: A water-based paint using egg yolk as a binder (a material that adheres pigment particles together). It was the most common medium for easel-size painting until the fifteenth century when oils became more prevalent. Egg tempera is fast-drying with bright, permanent colors and is suitable for small, detailed paintings.

Enclosing space: The interior area or other defined spaces in an architectural structure, as opposed to occupying space.

Environmental design: The organization and large-scale planning of streets, parks, buildings, highways or other usually outdoor areas (an enclosed shopping mall would be an exception to "outdoor"). Planning to make areas more habitable and pleasant.

Equestrian: Relating to horseback riding. Equestrian statues were common in the history of sculpture (dating back to antiquity). They usually consisted of an individual portrayed as a powerful leader with military prowess.

Etching: An intaglio (cut below the surface) printmaking process which makes use of the corrosive nature of acid to eat grooves into a metal plate. The plate is first coated with an acid-resistant wax called a ground. Then parts of the ground are removed with a needle to expose the metal plate. Next, the plate is placed into an acid bath which eats into the exposed areas, creating grooves. Then the grooves are filled with ink for printing. Etching also refers to the print obtained by this process.

Felt balance: A perceived equilibrium or balance in an artwork lacking precise symmetry. Also known as asymmetrical or informal balance.

Figurative: Art which portrays a recognizable human figure. Sometimes more generally used to indicate art that has recognizable objects or figures (as opposed to non-figurative or non-objective art).

Florentine: Of the Italian city of Florence, an important center for art in the Renaissance and home of Giotto, Michelangelo Buonarroti and Leonardo da Vinci.

Foreground: In a composition, the part of the scene closest to the viewer.

Form: The structural elements, plan or design of a work of art, as opposed to its subject matter. The manner in which an artist presents his subject matter or content. Also, a defined area or volume.

Freestanding sculpture: Sculpture not connected to architecture. Usually, it can be seen in the round (that is, from any point of view), although the term can also refer to sculpture in an architectural niche which limits viewing.

Fresco: A painting technique in which pigments in water medium are applied to fresh damp plaster. When the plaster dries, the color is a permanent part of the surface. The process is very difficult and requires great skill and dedication. Its durability makes fresco good for covering large areas such as walls and ceilings.

Futurists: Members of an early twentieth-century art movement originating in Italy in 1909 which celebrated motion, speed and dynamism and glorified the machine age, danger and war. They borrowed Cubism's multiple points of view and dissolution of form and added the feeling of motion.

Genre: A type, style or category of art characterized by a particular form or content, such as landscape, marine, or sports. Also, representations of scenes from everyday life, usually accompanied by a moral point of view.

Gestalt: A theory that the whole is an indivisible unit greater than the sum of its parts.

Glazes: Thin, semi-transparent layers of oil paint applied to dried layers of oil or tempera underneath to modify them slightly and provide luminosity, depth and a glossy finish. Also refers to the glassy coating on ceramic objects.

Gothic Style Architecture: A style prevalent in western Europe from the twelfth to the fifteenth centuries. The most impressive Gothic structures are the large cathedrals built in cross-shaped plans and characterized by ribbed groin vaults, pointed arches and flying buttresses—devices which enabled the building of structures with greater height, thinner walls and larger windows than the previous Romanesque style had allowed.

Graphic design: The applied arts as opposed to the fine arts (painting, sculpture, architecture). Work commissioned for use in commerce, advertising, and publication. This includes illustration, technical illustration, and graphic design found in newspapers, magazines, on billboards, record jackets, packaging of industrial products, and the like.

Graphite: A soft, black form of carbon used in writing and drawing pencils. The common lead pencil contains graphite rather than lead, a misnomer stemming from an early reference to the lead pencil as "black lead."

Ground: The surface (wood, canvas, etc.) onto which a painting or drawing is applied. Also refers to the substance used to prepare the surface for painting or drawing and to the prepared surface itself. In painting, grounds provide a manageable, even surface and prevent bleeding of colors.

Harmony: A sense of pleasing cohesiveness or unity in a work of art.

Hue: That property of a color that distinguishes it from others in the spectrum.

Impasto: Thick, opaque paint applied to a paint surface. Most common in oils and acrylics.

Implied movement: In a work of art, the suggestion of movement through visual organization of space as opposed to actual movement (as in kinetic art).

Kinetic energy: Actual energy as opposed to potential energy. In kinetic artworks such as motorized sculptures, actual energy and movement is displayed.

Light spectrum: The colors displayed when light is dispersed into separate components arranged in the order of their wavelengths.

Loom: Any machine used to interweave threads, yarn or other fibrous materials together at right angles.

Mannered: Having an artificial or stilted quality.

Medium (in art): The physical means or material through which the artist works (marble, clay, ink, pencil, oil paint, bronze, steel, etc.). Also, in paint-mixing, a liquid which is added to pigment to change its character and consistency (ie. drying time, durability, opacity, etc.).

Mobile: A kinetic sculpture (typically made of shapes and horizontal rods suspended by wire or string) that moves in response to air or touch. The shapes and supports balance each other physically as well as aesthetically.

Model: A small copy of something. Also, to shape or fashion a pliable material such as clay.

Monochromatic: Pertaining to images produced using a single hue with different values obtained through mixing the color with black or white. Often used less strictly to apply to an image with small color differences, but predominantly of one hue.

Monumental: Something serving as or having the size and greatness of a monument.

Mosaics: Pictures made by setting small, usually irregular pieces of stone, glass or ceramic materials into cement or plastic. Mosaics were the most prominent expression of Byzantine art.

Naturalism: A kind of representational art that comes close to observed reality with little stylization or distortion.

Neoclassical: An art movement beginning in the late eighteenth century and continuing into the nineteenth that was characterized by a revival of classical ideals of reason and order, reflected in stage-like compositions, austere in tone, lacking in background detail and with an emphasis on verticals and horizontals.

Non objective art: Art without any reference to objects from nature. Also known as non-representational art.

Normative philosophy: Any system of thought which prescribes, relates or conforms to an authoritative standard (norm).

Opacity (opaque): The quality of being impenetrable to light. The ability of a layer of paint to block out previous layers as in certain paint media such as egg tempera and acrylic.

Organic shapes: Shapes that have the characters of living organisms (plants and animals), as opposed to geometric shapes.

Palette: The various colors an artist uses in a painting. Also, the surface the painter uses to place and mix colors before applying them to the paint surface.

Patron: Someone who uses his or her time, money and/or influence in support of a cause, institution or individual. For example, a patron of the arts.

Perception (perceptive, perceptual): The awareness of the environment by way of the senses, usually implying understanding and insight.

Perspective rendering: Drawing in perspective, a system for the representation of three-dimensional space on a two-dimensional surface; based on the perception that objects diminish in size and appear less sharp as they recede from the foreground and that parallel lines appear to converge to a point or points on the horizon line.

Phosphorescent: Characterized by the emission of glowing light without any indication of the presence of heat.

Pictorial: Pertaining to an image (painting, drawing, photograph, etc.). For example, pictorial space or pictorial depth.

Picture plane: The two-dimensional surface on which an artwork is created. Also, an imaginary window through which a scene is viewed and onto which the scene is projected for the purpose of rendering the illusion of three-dimensionality on a two- dimensional surface.

Pigment: A natural or synthetic color particle mixed with a liquid vehicle or medium (water or oil, for example) to form paints or inks.

Polychromatic: Descriptive of images consisting of many colors.

Primary colors: Hues (red, yellow and blue) that cannot be produced through mixing any others. Theoretically, all other colors can be produced from various combinations of these three hues.

Primed canvas: Canvas that has been coated with a layer of paint or sizing to make the surface less porous and less subject to deterioration.

Relief sculpture: Three-dimensional forms that project from a surface to which they are attached, as opposed to free-standing sculpture. It can vary from almost two-dimensional low or bas relief to high or haut relief.

Representational art: Art that portrays objects or figures in a recognizable form, as opposed to nonobjective or totally abstracted works where the figures or objects are still discernable. Realistic art and naturalistic art are representational art.

Rococo: An eighteenth-century, late Baroque style of art characterized by playful, witty, frivolous, romantic scenes painted loosely with soft pastel colors.

Romantic: Stressing the exotic, the dangerous, the heroic or the mysterious. Also, pertaining to an art movement of the nineteenth century that rebelled against the academic austerity of the concurrent Neoclassical movement. Romantic art stressed the dramatic, the emotional, the exotic and the dangerous, and tended to portray the power of nature, subjective experience and literary and historical subjects.

Secondary colors: The three colors orange, violet and green, each obtainable by mixing two particular primary colors together.

Sfumato: A soft, smoky effect in a work of art, resulting from a lack of sharp edges and a subtle blending of tones between forms.

Shade: A color whose value has been darkened through the addition of black, as opposed to tint, which refers to a color lightened in value through the addition of white.

Statuette: A small statue.

Style: A complex of characteristics which identify artwork with an individual, a school, an ideology, a time period or a geographical area. In painting, characteristics of style may include the artist's choice of subject matter, brushwork, color use, various procedural practices and techniques, as well as many less obvious elements related to individual temperament and personality.

Subordinance: In a composition, pertaining to areas or elements of less emphasis, as opposed to areas of dominance.

Tensile strength: The ability of a material to withstand stretching. For example, bronze and steel have greater tensile strength than stone.

Trompe L'oeil: A French phrase meaning "fool the eye." It refers to a painting or other art form that creates such a realistic image that the viewer initially wonders whether the image is real or a representation.

Two-dimensional: Having height and width but no depth. It can refer to flat media (painting, drawing, etc.), as opposed to sculpture or to the perception of flatness of space in a painting, as opposed to the illusion of depth.

Veneer: A thin surface layer of expensive material laid over a base of common material. Used to enhance the decorative beauty of a surface. For instance, the Romans typically used a fine layer of marble or other stone to face concrete structures.

Vermillion: A bright, vivid red or reddish-orange; or generally, various red pigments.

Warm color(s): Colors that (based on our associations with images such as fire and the sun) have a warm visual temperature. They tend to advance spatially when placed next to cool colors which tend to recede. Red-violet, red, red-orange, orange, yellow, yellow-orange and orange are warm colors.

Warp: The series of strands of yarn running lengthwise in a loom. The crossing thread or yarn is known as a weft or woof.

Weft: The filling thread or yarn in a loom that is woven in with the warp, crossing it at right angles. Also known as a woof.

Selected Bibliography

Barkan, M., L. Chapman, and E. Kern.
"Designing Units of Instruction." In Guidelines: Curriculum Development for Aesthetic Education, 32–55. CEMREL, Inc., 1970.

Bell, Clive.
"Significant Form." In *Introductory Readings in Aesthetics*, edited by John Hospers, 87–99. New York: The Free Press, 1969.

Broudy, Harry S.
Enlightened Cherishing. Illinois: University of Illinois Press, 1972.

Dewey, John.
"Criticism and Perception." Chapter Thirteen of *Art as Experience*, 1934. Reprint. New York: Capricorn Books, 1958.

Ducasse, Curt, J.
"The Subjectivity of Aesthetic Value." In *Introductory Readings in Aesthetics*, edited by John Hospers, 283–307. New York: The Free Press, 1969.

———. *Art, The Critics, and You*. Indianapolis: Bobbs–Merrill Co., 1944.

Feldman, Edmund.
"Mastering the Techniques of Art Criticism." Chapter Twelve of *Becoming Human Through Art*, 348–383. Englewood Cliffs, NJ: Prentice–Hall, Inc., 1970.

———. *Varieties of Visual Experience*. Englewood Cliffs, NH: Prentice–Hall, 1993.

Fry, Roger.
"Art as Form." In *Introductory Readings in Aesthetics*, edited by John Hospers, 100–115. New York: The Free Press, 1969.

Frye, Northrop.
"Polemical Introduction." In *Anatomy of Criticism*, 1957, 3–27. Reprint. Princeton: Princeton University Press, 1971.

Kaelin, Eugene F.
An Aesthetics for Art Educators. New York: Teachers College Press, Columbia University, 1989.

———. "The Visibility of Things Seen: A Phenomenological View of Painting." In *Art and Existence—A Phenomenological Aesthetics*, 153–182. Lewisburg: Bucknell University Press, 1971.

Langer, Susan.
"The Work of Art as Symbol." In *Introductory Readings in Aesthetics*, edited by John Hospers, 171–184. New York: The Free Press, 1969.

Lanier, Vincent.
The Arts We See: A Simplified Introduction to the Visual Arts, Chapter Three. New York: Teachers College Press, 1982.

Pepper, S. C.
The Basis of Criticism in the Arts. Cambridge: Harvard University Press, 1946.

About the Author

Dr. William T. Squires was born in Chelsea, Massachusetts. His education includes graduate study and degrees from Vanderbilt University (M.A.) and Florida State University (Ph. D.). Dr. Squires continues to study the philosophy and history of art, and art education. Currently, Dr. Squires teaches in the Lamar Dodd School of Art at the University of Georgia in Athens. He has authored articles exploring art teaching methodologies. His first and second books, *The Metal Craftsman's Handbook* and *Arc Welding,* reflect his interest in and commitment to metal working technology and sculpture. His third book, *Artwork: A Study Guide to Art Processes* is a learning tool which provides its user a conceptual grounding in the making of art.